The Birthright Lottery

THE BIRTHRIGHT LOTTERY

Citizenship and Global Inequality

AYELET SHACHAR

HARVARD UNIVERSITY PRESS
Cambridge, Massachusetts
London, England
2009

Printed in the United States of America

Library of Congress Cataloging-in-Publication Data

Shachar, Ayelet, 1966–
The birthright lottery : citizenship and global inequality / Ayelet Shachar.
p. cm.
Includes bibliographical references and index.
ISBN 978-0-674-03271-2 (alk. paper)
1. Citizenship. 2. Sociological jurisprudence. I. Title.
K3224.S53 2009
342.08'3—dc22 2008038983

Most of the things worth doing in the world have been declared impossible before they were done.

Louis D. Brandeis (American Supreme Court Justice, 1856–1941)

Contents

Preface

This book was conceived when I was nine months pregnant. Having completed a fellowship year as a Member of the Institute for Advanced Study in Princeton, I returned to Toronto, where, before rushing off to the delivery room, I was able to put the final touches to an essay written for *NOMOS* entitled "Children of A Lesser State: Sustaining Global Inequality through Citizenship Laws." As an immigrant and scholar of citizenship, I could not miss the irony of writing an essay on the birthright transmission of membership while awaiting the birth of my son, who was about to be given the gift of automatic and unconditional membership in our adoptive country, Canada (one of the most prosperous and peaceful societies in the world) simply by virtue of having been born on its soil.

Benefiting from a particular set of legal norms has not proven a sufficient reason to accept it without scrutiny, however. Nor did it lead me to abandon the aspiration to reorient the vital academic and political debate over citizenship by drawing the analogy to inherited property. If anything, it provided an added impetus—now with origins planted not only in the world of ideas but rooted in lived experience as well—to explore, comprehend, and reveal the manifold ways in which birthright access to citizenship operates as a distributor (or denier) of opportunity on a global scale. Although the notion of gaining privilege by such arbitrary criteria as one's birthplace or bloodline is discredited in virtually all fields of public life, it still reigns supreme when it comes to the assignment of political membership—

the realm we associate with democracy, participation, and accountability—perhaps the domain where we would least expect to see a continuation of inherited entitlement.

Yet birthright not only survives but thrives in the realm of citizenship. Access to affluent polities in our unequal world is still reserved primarily to those born in a particular territory or to a particular ancestry while at the same time shutting out everyone else born on the wrong side of the border of security and prosperity. By offering a new way of thinking about political membership, I have throughout this book tried to identify and articulate the striking conceptual and legal commonalities between intergenerational transfers of citizenship and property. This has permitted me to move beyond the standard emphasis in the study of citizenship on status, rights, and identity. Instead, we can expand our conversation beyond these familiar categories simply by exploring the justifications for and consequences of our almost universal acceptance of *birthright* citizenship as a presumably natural and apolitical way to allot the precious good of political membership. Fertilized at the intersection of law, economics, and political philosophy, this book emphasizes the problem of unburdened intergenerational transmission of citizenship. Rejecting calls for either abolishing or resurrecting borders, I have sought to develop new legal concepts and innovative institutional designs to mitigate the voice and opportunity disparities that currently attach to birthright citizenship in an unequal world.

In my earlier work, I focused on the significance of family law and the social regulation of women's bodies and procreation as markers of identity and membership, particularly among religious minority communities that do not possess the power to control the formal (statehood-like) tools of membership definition, such as issuing passports, levying taxes, or controlling mobility. The focal point of *Multicultural Jurisdictions: Cultural Differences and Women's Rights* (Cambridge University Press, 2001) was to expose the "paradox of multicultural vulnerability," highlighting the complex ways in which state accommodation policies designed to improve relations between majorities and minorities in diverse societies may end up serving as a license for perpetuating inequalities within them, especially along gendered lines. That book proved influential in the vibrant debates about feminism and multiculturalism. Its core ideas and institutional designs also had an impact beyond academia, intervening in actual public policy and legislative debates over citizenship, women's rights, and religious accommodation in various countries the world over. In this book, I shift the gaze to sovereign polities that hold the sole official power to define inclusion in and exclusion from membership in a particular state, and derivatively, continue to control access to membership in supranational entities (such as the European Union). I can only hope that *The Birthright Lottery,* just like *Multicultural Jurisdictions,* meets with the same response: ideally nourishing and fueling its readers' passion and commitment to take action and make our world a more just and fair place for all of its inhabitants.

Writing a comprehensive and iconoclastic book like this one would have never been possible without the immense trust and support that I received from the following people and institutions: Michael Aronson of Harvard University Press believed in this project long before it deserved his confidence in it. Ian Shapiro and Seyla Benhabib gave me an early opportunity to present an embryonic version of the citizenship-as-inherited-property analogy at a conference gathering of some of the world's leading citizenship and immigration scholars at Yale University. Chris Eisgruber of Princeton facilitated my six-month visit as a Senior Visiting Scholar at the Program in Law and Public Affairs (LAPA), which he directed at the time, allowing me the freedom to formulate on paper many of the ideas that eventually came to fruition in the final manuscript. Joseph Weiler's entrepreneurial spirit matched mine when he opened the doors of his Jean Monnet Seminar to my presentation of an early version of the book's arguments to his students and colleagues at NYU. I was later fortunate to receive an invitation from Ron Daniels and Karen Knop to present the inaugural lecture at the Globalization, Law and Justice Workshop of the University of Toronto Faculty of Law, my home institution. In 2006-07, I enjoyed the privilege of serving as the Leah Kaplan Visiting Professor of Human Rights at Stanford Law School. During that academic year, Barbara Fried and Tom Gray gave me the opportunity to try out and receive constructive criticism on the proposed birthright privilege levy at their acclaimed Legal Studies Workshop; Josh Cohen and Rob Reich generously put together a joint meeting of their Global Justice and Political Theory Workshops, where Eamon Callan provided insightful commentary.

At Harvard Law School, where I spent the 2007–08 academic year as the Jeremiah Smith Jr. Visiting Professor of Law, I benefited greatly from conversations about different parts of the manuscript with Gerry Neuman, Yochai Benkler, Joe Singer, Martha Minow, and Bill Stunz. I also owe a debt of gratitude to Philippe Van Parijs (himself visiting in Harvard's Philosophy Department), who, over a lunch meeting in the Harvard Law School's faculty dining room, pressed me to find a more elegant title for the genuine-membership principle that I advocate in this book. When Charles Fried joined our table to contribute his mastery of Latin, it was clear that something special was brewing. Then, Van Parijs came up with the term "*jus nexi*" (replacing the cluckier "jus connexion") and the rest, as they say, is history. I thus owe him dividends on any returns the term might yield, especially if and when implemented in the real world. Finally, I had the privilege of presenting sections of this work at the annual meetings of two of the major academic communities in which I am a member: the American Political Science Association (APSA) and the American Association of Law Schools (AALS). I thank Casiano Hacker-Gordon and Naomi Mezey, respectively, for these invitations.

I would also like to single out additional friends, editors, and colleagues who have provided immensely valuable commentary on various parts of the book (at different stages of their incarnation), including: Rogers Smith, Rainer Bauböck, Steve Macedo, Geoffrey Levey, Joseph Carens, Jorge Valadez, Brooke Ackerly, David Owen, Craig Calhoun, Guy Mundlak, Chandran Kukathas, Veit Bader, Reva Siegel, Barbara Fried, Jackie Bhabha, Mark Elton, Emilie McLachan, Martin Scheinin, Peter Schuck, Tsilly Dagan, Jennie Rubio, Kate Brookson-Morris, Helena Likwornik, Debra Satz, Iris Marion Young, Bruce Chapman, Jean-Francois Gaudreault-DesBeins, Daniel Weinstock, Yoav Peled, Linda Bosniak, and Leti Volpp. I also thank Harvard University Press' anonymous reviewers for their detailed and generous engagement with the text. My greatest, indeed irredeemable, debt of gratitude is reserved for Ran Hirschl, my better half, without whom this book would have never seen the light of day. His intellectual involvement and rigor, as well as loving support, made this endeavor possible.

This book reflects my faith in the prospect of achieving greater redistributive justice and democratic inclusion even in the face of steep inequalities and entrenched legal norms in a nonideal world. For, as I hope to show in what follows, once we draw the analogy between birthright citizenship and inherited property, pressing questions of justice and distribution on a global scale cannot but ensue. In the end, as Oscar Wilde's Selfish Giant came to learn, it is not the walls that surround our gardens (or our communities) that make them flourish. Rather, it is the hustle and bustle of the diverse human activity that takes place within them, crisscrossing once fixed and ascriptive boundaries, which breeds life and blossom, and makes worth preserving, a revised and revitalized interpretation of citizenship for a more cosmopolitan world.

I AM GRATEFUL to the following journals and publishers for permission to reprint in modified form several of the themes that appear here: "Citizenship as Inherited Property" (co-authored with Ran Hirschl), *Political Theory*, Vol. 35, No. 3, 2007, 253–287, copyright by Sage Publications; "Children of A Lesser State: Sustaining Global Inequality through Citizenship Laws," in *NOMOS XLIV: Child, Family, and State,* edited by Stephen Macedo and Iris Marion Young, NYU Press, 2003, 345–397; "The 'Worth' of Citizenship in an Unequal World," *Theoretical Inquiries in Law*, Vol. 8, No. 2, 2007, 367–388, copyright of the Cegla Center for Interdisciplinary Research of the Law; "Against Birthright Privilege: Redefining Citizenship as Inherited Property," in *Identities, Affiliations, and Allegiances*, edited by Seyla Benhabib, Ian Shapiro, and Danilo Petranovic, Cambridge University Press, 2007, 257–281. I would also like to thank Hilda K. Britt for permission to reprint in full her poem, "Plane Love," copyright of Hilda K. Britt.

The Birthright Lottery

Introduction: The Puzzle of Birthright Citizenship

> Give me your tired, your poor,
> Your huddled masses yearning to breathe free,
> The wretched refuse of your teeming shore.
> Send these, the homeless, tempest-tost to me,
> I lift my lamp beside the golden door!
>
> EMMA LAZARUS, *The New Colossus* (1883)

IN 2003, five men from the Dominican Republic hid themselves on a ship headed for Houston, Texas, in search of the "golden door." When the ship was about half-way to Houston, one of the stowaways became ill. The five men decided to call upon the human compassion of the crew, and made their presence known. The vessel's crew knew they were bound by the rules of the International Maritime Organization "to protect, feed, and repatriate stowaways." But they also knew that they would receive special bonuses from the vessel's owner if they reached the shores of the United States stowaway-free. America's current immigration policy imposes significant monetary fines on vessels arriving with unwanted and undocumented migrants, like the five men in our story, who were from "the wrong side of the tracks" of prosperity and security. So the crew members acted swiftly. Showing no compassion at all, they threw two of the stowaways overboard and left the other three on a raft in the sea. After four hours of dangerous navigation, the three men were picked up by another vessel. The two others were less fortunate. Their shark-eaten bodies were found some time later.[1]

The stowaways apparently believed that boarding a vessel bound for the United States, without any proper documentation or permission to enter, represented their only hope to fulfill the American dream. As the Texas court that heard the survivors' legal claim against the vessel's owner (the person responsible for issuing the bonus reward for stowaway-free arrival) sympathetically noted, the five men's belief was in fact shared by "countless immigrants who have—legally and illegally—entered our great country almost since it gained independence."[2] The problem nowadays, for those who hold this belief, is that the golden door is not often left ajar. In fact, it is increasingly shut tight. This is true in the United States, as well as in most other prosperous nations.[3]

When we place the sad story of the stowaways in this broader context, we soon realize that despite jubilant predictions by post-nationalists of the imminent demise of citizenship, the legal distinction between member and stranger is, if anything, back with a vengeance.[4] This distinction has gained a renewed, and at times draconian, significance in the post 9/11 years. It is this realization that informs my assertion in this book that we must step back and account for the *persistent* importance of citizenship, *especially* in our current era of globalization. This last point requires further elaboration. There is no doubt that growing transnational flows of people across borders have created a wealth of new levels of membership and affiliation, operating within and across territorial borders, as well as above and below the traditional organizational framework of the nation-state.[5] Such multilayered and potentially overlapping sources of identity and authority provide meaningful rights and obligations that operate on a variety of levels, but they hardly correspond to, nor do they erase, the significance of citizenship as full membership in a political community of equals. As one author eloquently observes, we might use "the term *citizen* in other contexts, but only as a metaphor . . . Cities, provinces, and territories have residents; . . . corporations and communes have stakeholders; the global village has its cosmopolitans and its humanists who dream of a day beyond territorial divisions. But only nation-[states] have citizens."[6]

This situation may, of course, change in the future. But in today's world, as I will explain in the following pages, there are strong forces that explain not only the persistence of regulated membership (at the national or supranational level) but also the preservation of its archaic mechanism of conferring citizenship by virtue of birthright. Indeed, we cannot understand the resilience of bounded membership—which defies the vogue predictions of its demise—unless we revisit the legal and political institution of *birthright* citizenship. This institution provides a state-sponsored apparatus for handing down from generation to generation the invaluable security and opportunity that attach to membership in a stable, affluent, and rule-of-law society. It also allows members of well-off polities an enclave in which to preserve their accumulated wealth and power through time. If we focus on these *transfer* mechanisms, we soon realize with some surprise that today's birthright citizenship laws resemble ancient property regimes that shaped rigid and tightly regulated estate-transmission rules. Birthright citizenship operates not merely *as if* it were any other kind of inherited property; rather, it moves down the generations like an entail form of untaxed inherited property.[7] Today, such "entailed" transfer of property is deeply discredited: it is banned in most jurisdictions and, indeed, is largely associated with a bygone feudal system. At the same time, we still find strict reliance on birthright transmission of entitlement in the assignment of the valuable good of *political membership*.

It was none other than Alexis de Tocqueville who, in *Democracy in America,* famously warned about the social and political dangers of inherited property becoming the basis of enduring privilege. A similar cautionary tale is worth telling about birthright citizenship in an unequal world like our own. This book does just that: in confronting the complexity of the current system of citizenship transfer, I aim to offer a new way of thinking about political membership by drawing a conceptual analogy between birthright citizenship and inherited property. This perspective creates a space in which to explore membership entitlement in the broader context of today's urgent debates about global justice and the distribution of opportunity.

For those granted a head start simply because they were born into a flourishing political community, it may be difficult to appreciate the extent to which others are disadvantaged due to the lottery of birthright. But the global statistics are revealing. Children born in the poorest nations are five times more likely to die before the age of five. Those who survive their early years will, in all likelihood, lack access to basic subsistence services such as clean water and shelter, and are ten times more likely to be malnourished than children in wealthier countries. Many will not enjoy access to even basic education, and those out of school are more likely to be girls than boys.[8] The odds that they will either witness, or themselves suffer, human rights abuses are also significantly increased. What is more, these disparities that attach to birthright citizenship are not a matter of individual desert or fault; rather, they represent systemic and structural patterns. In such a world, citizenship laws assigning political membership by birthright play a crucial role in the distribution of basic social conditions and life opportunities on a global scale.[9]

My intention is not to belabor the familiar argument that such extreme inequality of actual life chances is morally and ethically troubling. Rather, the point here is more subtle: by focusing on the often neglected angle of membership transfer, I wish to call attention to the crucial role played by existing legal regimes for allocating entitlement to political membership (according to birthright) in restricting access to well off polities and sustaining the privilege of inherited entitlement. I further wish to destabilize the notion that such reliance is "natural" and, in this sense, apolitical. This latter notion serves to legitimize (and make invisible) the significant intergenerational transfers of wealth and power, as well as security and opportunity, which are currently maintained under the seal of the birthright regime of membership allocation. By highlighting the analogy to inherited property regimes, it becomes possible to call attention to the manifold ways in which reliance on birth in the assignment of citizenship regularizes, naturalizes, and legitimizes distinctions not only between jurisdictions, but also between vastly unequal bequests. Framed in this way, we can begin to acknowledge the massive estate-preserving implications of inherited citizenship regimes as they exist today. Drawing upon the rich body of democratic theory and property jurisprudence, this book sets out to expose—and challenge—the moral problem of unburdened intergenerational transmission of citizenship.

It seems unlikely that circumstances of birth would serve today as the core determinants of entitlement to full and equal membership in the citizenry body, given the extent to which it has been rejected in so many other domains of public life.[10] And yet, reliance upon the accident of birth is inscribed in the laws of all modern states and applied everywhere. In fact, the vast majority of the global population has no way to acquire membership *except* by circumstances of birth.[11] To the extent that citizenship is a valuable resource, it is currently secured on the basis of a morally arbitrary set of criteria. Birthright membership principles that sanction such distribution deserve the same critical analysis appropriate to any other social institution that stands in the way of the equal realization of opportunities. Such analysis is, however, conspicuous for its absence. The almost casual acceptance of ascription as a basis for assigning political membership is so prevalent that we tend to simply take it for granted.[12] Even those who propose to tighten the circle of membership do not contest the basic principle of hereditary entitlement; instead, they quibble about the scope of its application. What remains unchallenged, and remarkably so, is the entrenched assumption that reliance on birth is somehow an unquestionable component of assigning political membership. This (misguided) assumption is, in part, to blame for the scant attention that has been paid to the puzzle of birthright citizenship even by progressive scholars interested in "rethinking" the political community.[13]

This is a serious omission: the bulk of the world's population acquires citizenship on the basis of transmission at birth based on parentage or territorial location at time of birth. The harsh facts on the ground are such that most people alive today, especially the huddled masses yearning to breathe free, remain largely "trapped" by the lottery of their birth.[14] This acknowledgment motivates (in the book's latter chapters) the uneasy task of envisioning viable and realistic possibilities for reforming the existent birthright-allocation system. These possibilities involve enlarging our scope of analysis beyond the standard accounts of political membership as a repository of legal status, rights, and collective identity.[15] Although each of these aspects remains a vital part of citizenship's domain, together they do not capture the full range of its purpose. Instead of dwelling on these familiar categories, my interest lies in *expanding* our understanding of citizenship by adding a thus-far missing aspect: thinking about birthright access to citizenship as a distributor, or denier, of security and opportunity on a global scale. To unearth the more complex and multidimensional functions of birthright citizenship, we need to take a hard look at the entrenched legal connection between birth and political membership.

A hypothetical illustration sets the stage for our inquiry. Imagine a world in which there are no significant political and wealth variations among bounded membership units. There are no resource scarcities of any kind, and there are also no conflicts based on social factors such as class, ethnicity, or nationality. In such a world, nothing is to be gained by tampering with the existing membership structures. In this imaginary and fully stable world system, there is no motivation for change or migration. Each political entity offers a safe and welcoming space in which people live, love, work, and eventually pass away. Assuming there are no natural or human-made disasters, children and grandchildren may well pursue the same membership path as their progenitors. More important still, the specific collective in which a child belongs does not matter; roughly equal opportunities attach to citizenship entitlement in whatever political community she happens to have been born.

When we relax these assumptions in order to fit them more closely to the reality of our own world, with its omnipresent struggles and conflicts—a world where political instability, human mobility, and material inequality continue to persist—things begin to look quite different. In our world, membership in a particular state (with its specific level of wealth, degree of stability, and human rights record) has a significant impact on our identity, security, well-being, and on the range of opportunities realistically available to us. When analyzed in this broader context, full membership in an affluent society emerges as a complex form of property inheritance: a valuable entitlement that is transmitted, by law, to a restricted group of recipients under conditions that perpetuate the transfer of this precious entitlement to "their body," specifically, their heirs. This inheritance carries with it an immensely valuable bundle of rights, benefits, and opportunities.

Although they have a pernicious effect on distributing life prospects and human security, birthright entitlements still dominate our laws when it comes to the allocation of political membership to a given state. In fact, material wealth and political membership (which are for many the two most important distributable goods) are the only meaningful resources whose intergenerational transfer is still largely governed by principles of heredity.[16] Whereas the normative foundations of these principles have been thoroughly discussed in terms of the intergenerational transmission of property, they have seldom been considered in terms of citizenship. This omission is as surprising as it is disturbing: academics and policymakers pay a great deal of attention to questions of citizenship, immigration, the claims of minority groups, concerns about civic integration, and how to make political membership meaningful in a world of overlapping and competing affiliations. These vibrant debates engage primarily with the trilogy of status, rights, and identity. What remains conspicuously absent from these discussions, however, is a serious analysis of the global-distributive implications of the entrenched norm and legal practice of designating membership on account of pedigree or birthplace, and its accompanying protections and benefits.[17] When it comes to any other legal entitlement generated and distributed by the state, reliance on birth status has been deeply discredited. To date, however, birthright citizenship laws have largely escaped similar scrutiny. It is my conviction that it is time to redress this imbalance: we must start to critically examine the connection between birth, the *demos* definition, and the unequal distribution of voice and opportunity on a global scale.

Although there have been many significant efforts to problematize citizenship and to counteract problems of global inequality and deficits of democratic legitimacy, the typical strategy has been to focus almost exclusively on the situation of nonmembers, pressing hard to expand their rights and to open up the regimes that make it possible for newcomers to join the circle of members.[18] Undoubtedly, these are important objectives, which have become ever more urgent in recent times. The years following 9/11 have seen governments throughout the world expand and deepen their regulatory control over territorial access and membership admission as part of a larger strategy to regain control over borders.[19] Yet, as an analytical matter, to frame the question of political membership in this way is to omit something important. It is not enough to focus only on the situation of those who do not belong; the basis for entitlement of those who "naturally" belong must also be examined. How is full membership acquired in the absence of migration? On what basis is the coveted entitlement to citizenship conferred upon some, while denied to others? Who benefits and who loses out when birthright principles are entrenched in citizenship laws? These are the fundamental questions that will concern me in the discussion that follows. To address them, we must shift our gaze from the immigrant to the citizen, and expand the discussion of membership beyond the familiar lens of identity and belonging to account for the transfer mechanism of citizenship by birthright with its pernicious effects on the distribution of voice and opportunity on a global scale.

Birthright Attribution: The Legal Frameworks of Citizenship and Property

When we talk about birth as a source of citizenship, we must distinguish between two principles that define membership in a state in the modern era: *jus soli* ("the law of the soil") and *jus sanguinis* ("the law of blood"). While *jus soli* and *jus sanguinis* are typically presented as antipodes, it is important to note that both rely upon, and sustain, a conception of bounded membership. They share the basic assumption of scarcity: only a limited pool of individuals can automatically acquire citizenship in a given polity. Once the idea of scarcity is introduced, we are faced with the dilemma of allocation, or boundary making: put another way, how do we determine whether a person is to be included within the circle of members or left outside its parameters? Both principles resolve this dilemma in a similar fashion: by reliance on *birthright transfer of entitlement.* The distinction between them lies in the connecting factor used to demarcate a respective polity's membership boundaries: *jus soli* relies on birthplace; *jus sanguinis* on parentage. It is tempting to think that a rule that makes citizenship "contingent upon the place of a child's birth is somehow more egalitarian than a rule that would make birthright citizenship contingent upon the legal status of the child's parents."[20] But this distinction can easily lead us astray. Both criteria for attributing membership at birth are arbitrary: one is based on the accident of birth within particular geographical borders while the other is based on the sheer luck of descent.

By focusing selectively on the event of birth as the sole criterion for allocating automatic membership, existing citizenship laws contribute to the conceit that this assignment is no more than an apolitical act of membership demarcation. It is in this way that the potential distributive implications are obscured from view.[21] In practice, however, birthright-attribution rules do far more than demarcate who may be included in the polity. Like other property regimes, they also define access to certain resources, benefits, protections, decision-making processes, and opportunity-enhancing institutions which are reserved primarily to those defined as right-holders. In this respect, birthright citizenship exhibits the definitive features of property regimes, which can broadly be characterized as a system of rules that govern access to, and control over, resources that are scarce relative to the human demands made upon them.[22]

As William Blackstone already observed more than two hundred years ago, "there is nothing which so generally strikes the imagination, and engages the affections of mankind, as the right of property."[23] Invoking a conceptual analogy to property and inheritance thus requires vigilance and clarification of the intended use of these charged concepts, a task that I undertake in the following chapter; at this point, suffice it to say that citizenship clearly differs from the narrow and atomistic (indeed, "Blackstonian") conception of property that has become synonymous with the values of tradability, alienability, or "sole and despotic" ownership.[24] Rather, it is a competing vision of property, one which emphasizes stewardship and mutual responsibility, that I wish to bring to the fore in the context of citizenship. As a collectively generated good that creates a complex set of legal entitlements and obligations among various social actors, citizenship offers an excellent example of more contemporary interpretations of property as a web of social and political relations imbued with obligations to promote the public good and not just to satisfy individual preferences.[25] This broader perspective permits us to see citizenship regimes not only as generating intricate rules that define the allocation of membership, but also as bearing considerable effects on the distribution of power, wealth, and opportunity. These latter implications are particularly disturbing given that access to the said social good is determined almost exclusively by circumstances beyond our control. To draw the analogy to inherited property and to acknowledge birthright entitlement to citizenship as a human construct not impervious to change is to open up the existing system of distribution to critical assessment. Once we categorize certain relationships under the rubric of property and inheritance, the classic questions of distributive justice—that is, of *who* owns what, and on *what* basis—cannot but follow.

Birthright Citizenship and Global Inequality

Birthright citizenship does more than define the formal boundaries of membership. It also closely corresponds to strikingly different prospects for the well-being, security, and freedom of individuals. For most legal scholars (as well as most political philosophers), however, the question of which state would guarantee membership to a particular individual has been seen as largely irrelevant. In this respect, notes Benedict Kingsbury, "the system of state sovereignty has hitherto had the effect of fragmenting and diverting demands that international law better address inequality."[26] This may explain why theories of law and morality have too long been blind to the dramatically unequal voice and opportunity consequences of birthright citizenship; but it does little to justify it.

Even thinkers who defend a moral or basic human right to membership typically do so at a general, abstract level, while relegating "the specific content of the right to citizenship in a specific polity . . . [to the] specific citizenship legislation of this or that country."[27] This division of labor may well be motivated by the idea of sovereign autonomy or democratic self-determination. Alas, it unwittingly strengthens the notion that all that matters is that one gain a right to access citizenship "in this or that country" rather than exploring the dramatically unequal life prospects that attach to membership in this or that country. It is this slippage between an abstract right to membership and its concrete materialization that demonstrates how the focus on *formal equality of status* makes invisible the *inequality of actual life chances* attached to citizenship in specific political communities.

The typical response of liberal and democratic theory to the inequality of opportunity caused by ascriptive factors is to work hard to ensure that "no child is left behind." While this slogan has never fully materialized in any country, it reflects an aspiration to overcome social hierarchies and economic barriers that are caused by morally arbitrary circumstances or structural patterns of disadvantage. It is therefore surprising that the global-distributive dimension of birthright membership has largely escaped critical assessment. This paucity of analysis is explained at least in part by the fact that the study of citizenship laws has traditionally been the province of domestic and often parochial scholarship, which tends to concern itself with the particular features of its own country's norms and procedures for defining membership and admission.[28] International law, for its part, has focused primarily on attempts to resolve the problem of statelessness. This account calls our attention to the fact that it is better for the individual to enjoy a special attachment to a given polity than to remain with no state protection at all.[29] This is clearly a potent argument. However, this formulation focuses only on formal equality of status. It says nothing about rectifying inequalities that correlate with the birthright assignment of membership in "this or that" particular country.

Moreover, the familiar focus on formal equality of status (requiring that all individuals belong to one state or another) itself relies on a schematic picture of an orderly world comprised of clearly delineated political communities. This conception of the world is described by Rainer Bauböck as having, "a quality of simplicity and clarity that almost resembles a Mondrian painting. States are marked by different colors and separated from each other by black lines . . . [This] modern political map marks all places inhabited by people as belonging to mutually exclusive state territories."[30] In such a world, with its clear and exhaustive division of the global political landscape into mutually exclusive jurisdictions, it appears "axiomatic that every person ought to have citizenship, that everyone ought to belong to one state."[31] By focusing on the Mondrianesque picture of citizenship, it becomes possible to emphasize the artificial symmetry between states (represented as different color-coded areas on the world map) while ignoring inequalities in the actual life prospects of citizens who belong to radically different (yet formally equal) membership units.[32]

On this score, the stowaways knew better. It must have required an acute awareness of the actual inequalities in life prospects to embark on their fatal trip, risking everything, including their very survival, for the goal of attaining a better future in a more affluent and stable country to which they did not legally belong.[33] It is in this context that the relationship between birthright citizenship and inequality of opportunity comes to the fore. Although existing citizenship laws do not create these disparities, they perpetuate and reify dramatically differentiated life prospects by reliance on the morally arbitrary circumstance of birth. At the same time, they camouflage these crucial distributive consequences by appealing to the presumed "naturalness" of birth-based membership. There is, however, nothing apolitical or neutral about these birthright regimes.[34] They are constructed and enforced by law, advantaging those who have access to the inherited privilege of membership, while disadvantaging those who do not—just like hereditary regimes of property transmission in the past preserved wealth and power in the hands of the few.

The Importance of Citizenship's Global Distributive Dimension

We can now see membership boundaries in a more complex light: not only are these boundaries sustained for symbolic identity and belonging purposes (as the conventional argument holds), they also serve a crucial role in preserving restricted access to the community's accumulated wealth and power. The latter is jealously guarded at the juncture of transfer of "ownership" from the present generation of citizens to its progeny. In other words, birthright citizenship mechanisms provide cover through their presumed naturalness for what is essentially a major (and currently untaxed) property/estate transmission from one generation to another. Ours is a world of scarcity; when an affluent community systemically restricts access to membership and its derivative benefits on the basis of a strict heredity system—akin to an entail structure of transmission—those who are excluded have reason to complain.[35]

If we wish to revisit these automatic transmission principles and to consider how to better allocate across borders the social benefits that presently attach to citizenship in a bounded community (as I believe we should), the first order of business is to draw attention to the entrenched connection between birth and political membership. Despite its pervasive effects, this connection has largely escaped attention in both academic and public policy circles. Once subjected to scrutiny, this system of allocation can no longer be taken for granted, nor can it be ignored.[36] This is so for at least three reasons.

First, the scope and scale of citizenship distribution is truly grand: it affects every single human being on this earth. Although the topic of immigration nowadays attracts considerable attention, it is still by means of ascriptive birthright that individuals attain their initial political membership in "this or that" particular country. And despite the public attention paid to those who go on to reside outside the polity in which they were born, they represent less than three percent of the global population. Everyone else—namely, ninety-seven percent of the global population, or more than six billion people—is assigned the life-long good of membership by the lottery of birth and either chooses, or is forced, to keep it that way.[37]

Second, the consequences of this membership-transfer system are profound, going far beyond the familiar emphasis in citizenship studies on questions of identity, diversity, and civic virtue. In an unequal world like our own, birthright citizenship does more than demarcate a form of belonging. It also distributes voice and opportunity in a vastly unequal manner. By legally identifying birth, either in a certain territory, or to certain parents, as the decisive factor in the distribution of the precious property of membership, current citizenship principles render membership in well-off polities beyond the reach of the vast majority of the world's population. It is in this way that citizenship may be thought of as the quintessential inherited entitlement of our time.

And what a significant inherited entitlement it is: in our world, the global disparities are so great that under the present regimes of birthright citizenship, "some are born to sweet delight" as William Blake memorably put it in the *Auguries of Innocence,* while others (through no fault or responsibility of their own) are "born to endless night."[38] The reality of our world is that the endless night is more prevalent that the sweet delight. More than a billion people live on less than a dollar a day; about 2.7 billion live without access to adequate sanitation and more than 800 million are seriously malnourished.[39] Add to this the almost incomprehensible fact that eight million will die each year, as one author piercingly remarks, "because they are simply too poor to live."[40] Or think of the shocking atrocity that we casually permit to continue every day: more than ten million children under five years of age perish each year in the world's poorest nations—most from entirely preventable causes of death.[41] To this we must add the stinging realization that—contrary to the conventional optimistic story of breaking down ascriptive barriers and replacing them with mechanisms of choice and fair distribution—under the current system of birthright, gaining access to citizenship's goods is clearly not open to anyone who voluntarily consents to membership or is in dire need of its associated benefits.[42]

Once this more critical perspective is taken into account, with its profound emphasis on global disparities coupled with a sharp recognition of how tightly our membership boundaries are regulated, the existing correlation between inherited citizenship and general well-being is impossible to ignore. The quality of services, safety, and scope of freedoms and opportunities enjoyed by those born in affluent polities are far greater, ceteris paribus, than the opportunities of those born in poorer or less stable countries.[43]

When our citizenship laws effectively become intertwined with distributing shares in human survival on a global scale—designating some to a life of relative comfort while condemning others to a constant struggle to overcome the basic threats of insecurity, hunger, and destitution—we can no longer silently accept this situation. These dramatically differentiated life prospects should disturb not only the expectant crowd of moral universalists but also free-marketers who believe in rewarding effort and distributing opportunity according to merit, rather than on the basis of station of birth. The problem of unequal allocation and transfer, which has gained plenty of attention in the realm of property, is, in fact, far more extreme in the realm of birthright entitlement to citizenship.

The third reason why we must pay careful attention to the puzzle of birthright citizenship is that, astonishingly, we continue to have no coherent theoretical explanation for the continued reliance on circumstances of birth in the assignment of political membership. This is despite the fact that the vast majority of the global population is assigned political membership by ascription (the scope of the studied phenomenon), and the dramatic global distributive implications that result from this entrenched system of allocation of unequal opportunity (birthright's consequences). If anything, the persistence of ascription in this most unlikely of social arenas—namely, the definition of who is included and who is excluded from the *demos* (the citizenry body), flies in the face of our standard liberal and democratic accounts of citizenship as reflecting the choice and consent of the governed.[44] It also reveals serious cracks in the conventional argument that we can divide the world neatly into countries that fall into the "civic" or "ethnic" ends of the spectrum of conceptualization of membership. Similarly, the prevalence of birthright membership stands in tension with the conventional characterization of citizenship as reflecting a social contract between the individual and the political community, or what various French authors refer to as *"le lien politique et juridique."*[45] This post-Enlightenment vision is often contrasted with the older, Roman law conception of citizenship as an assigned status, with rights and obligations following automatically as a consequence of birth, not choice. Many of the giants of social and political thought recount and reify this (largely fictitious) distinction, according to which the modern state's allocation of citizenship operates as a matter of choice and consent, marking an important improvement on the prior, status-based definition of one's standing in the community. These triumphant themes are perhaps most famously captured in John Locke's *Second Treatise of Government* and in Henry Maine's catch-phrase thesis in *Ancient Law,* which describes the transition from the ancient world to the modern one as law and society's development "from status to contract."[46]

To recognize the surprising similarities in form and function between birthright citizenship and inherited property highlights a striking exception to the modern trend away from ascribed statuses in all other areas. The ascribed birthright-transmission mechanism, which is still exercised today, cannot be dismissed as a mere historical accident, given that the question of legitimizing political authority and property is central to the liberal, democratic, and civic-republican intellectual traditions. Such a startling observation only makes the persistent link between *political membership* and *station of birth*—a connection that has been both ignored and taken for granted—ever more puzzling and in urgent need of a coherent explanation. Addressing this lacuna is the challenge I take on in this book.

Placing the New Framework of Analysis in Context

My discussion is informed by, and in turn seeks to enrich, three different bodies of literature: citizenship studies in contemporary political and legal scholarship, global inequality debates, and sociological accounts of the demise of borders in the context of post-national theorizing. This literature is set against the actual, restrictive policy changes undertaken by most advanced industrial nations in recent years in reformulating their citizenship and immigration regimes in response to perceived threats of increased cross-border mobility and global insecurity. In juxtaposing these different lines of inquiry, I highlight the paucity of attention paid to *birthright* membership. I further contend that we need to take into account these partly intersecting discourses if we wish to find a justifiable balance that permits the preservation of the enabling properties of citizenship in a self-governing polity while at the same time aggressively responding to the global injustices perpetuated by the current system of entail-like transmission of membership by birthright. This mode of enquiry also illustrates the gaps and inconsistencies in each body of literature.

Consider the following: most of the writings on citizenship in recent years engages in a nuanced account of the rights of minorities in diverse societies, the civic virtues of citizenship, the ideals of deliberative democracy, and the prospects of creating a world without borders, or at least with more porous ones. This welcome renaissance-of-sorts in citizenship studies has dramatically enriched the field, highlighting the manifold ways in which political membership means much more than "the narrow passport-holding sense of having a formal legal connection to a particular [state]."[47] Remarkably, however, sparse attention has been paid to analyzing the *transfer* mechanism of membership by birthright and its pernicious effects on the distribution of voice and opportunity on a global scale.

The literature on global inequality, in contrast, suffers from an opposite shortcoming. Although encompassing tremendously rich debates about the effects of globalization on both inter-country and intra-country inequalities, the units of analysis themselves, that is, bounded membership communities (in their present incarnation as sovereign political entities in the interstate system), are often taken for granted. Therefore, no attention is paid to the type of questions that concern me here: how the boundaries of inclusion and exclusion are defined in the first place, what sustains them, and why polities in the real world continue to rely upon morally arbitrary circumstances of birth in deciding who falls on what side of the border of prosperity and security. In spite of the academic fanfare of post- and transnationalists, who happily predicted the demise of regulated borders and the eventual devaluation of bounded membership, citizenship is enjoying an unmistakable resurgence of authority at present.[48] This makes the study of citizenship's birthright transfer mechanisms—the lost dimension of law's construction of formidable walls that establish (and then protect) the membership boundaries they helped create—ever more pressing.

Highlighting this tremendous gap between theory and practice is part of my endeavor here, but it takes place as part of a larger project of merging the critical account of existing citizenship laws with a constructive exploration of the real possibilities for making our world a better place for all of its inhabitants. I do this by reformulating the very birthright principles that currently allocate political membership on the basis of an unrestricted form of inherited entitlement. I argue throughout this book that we must consider the two topics together—birthright citizenship and global inequality—in order to better comprehend the former and tackle the latter.

Thematic Overview

My discussion proceeds in two major stages. In the book's first part, I develop the analogy between birthright citizenship and inherited property in the context of a world of severe inequalities of wealth and opportunity. This analogy permits deploying qualifications found in the realms of property and inheritance theory in the membership context; in so doing I propose a model that has the potential to impose restrictions on the unlimited and perpetual transmission of membership—with the aim of ameliorating the most glaring inequalities of opportunity perpetuated by the system of birthright citizenship. This goal informs the idea of a *birthright privilege levy* as an obligation borne by windfall recipients of membership entitlement in well-off polities to improve the life prospects of those alloted less under the birthright lottery.

Since birthright citizenship involves the transfer of a lucrative entitlement to resources and opportunities, it invites a legal response that mitigates these presently unburdened intergenerational transfers. If affluent political communities wish to continue to bestow membership according to birthright, thereby shaping the life prospects of recipients in a fashion that conceptually resembles the inheritance of entailed fortunes, they must accept a corresponding obligation. In this way, the imperative to provide for those less fortunate in their citizenship assignment is not a matter of charity but of legal duty. The basis for this obligation is rather straight forward. Even avid defenders of property rights resist endorsing automatic transmission of entitlement from one generation to another in perpetuity: such inheritance regimes are treated as morally weak and objectionable. Taking the existing constraints on the power to convey property through inheritance as our model for taxing the birthright recipients of hereditary citizenship in affluent polities, the privilege levy offers a creative way in which to denaturalize the entail-like mechanisms that presently permit the uncurtailed concentration of wealth and power in certain bodies politick. Although many details need to be addressed in respect of the actual design and administration of such a birthright levy on citizenship inheritance in affluent polities, we can envisage distributing these revenues to specific projects designed to improve the life opportunities of children in the world's poorest nations—regardless of their (unchosen) birthplace or ancestry.

In the book's second part, I shift the focus from the global to the domestic, exploring the in-state problems of overinclusion, underinclusion, and democratic legitimacy, articulating their connection to the current regime of birthright citizenship. As with the discussion of citizenship and global inequality, I begin my exploration of the deficiencies of reliance on birth in defining membership in the polity by first mapping the legal terrain, placing it in a broader comparative and historical perspective. This is followed by a critical evaluation of the normative defenses that favor the preservation of a connection between birth and political membership. This critique is followed by the development of an alternative framework to define access to citizenship. Under this framework, emphasis is put on the significance of actual membership in the community, over and above any privileges obtained by inherited entitlement. I call this genuine connection principle *"jus nexi"* because, like *jus soli* and *jus sanguinis,* it conveys the core meaning of the method through which political membership is conveyed: by connection, union, or linkage.

The two-pronged analysis adopted in the book leads to unexpected results. For instance, it brings to center stage the importance of citizenship's enabling capacities and highlights its complex relationship to the gatekeeping function of membership. And although I fiercely criticize the transfer mechanism of citizenship, my conclusion is not that we must abolish the collective good of membership. Rather, I argue that a more productive balance can (and must) be found between protecting the valuable properties of membership and improving the well-being of those excluded from gaining access to such benefits solely because of where or to whom they were born. Although there is no one-size-fits-all solution, the birthright privilege levy supports the creation of a transnational transfer system of knowledge, services, and infrastructure (or what we might call a "worldwide safety net"), which is designed to address the morally unjustifiable disparities in life prospects that currently attach to perpetual membership transmission. It represents a concrete institutional measure to restrict birthright's presently uncurtailed transmission of privilege. This potentially far-reaching idea finds its roots in emphasizing the global-distributive aspect of citizenship and the analogy to inherited property.[49]

Importantly, the proposed reconceptualizing of citizenship as analogous to inherited property does not require rejection of the premise that special, or more extensive, obligations are owed to those defined as fellow members in the political community.[50] It simply means that bearing such special obligations does not tell against having a parallel general duty to provide a basic safety net of well-being and opportunity to those who remain barred from membership through accidents of birth.[51]

As anyone with an interest in domestic and international affairs would surely acknowledge, the importance and timeliness of the topics discussed in this book cannot be overstated. Citizenship and immigration are notorious hot-button political issues in the world's most affluent countries and, increasingly, in many emigrant-sending polities as well. Human mobility as well as pressing concerns about justice, equality, and development are becoming increasingly global issues. Yet our laws and conceptual imagery that define who gains access to the life-long good of citizenship and according to what criteria are still conducted in feudal-like terms of birthright entitlement, which simply no longer fit the bill; the social world that spawned these categories has long been succeeded by other relationships and values. In the same way, the political reality around us has changed radically in recent years, particularly in terms of the ever deeper economic and global security interdependence. These transformations are, of course, making their mark on the ground. What is lacking, however, is a fitting vocabulary to capture and assess the new political economy of citizenship in a world that is still riven with stark inequities.[52]

It is time to revise our already tired and familiar methods of defining who belongs to the political community, and on what basis. An equally pressing task is to respond to the concerns and demands of those who remain outside the circle of membership due to nothing more than accidents of birth. This book further highlights the need to place the debate about membership allocation in a broader context of consideration of inequality of life prospects and the possibilities for providing a basic safety net globally, irrespective of the political community into which one happens to have been born. Such an inquiry is particularly urgent given that mounting fears about the overcrowding of affluent countries by unwanted immigrants seem to drive much of the restrictive policies recently adopted in this sphere. Thinking about citizenship as if it were a form of inherited property is one way to defract our current limited reality into a new set of possibilities.

The following chapters attempt to respond to some of the most crucial problems in today's citizenship law and practice: overcoming the blind reliance on birthright regimes, which, beyond their severe global distributive consequences (the subject of discussion in the book's first part), are also proving to be poor predictors for defining who will actually belong in the circle of members (the book's second part) based on their real and substantive ties rather than any status-based, ascriptive factors. I further contend that once the analogy between birthright citizenship and inherited property has been drawn, foundational questions of access, transfer, and distribution become pertinent to the discussion of citizenship's domain. Although our theories of justice and property allow for unequal accumulation of wealth and other resources, they devote considerable thought to providing justificatory grounds for defending such inequity in the distribution of holdings. More important still for the purposes of our discussion is the recognition that these theories impose significant restrictions on social institutions that generate inequality. This is precisely what is missing in the prevalent framework of birthright citizenship.

The Road Ahead

The reliance on ascription in the conferral of citizenship—perhaps the most celebrated feature of the modern landscape—is at the heart of my inquiry in this book: how could it be that political membership, something which is so crucial for our identity, for our rights, for our political voice and for our life opportunities, is distributed on the basis of accidents of birth? Weaving together pertinent fields of inquiry (including law, political philosophy, institutional design, development economics, citizenship and globalization studies, and critical social theory) this book offers a comprehensive, yet surprising, answer to this question.

Let the flow of ideas speak for itself.

PART ONE

BIRTHRIGHT CITIZENSHIP AND GLOBAL INEQUALITY

CHAPTER ONE

Reconceptualizing Membership: Citizenship as Inherited Property

> I am astonished that ancient and modern writers on public matters have not ascribed greater influence over human affairs to the laws governing inheritance. Such laws belong, of course, to the civil order, but they should be placed first among political institutions because of their incredible influence on a people's social state; . . . in a sense, they lay hold of each generation before it is born. Through them, man is armed with an almost divine power over the future of his fellow men. Once the legislator has regulated inheritance among citizens, he can rest for centuries. Once his work has been set in motion, he can remove his hands from his creation. The machine acts under its power and seems almost to steer itself toward a goal designated in advance. If construed in a certain way, it collects, concentrates, and aggregates property, and before long, power as well.
>
> ALEXIS DE TOCQUEVILLE, *Democracy in America* (1835)

THE VAST MAJORITY of today's global population (97 out of every 100 people) have acquired their political membership solely by virtue of birthplace or "pedigree."[1] Even in the current age of increased globalization and privatization, there is little doubt that securing membership status in a given state or region (with its specific level of wealth, degree of stability, and human rights record) is a crucial factor in the determination of life chances. However, birthright entitlements still dominate both our imagination and our laws in the allocation of political membership to a given state. In fact, material wealth and political membership (which are for many the two most important distributable goods) are the only meaningful resources whose intergenerational transfer is still largely governed by principles of heredity entitlement. Whereas the normative foundations of these principles have been thoroughly discussed in terms of the intergenerational transfer of property, they have seldom been considered in terms of citizenship.

This omission is especially disturbing in light of recent heated debates in political and legal theory concerning the claims of minority groups, the narratives of collective-identity formation, and the ethics of political boundaries.[2] These debates involve what can be referred to as the "identity-bonding" dimension of citizenship. However, what remains conspicuously absent from these discussions is a serious analysis of what we might call the global-distributive implications of the entrenched norm and legal practice associated with automatically allocating political membership according to parentage *(jus sanguinis)* or territoriality *(jus soli)* principles. This chapter begins to address this considerable gap: it conceptualizes birthright citizenship laws, which construct and govern the *transfer* of membership entitlement, as analogous to a complex form of inherited property. This analysis in turn opens the door to fresh ideas for mitigating the profound distributive consequences that follow from reliance on circumstance of birth in allocating political membership.

Unlike advocates of world citizenship who seek to abolish bounded membership altogether, I believe that greater promise lies in diminishing the extreme inequities in life prospects that are presently attached to ascribed membership status under the existing birthright regime. This approach strikes a new balance between political membership and global justice without substantively detracting from the participatory and enabling qualities of membership in a self-governing polity. Although there are a number of responses that might get us closer to accomplishing this vision, I will focus here on the *obligation* to impose certain property-like and justice-based restrictions on the presently uncurtailed citizenship inheritance. Whether to interpret this obligation as a strong egalitarian commitment or a weaker international baseline welfarism is, of course, open to debate and will eventually have to be worked out through various democratic deliberations and reiterations across and between membership communities.[3] But the crux of my argument is this: once the analogy to inherited property is placed at center stage, it becomes far harder to justify the wealth-preserving aspect of citizenship that has long been cloaked under the cover of birthright's "naturalness." Once we see this complex system for what it is, the justice of requiring well-off hereditary title holders to provide at least a minimal threshold of well being (or subsistence) to those excluded from membership in an affluent and stable polity by accident of birth becomes more manifest.[4]

Theorists and policymakers shall undoubtedly have a heyday debating where precisely to draw this threshold. The more important point for our discussion is, however, to establish and defend the global redistributive obligation as a binding *corollary* to the right of birthright recipients to maintain their own entitlement to citizenship in a well-off polity. (In the course of this book I will be exploring some institutional options to facilitate that obligation.) In Hohfeldsian terms, the duty toward those who are excluded from citizenship by circumstances that are absolutely beyond their control is seen as correlated to the recipients' right to uphold their windfall membership. The analogy to inherited property further provides a foundation for avoiding "malfare" worldwide, yet without jumping to the quasi-tyrannical conclusion that we must abolish *tout court* the space in which semibounded, self-governing political communities can flourish.[5] This permits the preservation of the social relations aspect of citizenship, while counterbalancing the inequities sustained under the seal of natural transmission of entitlement by virtue of birth. It is here that the analogy to inherited property proves most useful. After distinguishing between a narrow and broad conception of property, I turn to a description of the main insights that can be applied from the realm of intergenerational transfer of property to the study of intergenerational transfer of citizenship.

My analysis in this chapter proceeds in four parts. (1) I begin my discussion of birthright-citizenship transfers as resembling property and wealth transfers by highlighting the disparities in the living conditions and opportunities offered to citizens born into unequal political communities across the world. (2) I survey a few key concepts in property theory that serve as a basis for my conceptual analogy between property and citizenship regimes. (3) I show that a broad conception of property corresponds with two core functions of bounded membership in the world today: "gate-keeping" and "opportunity-enhancing." (4) I venture into an exploration of the early common-law mechanisms of *fee tail* or *entailed* estates. This discussion shows the surprising commonalities in both form and function between these antiquated approaches to property transmission and present-day birthright principles that regulate access to bounded membership. Both these mechanisms serve to preserve and disguise as natural the immensely advantageous starting points in life to those who benefit from the birthright transfer. The analogy between inherited citizenship and the intergenerational transfer of property also helps reveal the pacifying role that legal norms and institutions play in legitimizing these transmission patterns. No less significantly, it permits us to deploy existing qualifications found in the realm of inheritance as a model for imposing restrictions on the presently *un*curtailed transmission of membership—with the aim of ameliorating its most glaring inequalities of opportunity.

Although I criticize the *transfer* mechanism of citizenship (by way of automatic birthright), my conclusion is not that we must abolish the collective good of membership. Rather, a new balance can and must be found between protecting the valuable features of political membership and improving the well-being of those who currently remain outside the legal walls surrounding well-off polities. I am not suggesting or implying that wealth-preserving is the sole or even core function of birthright citizenship. There are other plausible functions or explanations, such as identity-bonding, democratic self-governance, administrative convenience, respecting cultural differences or constitutive relations. I address these in Chapter 5, but bracket them for now in order to highlight the global distributive dimension that often goes unnoticed in our familiar discussions about citizenship. Ultimately, once the analogy between property and citizenship is drawn, the rich body of literature on inheritance becomes relevant to our discussion of the intergenerational transmission of citizenship. This enables me to defend the protections that citizenship guarantees to those included within a given membership circle, while at the same time targeting the unequal effects of this transmission system on those who remain excluded by its rigid, birth-based entitlement structure. Viewed through this prism, a redistributive *birthright privilege levy* (described in Chapter 3) might provide a model solution for addressing the severe inequalities of starting points that currently attach to inherited membership. Given that "*all* reasonable moral theories give us a sound basis for condemning the status quo," placing this kind of burden on the presently uncurtailed inheritance of citizenship permits establishing a binding legal obligation on the fortuitous birthright recipients.[6]

What Is Citizenship Worth?

Much has been written about global inequality. Everybody knows that the living conditions of a child born in Swaziland are, other things being equal, far worse than those of a child born in Switzerland. Publications such as the UNDP's *Human Development Report* or the World Bank's *World Development Report* reveal just how tremendous global disparities in life opportunities, chances, and choices actually are.[7] Consider, for example, measurements reflecting absolute deprivation: that is, the number of people falling below a threshold that enables them to function in a decent manner, such that the possibility of autonomous human action is severely restricted if not removed outright.[8] According to recent World Bank statistics, approximately 1.1 billion people live in extreme poverty with an income of less than $1 per day per person, measured at purchasing power parity.[9] Another 1.6 billion live in moderate poverty, defined as living on between $1 and $2 per day. In other words, over 2.7 billion people—approximately 45 percent of the world's population—survive on less than $2 a day. Virtually all of the world's extreme and moderate poor live in Asia, Africa, and Latin America. The overwhelming share of the extremely poor live in Southeast Asia and sub-Saharan Africa. At least 25 percent of the households in almost all sub-Saharan Africa or East Asian countries subsist on less than $1 per day per person at real purchasing power levels. As of the early 2000s, the average annual per capita income in the United States exceeded $30,000, with an average annual growth of 1.7 percent over the last two centuries. In contrast, the per capita annual income in Africa is just over $1,300 (far lower in sub-Saharan Africa), with an average annual growth rate of 0.7 percent over the last 200 years. Global inequalities in terms of income are even more striking when gender is factored in. Whereas in most industrialized polities, significant strides have been made toward the elimination of at least formal gender inequality, in other parts of the world women continue to lag far behind their fellow countrymen in terms of income and meaningful life choices.

But global inequalities in opportunity go far beyond income and expenditure. The mean years of educational attainment for the world have almost doubled from 3.4 in 1960 to 6.3 in 2000. However, disparities in educational attainment and achievement between students in developing countries and those in Organization for Economic Co-operation and Development (OECD) countries remain strikingly large. In many developing countries, literacy rates are still unacceptably low. According to the 2006 *World Development Report,* developing countries constitute the lower tail of the learning distribution. Students in these countries fare, on average, far worse than students in even the poorest-performing OECD countries. A recent study found that for children in Argentina and Chile average performance is two standard deviation points below that of children in Greece, one of the poorest performing countries in the OECD. Another recent study found that the reading ability of an average Indonesian student is equivalent to that of a French student at the seventh percentile.

Global inequalities also exist in health expenditures and health care. Whereas in 2002 the health expenditure per capita in Switzerland and Norway was roughly $3,500 (PPP US$), the equivalent health expenditure in Sri Lanka in the same year was $131, and a meager $15 in the Congo. Alternatively, take the crucial indicator of access to clean water. In 2002, 100 percent of Australia's population had permanent access to safe water sources. But only 70 percent of Australia's neighboring Solomon Islands' population, and approximately 39 percent of neighboring Papua New Guinea's population had sustainable access to safe water sources. Another revealing disparity is found in health care provision. Even health outcomes of the rich citizens in poor countries remain well below the OECD average. For all countries with average per capita GDP below $2 a day, the infant mortality rate of the richest quintile of the population is more than 10 times higher than the OECD average. Basic sanitation standards seem to be a long way off throughout the developing world. The availability of appropriate medical services and drugs is sporadic. And we have not yet taken into account the HIV/AIDS pandemic, with its clear regional concentration and impact on infant mortality.

A baby born in 2001 in Mali (one of the world's poorest countries) had a 13 percent chance of dying before reaching the age of one year, with his or her chances improving a mere 4 percent, to 9 percent, if the baby was born to a family in the top quintile of Mali's asset distribution. It is further estimated that approximately one in four children (24 percent) born in Mali will not reach age five. By contrast, a baby born in the United States the same year had less than 1 percent chance of dying in its first year or first five years. The probability at birth of not surviving to age 40 (for the 2000–2005 cohort) in Mali was 37.3 percent. In other words, at least one in every three people born in Mali between 2000 and 2005 will die before reaching the age of 40. As of 2003, only 48 percent of Mali's population had sustainable access to an improved water source (100 percent had such access in the United States). That year, over 70 percent of Mali's population lived on less than $1 a day, and over 90 percent of Mali's population lived on less than $2 a day. Although the average American born between 1975 and 1979 has completed more than 14 years of schooling (roughly the same for men and women, in both urban and rural areas), the average attainment of the same cohort in Mali is less than two years, with women's attainment less than half that of men, and virtually zero in rural areas. Not surprisingly, the illiteracy rate in Mali (percentage of those aged 15 and above as of 2003) was 81 percent. Taking into account the actual quality of education in the two countries is likely to yield far greater differences.

In short, the general well-being, quality of services, safety, and scope of freedoms and opportunities enjoyed by those born in affluent polities are all far greater, other things being equal, than the opportunities of those born in poor countries. Ours is a world in which disparities of opportunity between citizens of different countries are so great that about half of the population of the world, according to the World Bank, lives "without freedom of action and choice that the better-off take for granted."[10] Although extant citizenship laws do not create these disparities, they perpetuate and reify dramatically differentiated life prospects by reliance on morally arbitrary circumstances of birth, while at the same time camouflaging these crucial distributive consequences by appealing to the presumed naturalness of birth-based membership.

These dramatically differentiated life prospects should disturb not only moral egalitarians, but also free-marketers who believe in rewarding effort and distributing opportunity according to merit, rather than station of birth.[11] As the data provided here documents, the problem of unequal allocation, which has gained plenty of attention in the realm of property, is far more extreme in the realm of hereditary or territorially attributed citizenship. Remarkably, in spite of the conceptual affinity between the intergenerational transfer of property and birthright citizenship, and irrespective of the thousands of pages devoted to debating the justifications for inheritance in property law, there have been few, if any, scholarly attempts to scrutinize the justifications for automatic inheritance of citizenship by birth. The muteness of political and legal theory with respect to the intergenerational transfer of citizenship by the fortuitous location or station of birth becomes all the more astonishing when we consider the incredible gaps in life opportunities perpetuated by birthright citizenship regimes. Such disparity runs far deeper and is infinitely more multifaceted than the material inequalities perpetuated through the intergenerational transfer of fungible wealth. By drawing the analogy from inherited citizenship to intergenerational transfer of property and privilege, we open up a new avenue for the development of just such debate.

Property Theory: Some Key Distinctions

Property as State-Enforced Relations of Entitlement and Duties

Property is notorious for escaping any simple or one-dimensional definition. It is commonly recognized that "although property has to do with tangible and certain intangible 'things' property is not the thing itself."[12] Rather, it is a human-made and multifaceted institution, which creates and maintains certain *relations* among individuals in reference to things.[13] These relations have a special validity in law; a property owner has rights that are valid against the world (rights *in rem*), as distinct from rights *in personam* which are only valid against a specific set of individuals such as those with whom one has contracted. The *in rem* quality provides strong protection to entitlements that get defined as property. This protection, in turn, relies upon collective recognition and enforcement. The collective dimension is important: property rights gain meaning only when they are connected to a system of law and governance that can enforce them.[14] In the modern era, the enforcing body has typically been the state.[15] As Thomas Gray aptly observes, "property must be seen as a web of state-enforced relations of entitlement and duty between persons, some assumed voluntarily and some not."[16] Given its currency in the contemporary moral and legal landscape, the specific content and protection given to a property entitlement has always been (and still is) subject to political contestation. Property relations are thus never immune to reconstructive inquiry whether in law or in philosophy.

Property relations establish a range of enforceable claims. As stated in Wesley Hohfeld's seminal work, these enforceable claims are often described as a "bundle" of rights.[17] Some of the most notable sticks in the bundle include the right to use, to transfer, to delimit access, and so on.[18] As Guido

Calabresi and Douglas Melamed observe in their classic "view from the cathedral," each society or legal system must define who has an enforceable claim in a given entitlement and must further determine which protections, opportunities, and decision-making processes become available to the right-holder.[19]

Modern theories of property extend the concept beyond concrete and tangible objects (my car, your house) to refer to a host of more abstract entitlements (shares in a company, intellectual property in the form of patents and copyrights, professional licenses, genetic information, even folklore practices). Changes in human relations and social values constantly modify our understanding of what counts as protected property.[20] Important questions of allocation come up when we begin to categorize certain relationships as legal property: who owns it, and on what basis? Ownership and possession of property affects people's livelihood, opportunities, and freedoms.[21] Conflicting interests concerning access, use, and control of goods are therefore likely to arise, particularly with respect to items that are scarce relative to the number of claimants or demands that human desires place upon them.[22] In this context, it is useful to draw on Jeremy Waldron's formulation of property relations as offering a "system of rules governing access to and control of [scarce] resources."[23]

When applying these understandings of property to citizenship, perhaps the most obvious parallel is that birthright and naturalization laws create precisely such a system of rules governing access to, and control over, scarce resources (in this case, membership rights and their accompanying benefits). I call this access-defining feature of citizenship its *gate-keeping function.* This function is well-recognized in the literature on political membership: "Every modern state formally defines its citizenry, publicly identifying a set of persons as its members and residually designating all others as noncitizens . . . Every state attaches certain rights and obligations to the status of citizenship."[24] Even in today's world of increased globalization and privatization, determining who shall be granted full membership in the polity still remains an important prerogative of the state.[25] As we shall see in latter chapters, gate-keeping is never absolute or unrestrained. But at present, it does not generate (legally or ethically) an obligation to make the global minimum a correlating duty to the existence of bounded membership. Establishing such a duty as a restraint on the right to exclude is part of what this books aims to achieve.

Although there is a lively discussion among citizenship theorists about the expansion of rights accorded to noncitizens (postnational citizenship), the embryonic development of regional citizenship (the European Union is the prime case study in the literature), and the normative vision of global (or cosmopolitan) citizenship, it is all too easy to ignore the facts on the ground: gaining access to membership status remains crucially important for defining our scope of opportunity, security, and sense of belonging. This observation, which highlights the continued significance of regulated citizenship in today's world, is fully compatible with acknowledging that at some point in the future we might have a different system of dividing political and juridical authority over people and territory, a system that will not be so closely tied to secure membership in this or that country.[26]

Even enthusiastic advocates of post-Westphalian citizenship, such as Richard Falk, concede that at present "[d]espite globalization in its various impacts, the individual overwhelmingly continues to be caught in a statist web of rights, duties, and identities."[27] For instance, international travel still depends on passports issued by sovereign states, "borders are exclusively managed by governmental authority, and an abuse of rights in a foreign country is almost always dealt with by seeking help from one's country of citizenship." Even migration, "to the extent that it is 'legal,' rests on [bounded] notions of territorial sovereignty."[28] In short, although recent years have witnessed a surge in competing and overlapping sources of political authority (both above and below the national level), when it comes to citizenship, states have retained a relatively strong hold over the regulation of their membership boundaries.[29] This observation holds true even in the case that seems to contradict our focus on bounded membership, namely, European citizenship. Here, too, a close look reveals a surprising fact: access to membership at the regional or supranational (European Union) level is still entirely derivative. It is exclusively defined at the member-state level.[30] This reflects in part the existence of an institutional and international structure that privileges the power of interdependent states (even those bound to establish an "ever closer union") to define membership boundaries, which I take as a background condition for my analysis.

Returning to our property analogy, when we explore the realm of citizenship, we soon recognize that what each citizen holds is not a private entitlement to a tangible thing, but a relationship to other members and to a particular (usually a national) government that creates enforceable rights and duties. From the perspective of each member of the polity, reconceptualizing his or her entitlement to citizenship as a complex type of property fits well within the definition of *new property*, a phrase famously coined by Charles Reich referring to public law entitlements as serving the traditional private law purposes of ensuring a baseline of security and dignity to citizens under market-based economies.[31] Unlike traditional forms of wealth, which were held as private property, valuables associated with the public title of citizenship derive specifically from holding a legal status that is dispensed by the state alone. Such entitlement to the status of membership in turn bestows a host of privileges and benefits (as well as certain civic obligations) upon its holders.[32]

Although the value of citizenship is communally generated, the entitlement conferred upon each member is individually held.[33] This intricate combination of individual and collective aspects makes citizenship a particularly complex type of property-like entitlement, with "priceless benefits" as the U.S. Supreme Court memorably put it, adding that "it would be difficult to exaggerate its value and importance."[34] In this legal structure, the state operates as generator and trustee of membership titles, with their critical enabling implications on the life opportunities of its individual members.[35] Each insider differs from the outsiders by virtue of his or her share in the protection conferred only on those counted as citizens and by their right not to be deprived of the valuable good of membership itself.[36] For each member, citizenship further entails a share of ownership and governance of that polity's communal and pooled resources. As such, citizens stand in a special relation to each other and to the collective that they govern. When citizenship is conceived in this way, the distinction between "narrow" and "broad" conceptions of property becomes highly relevant.[37]

The Narrow and Broad Conceptions of Property

The narrow (or "rivalrous") conception treats property as a market commodity that can be sold, traded, or alienated, through voluntary transactions.[38] According to this notion of property, each owner has a near absolute dominion over his or her assets, and is free to dispose of these as he or she sees fits.[39] This vision of property rests on a particular conception of social life, according to which all interpersonal interactions are characterized as "trades," and thus everything may in principle be subject to market transaction.[40] This in turn relies on a possessive individualism worldview, whereby social atomism and unrestricted commodification rule, and where self-interest is the core motivation for human action.[41] In this view, maximum freedom ought to be granted to the right-bearer, whose preferences may only be limited by compelling state interests (in the form, for example, of compensated "takings"), or certain *ex ante* (rather than *ex post*) legal constraints.[42]

In contrast, the broad (or "trusteeship") conception of property views property as part of a web of social and political relations, wherein people depend upon others "not only to thrive but even just to survive."[43] This view of human flourishing dates back to Aristotle and treats property not as an end in itself but as a means toward advancing the commonweal and building relations of trust.[44] Closely related to the distinction between the narrow and broad conception is a disagreement over how best to characterize property's core. For those who emphasize self-interest (the narrow conception), property is understood primarily as entailing the right to exclude others from the use and benefit of what one owns.[45]

This right to exclude privileges the possessive individual who presumably stands solely in market relations to other traders in a laissez-faire society. It allows each person to erect high and enforceable legal boundaries of exclusion around her property, boundaries which operate as *in rem* rights, rights "against the world." In this conception, as Hanoch Dagan and Michael Heller sarcastically observe, each individual is seen as "cloaked in the Blackstonian armor of 'sole and despotic dominion.'"[46] Given its fend-for-yourself ideological bent, the narrow account of property fails to explain situations in which individuals form relations of co-ownership or interdependence. This is a remarkable shortcoming given the current social and economic reality in which co-ownerships, partnerships, shareholding structures and the like, constitute a growing proportion of property relations.

The literature on property, which is mostly dominated by the proponents of the narrow conception, holds in stock plenty of arguments in favor of protecting exclusive and sole ownership. It is argued that this arrangement fosters the owner's independence, dignity, and freedom by creating a zone of privacy within which he or she is protected against the power of the state or a majority of fellow citizens.[47] Even the harshest critics of the narrow version of property, such as Jennifer Nedelsky, concede that it has valuable qualities: "we mean by property that which is recognized as ours and cannot be easily taken away from us."[48] In practice, however, the narrow vision has limited traction in explaining the rise of new property regimes that blend individualized and communal ownership in the co-governance of valuable resources.[49] For instance, there has been a dramatic surge in the number of common property institutions that emphasize cooperation and trust-building among diverse rights-holders by using the law of property to enhance mutually beneficial relationships rather than erecting zones of absolute privacy.[50]

A concrete illustration of this trend is found in the rise of common-interest communities in the United States. It is now estimated that approximately one-fifth of owners of residential housing have chosen to purchase property in housing communities with quasi-democratic governance structures, which typically involve exclusive rights to a dwelling unit and co-ownership of common areas.[51] The rise of organizations such as public corporations and shareholding provide further support for this idea. Such co-ownership calls for the development of institutions and procedures for decision making that take into account conflicts of interest among individuals who must together control or share collective resources. Furthermore, the "impoverished view of property," as the narrow conception is called by its critics, fails to seriously take into account power relations or distributional inequities that this conception of social relations is likely to generate.

The broad conception of property better addresses these complexities. Unlike the narrow vision, it is guided by an understanding of property that involves a two-fold legal mandate: the right to exclude and the right not to be excluded.[52] This interpretation of property is deeply grounded in the history of ideas. The combination of the right to exclude and the right not to be excluded is familiar to the various strands of classic and contemporary democratic, liberal, and republican thought. Although offering different normative visions of the polity, these traditions converge on the following conception: individuals possess inalienable rights to life, liberty, and property.[53] Along these lines, the U.S. Supreme Court famously described citizenship as "a right no less precious than life or liberty."[54] Citizenship is seen as a precious entitlement that is regulated and conferred by the state, and, as such, must receive the highest level of legal protection.[55]

No less significant, the right not to be excluded means that members of the political community are seen as equal partners in the common enterprise of governing the commonweal.[56] They stand in a special interpersonal relationship to each other; they are co-owners or partners in a shared political community. This special relationship represents for each member a right not to be excluded from whatever rights, powers, and privileges attach to such membership. Each member is entitled to enjoy those goods that society has declared for common use and to partake in the governance of the polity.[57] For each person, membership grants an equal share in the commonwealth and its governance. The broad conception further engages in the creation of a host of mechanisms for management, governance, and resolution of conflicts that may arise where more than one person has a stake in a given resource, reserving a wide host of decisions to democratic vote.

More important still for the purposes of our discussion, the right not to be excluded imposes a duty on joint owners to consult with one another, providing each a secured and inalienable "voice," in Albert Hirschman's influential terminology.[58] In the broad conception, we can see how the right not to be excluded imposes an active duty on government to consult with its citizens, as decision makers and stakeholders, in determining how to generate and allocate revenue for necessary government functions as well as how to implement its various redistributive and regulatory functions.[59] Understanding membership entitlement in these terms also enables us to think about the core democratic right of equal participation in collective decision-making processes (the franchise) as perhaps the strongest manifestation of a citizen's right not to be excluded. The franchise provides each right-holder with a concrete and enforceable claim to participate in the governance of the commonwealth, to share its burdens, and ideally, attain a threshold-level of well-being.

In contrast to the narrow interpretation of property that emphasizes despotic tendencies and possessive individualism, the broader conception sees property as a net contributor to our ability to blossom as individuals with dignity and opportunity and as a tool for governing shared resources and advancing the commonweal. This broad trusteeship or stewardship interpretation holds well not only for ourselves, but also for the larger community of members.[60] It is this broader conception that I take on board in asserting that various aspects of distributive justice come to bear once we think of citizenship as a complex form of inherited property.

Property and Citizenship: Several Analogous Functions

Citizenship shares several important characteristics with property, broadly conceived. To begin with, bounded membership provides a textbook example of the combination of a right to exclude and the right not to be excluded. Where citizenship is concerned, I will call the right to exclude "gate-keeping" and the right not to be excluded "opportunity-enhancing." I analyze each in turn.

The Gate-Keeping Function of Citizenship

To borrow from Waldron's definition of property, citizenship crafts a system of rules governing access to and control of a scarce resource, in this case, the precious good of membership in our human communities.[61] It demarcates who is included within the polity and who is excluded from gaining access to its bounty. States in the real world tend to be stringent, if not outright unyielding, in terms of drawing and enforcing the boundaries that distinguish those who belong from those who do not.[62] Every state currently limits access to its citizenship, typically granting automatic entitlement only to a select group of beneficiaries according to ascriptive principles of birthplace and bloodline (*jus soli* and *jus sanguinis* respectively). Even countries such as Canada and the United States, which both have a long tradition of welcoming immigrants, rarely fall below an average of eighty-five to ninety percent of their populations being "natural-born." Focusing on gate-keeping, it is notable that "citizenship is not only an instrument of closure, a prerequisite for the enjoyment of certain rights, or for participation in certain types of interaction. It is also an object of closure, a status to which access is restricted."[63] In other words, polities tend to follow through on their right to exclude. This is in part based on the rationale, explicated most eloquently by Michael Walzer in *Spheres of Justice,* that once a person is included in the actual community of membership, that person is entitled (or will eventually be entitled) to the complementary right not to be excluded from any additionally attendant rights and privileges. This simultaneous quality of the right to exclude and the right not to be excluded precisely corresponds to the twin elements I identified earlier as central to the broad conception.[64]

Despite much academic fanfare about the demise of borders, in practice, entry into a foreign land is still highly restrictive for most of the world's population, especially for those arriving from low-income or politically unstable countries.[65] Only citizens have an unconditional right to enter and stay in the state (and even this principle has been under pressure in the post 9/11 years); noncitizens do not.[66] In today's world, international mobility is anxiously guarded by border enforcement agencies whose main task is to monitor, regulate, and ultimately restrict unwanted admission.[67]

Just as with property, for citizenship the right to exclude is limited in practice. There remains a set of obligations on the admitting state to the individual seeking entry which are nonetheless balanced by the range of legal sanctions that can be imposed against a person who seeks to "trespass" or enter the territory without permission. The ultimate sanction for such breach, whether in property or citizenship law, involves physical removal from the estate/territory (unless such unauthorized admission is later regularized by the host country or the operation of its laws, a point to which I return in Chapter 6). Although certain restrictions apply, both systems create and maintain legal boundaries that are backed up by force. These boundaries are neither natural nor apolitcal. Instead, their erection and coercive enforcement protect the interests of those designated as legitimate title bearers, while imposing severe legal sanctions against those who are perceived (by these very same laws) as unauthorized entrants who breach them.

Both property and citizenship regimes share another important characteristic: they typically preserve unequal structures of holdings that tend to concentrate control over wealth. In the context of property, we find volumes of competing arguments that attempt to justify this unequal system of accumulation and transmission. No similar elaborations or theoretical justifications are found with respect to citizenship. There are also no convincing explanations for why a draconian system of legal exclusion can legitimately be perpetuated by reliance on the "natural" event of birth in the conferral of membership entitlement. Thinking through this analogy yields yet another surprising revelation: whereas the principle of automatic and irrevocable birthright has been roundly criticized as a basis for the intergenerational transfer of property, the entail-like transmission of citizenship has largely escaped similar scrutiny. That is the case despite the fact that such transmission is relied upon by governments (rather than a select class of estate owners)—thus inviting more rigorous, rather than more lenient, standards of review and accountability. More important still, citizenship as a form of inherited property affects a far greater number of individuals in the world, making it quantitatively and qualitatively far more crucial today for discussions of global justice and equality, than any antiquated—and in most countries now prohibited—form of perpetual transfer of landed estates.

The Opportunity-Enhancing Function of Citizenship

So far, I have emphasized citizenship's gate-keeping function, or the right to exclude. Fortunately, citizenship does more than delimit access and preserve unequal accumulation of wealth and power in the hands of birthright heirs. It also includes the right not to be excluded. Just as fiercely as it externally excludes nonmembers, citizenship can also act as an internal leveler of opportunity by providing the basic enabling conditions for members to fulfill their potential. The argument for such inclusion is simple yet powerful: citizens enjoy these entitlements, which are *of right,* on the basis of formal equality of status, which forms the bedrock of their membership in the community.[68] This I label citizenship's *opportunity-enhancing* (or enabling) function.

Like other types of property, citizenship allows its possessor to exercise freedom and autonomy through what is legally his or hers and to protect their rights against the world. But the right not to be excluded goes beyond this negative liberty. It involves a positive dimension as well. This positive component entails, just like property, a bundle of sticks. This translates, at minimum, into the security of holding an irrevocable membership status and its incumbent social and political benefits. Save in exceptional circumstances, this security of status cannot be denied or unilaterally taken away by one's government or fellow citizens.[69] This stands in sharp contrast to the vulnerable situation of nonmembers who have already become part of the social fabric of the community, but lack precisely the property-like protections that attach to citizenship.

But the enabling function of citizenship guarantees more than just protection from deportation.[70] For each member, it bestows the right to participate in the governance of the polity. It further provides, at least in its ideal type, the threshold condition of freedom-from-want as another classic expression of the right not to be excluded.[71] It is here that Reich's argument about treating governmental benefits as property to which citizens hold a rightful claim is connected to the idea of providing essentials (both substantive and procedural) for basic security and independence for members of the body politick.[72] Rather than merely operating to restrict access through its gate-keeping function, citizenship can be seen as an enabling institution that embodies our collective judgments about the shape of a fair society, offers members benefits and entitlements on an equal basis and, at the same time, assists in fostering their well-being.[73]

In many respects, the opportunity-enhancing function is far more powerful in the context of citizenship than it is for most other types of property, material or abstract. Such entitlement guarantees that each member will enjoy "a share in the protection conferred on the group as a whole over some asset and its wealth-potential."[74] Such a protection implies (even on the narrow reading) that each individual will gain a fair share of equal liberties, access to public goods, and nondiscriminatory participation in the economic and labor markets.[75] The broader conception would, however, likely endorse a more robust conception of enabling. Shared citizenship could include the duty to abolish absolute deprivation and seek a standard of relative prosperity in its place. Such a broad conception could further suggest that part of the state's role as creator and enforcer of membership entails the obligation to mitigate inequalities among social actors and that participation in a common polity entails an expectation of generosity by those citizens with greater authority and wealth toward those without it. This expectation flows from the basic premise that there is a joint responsibility of all citizens to their larger community. The idea of enabling might also lend support to an interpretation of full membership that requires the political community to provide each member with those basic life standards and infrastructure services (clean water, police protection, health, education, shelter, and the like) that are seen as preconditions for achieving a decent life.[76]

None of these markers of opportunity, which represent in their own ways different manifestations of the right-not-to-be-excluded, are premised on a strict idea of equalization of *results*. Instead, citizenship's enabling function is better understood as a means by which we can shift emphasis onto the goal of leveling the ground and achieving equalization of *starting points*. As such, it is fully compatible with the moral intuition that people can justifiably claim the rewards of their enterprise as a result of relevant efforts.[77] However, unlike the narrow conception of property, which emphasizes the self-interest of individual traders at the expense of losing sight of the existence of a community, the broad conception of property treats the success of individuals as being predicated, to some degree, on larger societal conditions.[78] In well-off polities, this is often translated into a robust set of conditions such as effective government, the rule of law, protection against foreign invasion, domestic peace and security, and stable markets, as well as additional supporting conditions such as public investment in infrastructure, higher education, arts and culture, and various social services.[79] Although the precise definition of what is included in the "basket" of citizenship's benefits may vary (even among OECD countries), a societal commitment to providing the basics differs sharply from the narrow, fend-for-oneself conception. The latter focuses on negative liberty as a way to restrict the encroaching state; the former treats citizenship's opportunity-enhancing function as corresponding with positive liberty as well as creating an environment that is conducive to fulfilling the capabilities of those who belong to the body politick.

Undoubtedly, meeting these requirements imposes a heavy burden that is not fully borne even by the world's most affluent and generous polities, let alone by resource-strapped or corrupt governments. But it serves as a normative yardstick against which we can measure how countries fare in their enabling commitment.[80] There's another message to be drawn from this as well, and one which is crucial to my central argument: automatic entitlement to political membership as encoded in today's birthright citizenship laws has *itself* become a valuable "property," generating for its holders secure access to certain common goods and the enjoyment of the basic infrastructures that permit human flourishing, in addition to establishing for those who count as members an enforceable right to participate in the governance of their shared polity.

Membership boundaries that extend across generational lines can now be viewed in a more complex light: not only are these boundaries sustained for cultivating bonds of identity and belonging (as the conventional argument holds), they also serve a crucial role in preserving restricted access to the community's prosperity and power. The latter is jealously guarded at the juncture of transfer of "ownership" from the present generation of citizens to its progeny. In other words, birthright citizenship mechanisms provide cover through their presumed naturalness for what is essentially a major (and currently untaxed) transmission of wealth and enabling resources from one generation to another. Ours is a world of scarcity; when an affluent community systemically delimits access to membership and its derivative benefits on the basis of a strict heredity system that effectively resembles an entail structure of preserving privilege and advantage in the hands of the few, those who are excluded have reason to complain.

Entailed Property and Birthright Citizenship: Analogous Transmissions?

If we were to look for a pattern that closely resembles the structure of birthright transmission of entitlement, we would find it, somewhat surprisingly, in the property inheritance regimes that date back to medieval England.[81] There, we find the now long discredited institution of the *fee tail* (or entail). In the language of the early common law, fee tail involved a landed estate that automatically descended from A to "B and the heirs of his body" and continued so passing through the descending line in order to keep the landed estates squarely in the hands of a small elite of powerful and wealthy families.[82] Technically, entail was a legal means of restricting future succession of property to the descendants of a designated person. It offered a tool to preserve land in the possession of dynastic families by entrenching birthright succession, while at the same time tying the hands of future generations from altering or alienating the estate they inherited from their predecessors.

The history of the entail dates back to the early medieval period. It was already in use by 1285, when the English Parliament enacted the *De Donis Conditionalibus* statute in response to petitions from "landowners who wanted to bestow on a child and the heirs of his or her body an inheritable estate in land that could not be alienated by fee simple."[83] The *De Donis* statute thus secured a special interest in land, which, as John Orth explains, created a distinctive pattern of succession whereby each successive holder was limited to use of the land for life without the power to alter the chain of transmission or to dispose of the property.[84] The purpose of the entail was to keep the estate strictly within the possession of the heirs of the landed aristocracy in a social order where the hold on land was intimately tied up with political authority.[85] Such birthright transmission of wealth and power was designed to be infinite in duration, transferring the land from one generation to another in perpetuity.

Successive generations, that is, the aristocratic progeny, were not always pleased with the restrictions that entail attached to the inherited estate. English lawyers eventually developed a method known as "common recovery," which permitted inheritors to "dock" (or "break") the entail and "seize" the estate, thus effectively removing the original restraint that ran to A for life, then to B and the heirs of his or her body, then to C and the heirs of his or her body, and so on.[86] Such legal maneuvering, which permitted the chain of transmission from one generation to another to be broken, was eventually approved by the English courts in the landmark 1472 decision of *Taltarum's Case*.[87]

Interestingly, the legal institution of entail later migrated to North America with the English colonists, who created estates in fee tail, primarily in the southern colonies such as Virginia, Georgia, and North Carolina.[88] One of history's little ironies was that it became harder for descendants of landed estates in the American colonies to dock or cut off the entail than for their counterparts in England to do so because certain colonies, such as Virginia, specifically enacted statutes that prohibited common recovery.[89] Thus, once an entail was created, the transfer of property to the heirs of one's body, and to them alone, "was of indefinite duration—the original perpetuity, in fact."[90]

It should come as no surprise that this aristocratic method for preserving land in the sole dominion of certain families, which perpetuated their disproportionate wealth and political power, sparked the ire of American revolutionary reformers. Thomas Jefferson, for example, led the effort to abolish the entail in his home state of Virginia by proposing the legal extinguishment of entailed estates to the Virginia Assembly in 1776. As many legal historians have observed, Jefferson counted the introduction of this legislation among his foremost achievements.[91] What is less well-known is that James Madison, the champion of property rights in the new republic, also supported the abolition of fee tail in Virginia and elsewhere in the United States.[92] Madison, like Jefferson, held that the "abolishment of fee tail [would] shorten the longevity of inherited wealth and thereby lesson the 'proportion of idle proprietors' in Virginia society."[93]

For American republican lawyers, the hereditary transfer of privilege in the form of the "entailment of land appeared to be [one of] the most glaring vestiges of a corrupt past."[94] It was associated with feudal encrustations on the common law that preserved and perpetuated England's social hierarchy. For Jefferson, explains John Hart, abolishing the entail "was a key part of a 'system' of reforms 'by which every fibre would be eradicated of ancient . . . or future aristocracy and a foundation laid for a government truly republican.'"[95] It was a central component of this project because entailed transfer of estates by creating a bloodline of land owners diminished opportunity for those who did not enjoy such inheritance. Such exclusivity therefore defeated the broader social and economic agenda of the "republican laws of descent and distribution," designed to gradually contribute to "equalizing the property of the citizens."[96] What is more, the concern was not only with accumulation of great wealth, but with the *permanence* of such riches in the hands of certain families. Such permanence was the result of the *birthright* nature of entail, which guaranteed entitlement to successive descendants simply by virtue of their status as "the heirs of [the original landholder] and his body." No other criteria were imposed, nor could a later generation alter this automatic grant. This led to a concern, already expressed by William Blackstone in his magisterial 1766 *Commentaries on the Laws of England,* that the Nth generation of heirs to an entail might become morally corrupt, lazy, and "disobedient when they knew they could not be set aside."[97]

In America, instead of cultivating a civic republican ethics of virtue, the perpetuation of property in certain families through mechanisms such as the entailment of land created a nascent American aristocracy.[98] What is more, as Blackstone predicted, heirs of such families knew that they could not be cut off from the chain of birthright transmission; the republican concern was that they would become disobedient and socially unproductive members of the polity.[99] If individuals were to be prevented from inheriting great wealth in perpetuity, irrespective of their talent, work ethic, and virtue, the entail would have to be replaced by a more egalitarian distribution of property.

Another dimension of the critique of entail focused not so much on the moral character of the birthright recipient, but on inefficiency; those who were guaranteed wealth as a matter of birthright, had little incentive to maximize the value of their estates. The preamble to the 1776 Virginia statute that abolished entailed estates did not shy away from explicitly expressing such concerns: "the perpetuation of property in certain families, by means of gifts made to them in fee taille, is contrary to good policy, . . . [it] discourages the holder thereof from taking care and improving the same [the estate], and sometime does injury to the morals of the youth."[100] An even more pointed argument about inequality is articulated in the 1784 legislative act of North Carolina that similarly abolished the fixed and perpetual transfer of wealth and opportunity by birthright. Its Preamble states that "entails of estates tend only to raise the wealth and importance of particular families and individuals, giving them an unequal and undue influence in a republic."[101]

This opposition to the perpetual birthright transmission of entitlement was extended, at least conceptually, into the realm of citizenship. As James Kettner argues, naturalization (the process of volitional admission to the polity rather than birthright membership) provided the model of republican citizenship in this period.[102] This vision was enacted into law relatively early in the history of the republic, in 1790, only a few months after ratification of the constitution.[103] Obviously, at this time the definition of eligibility for inclusion in the body politic was itself deeply laden with race and gender-based exclusions: full membership was reserved exclusively for the "free white person."[104] But the notion of acquiring (rather than inheriting) citizenship was not predicated only on racial and gendered categories. Something else had to be established. According to a new model, a nonmember who voluntary and affirmatively decided to join the republic was adopted into the polity as a full member after becoming part of its social and economic life and taking an oath of allegiance. This process of postbirth admission, which emphasized agency and volition, indeed seemed to better reflect the ideal of political membership as conceived by the republican and liberal traditions, which emphasized choice and consent of the governed as the root of legitimate authority.

This sentiment informs an oft-cited passage in John Locke's *Second Treatise of Government:* "a child is born a subject of no country or government." When that child comes to the age of discretion, continued Locke, "then he is a free-man, at liberty what government he will put himself under; what body politick he will unite himself to."[105] This rejection of imposed, or ascriptive membership, finds striking parallels in early American republican thought, and as Jefferson fittingly formulates in the context of access to volitional citizenship, "all men [have a right to] depart from the country in which chance, not choice has placed them."[106] Such insistence on severing the accidents of station of birth in assigning political membership (an ideal, which we must not forget, was initially conceived to apply merely to a small fraction of the population, namely free, white men) still remains a far cry from the reality that is in place under the current world system for the vast majority of the world's population. What is particularly surprising is that the alternative path that has been chosen (reliance on automatic and hereditary transfer of membership entitlement) resembles some of the most deeply criticized, and ultimately abolished, feudal mechanisms of inheritance: the entail.

Whereas the archaic institution of the hereditary transfer of entailed estates has been discredited in the realm of property, in the conferral of citizenship we still find a structure that strongly resembles it. Inherited entitlement to citizenship not only remains with us today; it is by far the most important avenue through which individuals are sorted into different political communities. Birthright principles strictly regulate the entail of political membership for the vast majority of the global population. Membership attributed through accident of birth secures the transmission of membership entitlement for a limited group of beneficiaries, either on the basis of bloodline or birthplace. These beneficiaries, in turn, gain the right to pass the benefit along to the next generation by inheritance, and so forth: it is this structure that effectively recreates the "fee tail" in the transmission of citizenship.[107]

To recognize the surprising similarities in form and function between birthright citizenship and inherited property of this particular kind is to identify a striking exception to the modern trend away from ascribed status.[108] This birthright-transmission mechanism, which is still exercised today, cannot be dismissed as a mere historical accident, given that the question of legitimizing political authority and property is central to the liberal, democratic and civic-republican intellectual traditions. This only makes the link that persists between political membership and station of birth—a connection that has been both ignored and taken for granted—ever more puzzling and in urgent need of a coherent explanation.

Whereas the delineation of enforceable membership boundaries (citizenship's gate-keeping function) has been challenged in recent years as an offense to the universality of our shared humanity, both proponents and opponents of bounded membership have paid scant attention to the crucial wealth-preserving aspect of hereditary citizenship—the dramatically differential opportunity structures to which individuals are entitled, based on the allocation of political membership according to predetermined circumstances of birth. This is a blind spot of citizenship theory. Unlike the critical accounts of entailed property regimes, from Blackstone to Jefferson to Madison, scholars of citizenship regimes have neglected to turn their gaze to the largely analogous form of strict intergenerational transfer that still persists in the realm of birthright transmission of membership entitlement. The account presented here, which establishes a conceptual analogy between property and citizenship, brings to the fore familiar criticisms that have been leveled against antiquated and unequal property transfer regimes in order to highlight the global distributive implications of prevalent structures of citizenship transmission. Such an inquiry is ever more urgent given that a transmission mechanism of this kind has, in a world like our own, the particularly pernicious effect of interfering with, and often capping forever, the life chances of individuals.

My critical account of birthright citizenship as a complex type of inherited property is not targeted against the political ideal and institution of citizenship. Full membership in a self-governing polity grants invaluable protections for the right-holder, especially so for the less advantaged: it guarantees for even the most vulnerable within a given society the fundamental security of an inalienable right to membership, the cultural and psychological benefits that attach to such a protected membership status, and the power to make claims in collective decision making as an equal stakeholder. In a world riddled with deep social and economic inequality like our own, the value of these protections cannot be overestimated.

Such recognition should not prevent us, however, from condemning the assumption that reliance on birth in the transmission of the political membership somehow resolves the serious boundary making and wealth-preserving dilemmas that attach to such entailed transfers. The crucial point here is that the analogy between inherited property and birthright citizenship permits us to see the latter in the light of the former: as a carefully regulated system for limiting access to scarce resources to those that "naturally" belong within its bounds as the heirs, not of "one's body," but of the *body politick* itself.

To treat birthright citizenship as if it were a special kind of property is to open the door to the application of core insights from inheritance theory to the citizenship arena. In this way, we can begin to address the inequality of starting points that attaches to the intergenerational transfer of membership entitlements according to birthright citizenship. Having formulated the puzzle of birthright citizenship and demonstrated that it hits hardest in perhaps the least expected realm of social life—namely, that of *political* membership, a realm we typically associate with participation, voice, and accountability, but certainly *not* inherited office or station of birth—it is now time to open up the debate, hearing the range of responses that could be leveled at the analogy between birthright citizenship and inherited property.

CHAPTER TWO

Abolishing versus Resurrecting Borders: Moving Beyond the Binary Options

> Our mind is capable of passing beyond the dividing line we have drawn for it. Beyond the pairs of opposites of which the world consists, other, new insights begin.
>
> HERMANN HESSE (1877–1962)

IN THIS CHAPTER, my focus shifts from framing and explaining the puzzle of birthright citizenship to seeking remedies for the acute distributional problems that attach to this strict system of membership allocation in an unequal world. The previous chapter showed just how the present allocation system has a very real effect on all our lives: it solidifies and naturalizes a system of unearned privilege, which, in turn, perpetuates stark global inequalities in life conditions, choices, and opportunities. I will explore several possible responses to these deep-seated problems, each staking out a different vision of the future of citizenship in a globalizing world.

I begin by elaborating on two visions that demarcate a rigid dichotomy: *abolishing bounded membership altogether* versus *resurrecting ever higher and less penetrable borders*. These positions define contrasting trajectories: one envisages a world without borders, where citizenship is seen as a global affiliation to which every person has access by virtue of membership in the larger family of humanity, whereas the contrasting vision adopts a strictly protectionist, or fortress interpretation of sovereign self-determination. After considering the options of abolishing or refortifying borders, I will explain why neither offers a fully adequate response to the challenges that are currently attached to birthright citizenship.

Abolishing bounded membership altogether risks forsaking the presently inalienable properties that attach to citizenship—a secure legal status, an enforceable bundle of rights, and a meaningful source of collective identity, to name but a few examples—without ensuring that a similar content will be replicated under an alternative regime of world citizenship. The resurrect-the-border option, for its part, artificially and dangerously ignores the reality of growing economic and political interdependence that binds us ever more closely to those beyond our immediate membership boundaries. It relies instead on an unrealistic and unstable, not to mention morally unappealing, fortress mentality of building ever more fearsome blockades around our jurisdictions and dispatching military-like brigades to aggressively exclude those deemed unwanted from our protected territory.

These serious shortcomings lead me to explore several alternatives that move beyond the binary logic of either erasing or re-erecting borders. Specifically, over the course of this chapter and the next, I identify four such options: (1) commodifying citizenship; (2) "unbundling" its components; (3) reallocating membership titles through more open admission policies; and (4) redistributing opportunity with the goal of improving the enabling function of citizenship everywhere. I will argue in Chapter 3 that the latter option—applied to the realm of citizenship through the idea of the birthright privilege levy—provides the most viable and balanced remedy to the problem at stake. In the final part of this chapter I analyze the options of commodification and unbundling, demonstrating that, despite their very different starting points, both lead to the erosion of the important role that democratic governance has in shaping membership and its associated benefits. In turn, this may lead to a splintering of the resources and protections that we currently enjoy as equal citizens. The main concern here is that once broken up, the collective achievements of citizenship, just like Humpty Dumpty, may never be put together again.

Two Extreme Solutions and their Limitations

Citizenship literature has witnessed the proliferation of prophetic arguments telling us that the deconstruction of national borders is imminent and that we shall soon bear witness to an alternative worldwide or cosmopolitan conception of political membership. Although there are significant variations on this theme, they ultimately thrust forward the conclusion that citizenship is being displaced within and beyond the nation-state level and, as a matter of justice, ought to be reallocated globally in the most expansive of ways: namely, world citizenship. At the other end of the spectrum we find the resurrect-the-border model of response, which embraces erecting ever higher walls to restrict the flow of those defined as noncitizens into predefined territorial and membership units. Various proposals stake out a middle ground, such as managed migration solutions, multilevel governance regimes, cross-border democratic participation, linking international mobility to development efforts, to name but a few. This range of options illustrates that presently there are no simple and widely accepted answers with which to respond to the challenge of "re-imagining the political community."[1] For the sake of analytical clarity, however, it is helpful for us to focus on the world citizenship and the resurrect-the-border models because they represent the two opposite ends of the spectrum: a vision of a utopian world without borders on the one hand and a fortress paradigm of sovereign self-determination that further locks in disparities between jurisdictions on the other.

World Citizenship

One alternative to the uncritical acceptance of the intimate alliance between birth and political membership is to advocate the abolition of borders and bounded membership, embracing instead a concept of world citizenship.[2] In theory, this option appears to offer a perfect resolution to the problem of the arbitrary nature by which citizenship is currently assigned. Instead of perpetuating privilege and disadvantage through inherited membership entitlement in different countries, all individuals would hold an equal status as members of a political authority of a specifically global kind. Thomas Pogge best describes this vision, which he calls legal cosmopolitanism, as being committed "to a concrete political ideal of a global order under which all persons have equivalent legal rights and duties, that is, are fellow citizens of a universal republic."[3]

A muscular vision of world citizenship stands in a zero-sum relationship to national (or any other level of bounded) membership; new forms of citizenship are seen as "actually or ideally displacing the old."[4] I later challenge this zero-sum assumption, but for now suffice it to say that this vision of world citizenship, which almost inevitably implies that there soon emerge a unified federal structure or a worldwide "bureaucratic command government," is unattractive for several reasons.[5] For one, the remedy is too drastic; it might well amount to throwing out the baby with the bath water.[6] To remove borders altogether is to lose an important feature of modern citizenship: namely, the entitlement possessed by each individual to enjoy secure legal standing in the home community to which she belongs as an equal and in which she has title as a full participant in the governance of the commonwealth.[7] While it is not impossible to imagine that such legal standing and participation might one day be replicated at the global level, it is not clear that world citizenship ought to be regarded as an aim. If we believe that the regulation and articulation of many aspects of our collective life properly belong at competing and potentially overlapping levels or layers of governance (the local, national, regional, transnational, cross-sectional, and so on), such a goal becomes even less attractive. In its ultimate manifestation, the ideal of world citizenship stands not as a complement to these other layers of membership and participation, but as its stark alternative.[8] Redrawing the world map de novo by diminution and erasure of the various membership lines that provide us meaning and context is not only an unrealistic option in a world of entrenched borders and interests, but also a dangerously top-down approach that may spectacularly backfire, unless we have some firm guarantees of its prospective success. Unfortunately, no such assurances are currently on offer.[9] The abrupt removal of citizenship's boundaries, may also remove many of its enabling capacities without guaranteeing a better mechanism of leveling opportunity globally.[10]

If all that citizenship stood for was the right to exclude (the narrow vision), without the complementary right not to be excluded (the broad vision), this outright abolitionist vision could arguably be defended as a worthy path toward eradicating the problem of "tying people to the land of their birth," as Joseph Carens memorably put it.[11] However, political membership cannot be so easily reduced to any single characteristic, as I seek to demonstrate over the course of this book. A vision based on a unitary, world government, in lieu of the panoply of more pluralistic membership communities is highly problematic.[12] What is more, transferring the weight of political membership from a bounded community to the global scale risks washing away the entire collective identity aspect embedded in the various "portals" of citizenship as we currently understand it. It may also lead to the disintegration of the social bonds and mutual responsibilities that, through joint action and decision making, help bind people together and motivate them to redistribute internally the benefits of membership in a relatively stable and self-ruling political community.[13] Another set of concerns relates to the potential cultural and social capital losses that are likely to occur if memories are all that remain of our rich and diverse forms of modern statehood. Each country's distinct and inevitably complex history, identity narratives, political struggles, social experiments, linguistic diversity, and so on, would potentially be lost. Some have further argued that the proper functioning of democracy itself to a certain extent relies on boundaries which help define who is representative to whom and who is accountable to whom.[14] Creating common institutions that serve the cross-sectional interests of a heterogeneous constituency is seen as equally important, thus addressing potential collective action problems of trust, risk, and the motivation to contribute to the larger collective.[15] Political economists, for their part, have stressed the importance of scale for economizing on the costs of administrating a political system, in terms of aggregating individual preferences in a democracy or executing a chosen public policy. These costs are likely to increase with the size of the territory and citizenry over which authority is exercised.[16]

Finally, arguments in favor of a world citizenship model remain notoriously abstract. Typically, they lack even the minimum level of institutional concreteness that is needed to enable this model of new world-state membership status to work in practice.[17] No answers are provided to even basic queries, such as what type of benefits and obligations global citizenship would bestow upon its members, which governance structures it would entail, what administrative procedures it would follow, what equality guarantees its citizens would enjoy, and so on. It also remains to be clarified whether (and if so, how) meaningful opposition could be articulated in the context of a mega-state bureaucracy of unprecedented proportions. Similar concerns arise when contemplating the level of autonomy that minority communities, or even smaller nations, would obtain in a global-citizenship structure, given that their limited numbers would make it difficult to win binding concessions through majoritarian politics.[18] Furthermore, where would we escape to if we deeply disagreed with the foundational political choices and actions adopted in our name by fellow members of the world polity? Ironically, we might find ourselves more exposed to the "tyranny of the majority" or "soulless despotism" (as Kant put it) in this brave new borderless world than in our current, imperfect, bounded polities.

It thus requires a great leap of faith to assume that a new concept of world citizenship will inevitably prove to be more democratic or egalitarian than the current alternatives. This is a serious concern that defenders of world citizenship from a legal cosmopolitan perspective are yet to convincingly address. Removing membership boundaries *tout court* may backfire miserably by crippling the opportunity-enhancing (or enabling) work that bounded citizenship currently supports within existing polities.[19] Changing the *locus* of citizenship does not guarantee, by itself, a more just distribution of wealth, voice, or opportunity worldwide. The concern here is that if citizenship were to become a "flat" membership status, then we might see a thinning out and watering down of the very contents associated with the concept rather than a global application of the relatively robust and successful formula of redistribution and mutual responsibility which characterize the self-governing polity that has been achieved (however imperfectly) at the domestic level.

Resurrect the Border

Diametrically opposed to the world-citizenship model is the position taken by those who seek to refortify existing borders and strengthen the distinction between "us" and "them." This resurrect-the-border argument uses the naturalizing masks of *jus soli* and *jus sanguinis* to reify the distinction between the legitimate property holder (the citizen) and the illegitimate trespasser (the alien). It is fueled by a deep sense of crisis or loss of control over borders, which requires in the eyes of its proponents the adoption of immediate and tough measures to regulate the international movement of people.[20] If borders are refortified, it is argued, each polity can then focus on its own challenges, instead of meddling in or trying to ameliorate the harms caused by other states' problems. *Prima facie,* this technique of isolation makes it possible to ignore, or treat as irrelevant, the needs and concerns of those who are legally and physically excluded (through the combined effects of hereditary citizenship, regulated admission, and guarded territorial borders) from our jurisdiction of membership, care, and responsibility.

In this respect, the resurrect-the-border option resembles a variant of the narrow conception of property; it highlights and almost exclusively prioritizes the right-to-exclude function of bounded membership. In this view, owners are perceived to hold absolute dominion, permitting them to ignore the social relations and web of interactions that ultimately maintain the security of their title. Citizenship regimes, just like regimes governing property, represent a form of power, however; the principles governing acquisition and transfer inevitably affect the interests not only of members but also of nonmembers.[21] In the current age, no country is an island. We do not live alone, and members of wealthy polities in particular must take account of the fact that their inherited membership entitlements do not exist in a vacuum. The barriers to admission erected through reliance on ascriptive factors of blood and soil in bestowing citizenship (combined with guarded and resurrected borders) create coercive effects on those trying to get in.[22] Given that the vast majority of the world's population remain excluded from well-off polities under the current birthright regime, it quickly becomes clear that neglecting their needs and interests simply because extant laws define them as nonmembers is not only morally wrong; it is also politically unwise. One can only hope that we will not have to learn this lesson the hard way. Of the many worse-case scenarios to ponder here, consider the possibility of experiencing a twenty-first–century worldwide economic crisis which will make the U.S.-lead depression of the 1920s and 1930s pale in comparison. The point here is not to scaremonger but to insist that, even from the perspective of those concerned about loss of control, a plausible argument can be made in favor of preempting such a crisis before it unravels rather than naively assuming that barricaded and resurrected borders can provide security and stability in case of a calamity on a global scale.

Instead of responding directly to these substantive challenges in a world of increased interdependence, proponents of the resurrect-the-border approach prefer to retreat behind a curtain of formalistic arguments. For instance, they emphasize the absence of an international human right to freedom of mobility across national borderlines (with the exception of providing immediate relief to asylum seekers escaping persecution) or the lack of any "hard law" commitment to establishing a worldwide safety net below which no one should be allowed to fall.[23] True, determining who shall enter and remain on its territory does remain an important prerogative of the state, although this is no longer seen as the impenetrable bastion of sovereignty that it was in the past.[24] Similarly, we face no shortage of visionary ideals and blueprints for establishing a global threshold of subsistence and development for the betterment of all. Perhaps the most familiar example here is the UN Millennium Declaration (ushered in in 2000 at the largest-ever gathering of world leaders), which has since been translated into a roadmap of concrete action goals. Known as the Millennium Development Goals, this eight-point plan includes core priorities such as eradicating extreme poverty and hunger, achieving universal primary education, promoting gender equality, reducing child mortality, and so on.[25] The sticking point remains whether to treat such commitments as voluntary or mandatory. Governments, multinational corporations, and various private and public actors may choose to assist the residents of other countries by means of foreign aid, trade, charity, and investment, if they so wish. But, at present, no norm of international law requires them to do so.

Ultimately, however, defenders of refortified borders cannot remain blind to the fact that we live in a world of increased interdependence in which no polity is fully immune to the effects of events occurring outside its borders—be they civil war, currency meltdown, or environmental disaster. It is perhaps the implicit acknowledgment of such interdependence that leads proponents to seek refuge behind increasingly high walls.[26] To erect such walls, many countries have in recent years adopted a set of interrelated policy measures: significantly restricting their immigration laws; allocating greater resources and personnel to land border control; tightening admission restrictions; entering regional agreements to establish "smart borders;" building virtual and actual fences along the perimeter of their territorial edges; and vowing to get tough on illegal immigration.[27] Clearly not designed to remedy the global-distributive deficit of birthright citizenship, these defensive measures are perhaps best interpreted as anticipatory responses to a potential scenario in which significant emigration pressures will be brought to bear by the world's less prosperous and less stable regions, where the bulk of the global population resides. As Bimal Ghosh observes, "no other source of tension and anxiety has been more powerful [in the west] than the fear, both real and perceived, of huge waves of future emigration from poor and weak states in the years and decades to come."[28] Many of these fears remain unfounded, but this is beside the point.[29] Refortified borders are perceived, in this context, as essential building blocks in the larger toolbox of strategies to insulate affluent, stable, rule-of-law countries from the threats of uncontrolled immigration, national security threats, ethnic and religious strife, poverty, disease, war, and despair, that seem to plague much of the world. As one scholar bluntly asserts, "the first world more and more sees the second either as a threat or a Pandora's box of insoluble problems, for whom nothing much positive can be done but from which one should above all be isolated, so as not to sink into its quick sands or be contaminated by its illnesses."[30]

These fears may nourish an extreme, Hobbesian-survivalist variant of absolutist exclusion. The obvious problem with this intense manifestation of the resurrect-the border approach lies in the real concern that it may be fueled by (and in turn inflame) xenophobic, often racist, anti-immigrant or antiminority sentiments. It may also create a rift among citizens, who may question the true membership standing of some (due to their ethnic or national background, religious affiliation, ideological leaning, and so on), and thus create what I have elsewhere called the "degrees of citizenship."[31] Concerns about such internal rift and discrimination or a category of second-class citizenship are among the oldest in the book; their study has occupied some of the brightest scholars from the fields of political science, sociology, law, and philosophy.[32] In the history of citizenship, the revolt against second-class citizenship has been a powerful tool for mobilization, leading, at crucial junctures, "to the extension of existing rights to new groups, thus broadening the body politic—the community of members."[33] Formal inclusion, however, has never been enough to guard against the painful experience of exclusion and alienation by members of minority communities who are subtly yet persistently categorized as alien, dangerous, and threatening; a "fifth-column," to refer to a familiar catch phrase.[34] In the post 9/11 era, the reality of these disturbing cracks in citizenship as a shared marker of identity and rights has become all too vividly apparent.[35]

Rejecting these divisive tendencies, others have argued in favor of regulated yet penetrable borders, which permit cross-frontier mobility so long as it is controlled by the relevant admitting entity. Under this approach, it is permissible for each polity to unilaterally seal the border under certain circumstances, such as an extreme national security crisis that may call for drastic though short-lived measures. A classic example of this pattern at work is the self-imposed blockade that the United States enforced on its borders immediately after the September 11 attacks.[36] The more complex judgment calls inevitably arise in times of peace, when no immediate threat is on the horizon. Here, we typically find those in favor of semiclosed borders appeal to ethical particularism or the priority of special ties and duties owed to fellow citizens and co-residents of our country—in whatever way such membership boundaries are defined.[37] Although presenting an array of arguments to make their case, the common strategy shared by defenders of regulated (but not impenetrable borders) is to minimize the extent to which current practices of inclusion and exclusion rely on the legal construction of citizenship's automatic transfer according to accidents of birth. In this way, the boundaries of the political community are implicitly reconstituted as a natural given. This allows for a shift in focus from the dilemma of the chance attribution of birthright citizenship to questions concerning how best to protect the prosperity, security, and freedom of those who already belong as full members of the collective. Under such conditions, little room is left for contemplating the arbitrariness or fairness of extant membership rules or the (in)justice of birthright principles. Similarly, debates concerning the potentially detrimental distributional effects of *jus soli* and *jus sanguinis* principles are generally inhibited.

Returning to the actual practice of polities in the real world, it is important to note that even taken on its own merits, the policy argument for resurrecting the borders suffers acute inconsistencies. First of all, the fortress mentality raises profound ideological difficulties for those liberal democracies that defend human rights values, support greater freedom in the exchange of goods and capital across national border lines, and also advocate increased openness to trade and democracy in societies traditionally governed by more centralized regimes. Second, most traditional immigrant-receiving countries do not actually wish to adopt a zero-tolerance immigration policy. Rather, they seek to better manage the definition of who may be included in their polities, and according to which criteria. Such attempts have led to reshaping the boundaries of inclusion through immigration; for example, by adopting stricter requirements for some (e.g., asylum seekers) and more relaxed admission procedures for others (e.g., skilled migrants). Furthermore, in spite of the general trend toward restricting the entry and residence of nonnationals, we are witnessing an increased reliance on professional-employment visas (including the H1-B, TN, or L visas in the United States, for example), along with fierce competition, or a global race for talent, among receiving polities to attract highly skilled immigrants to their respective markets.[38]

Third and lastly, we live in a deeply fragmented world, in which too many elected governments in too many countries fail miserably in the provision of security and freedom to their peoples, the protection of civil liberties, or even the most basic subsistence needs. Although leaders of such countries must be held to account, it would be naïve to believe that this alone can resolve the concerns of unequal distribution that go far beyond the action (or inaction) of any particular state. For the world's leading economies to play the blame game and do nothing to ameliorate the pressures of global inequality may prove imprudent, if not outright disastrous, in the long run.[39] This realization has not escaped several defenders of the resurrect-the-border argument. However, faced with a collective action dilemma, in which the benefits of do-it-alone restrictionism prevail in light of the significant barriers to international cooperation (at least in the short-term), it is not surprising that many countries in the North Atlantic region have become increasingly determined to adopt self-help measures. What is indisputable, however, is that any attempt to keep borders shut forever without addressing the tensions and pressures that encourage global migration patterns is hardly a compelling moral response to acute and persistent disparities of voice and opportunity.

Moving Beyond the Binary Options of Abolishing versus Refortifying Borders

The previous section identified the shortcomings of any simplistic solution that requires either the full-fledged abolition or resurrection of borders. Neither resolves the serious issues of unequal voice and opportunity raised by the current system of citizenship allocation. These extreme options do not, however, exhaust all possible resolutions. The following pages are devoted to exploring alternative models of response, none of which make the assumption that we will see either the abolishment of citizenship or the rise of impenetrable borders in the immediate future.

Although there are many alternatives to consider, I have chosen to elaborate on those that offer important and innovative visions for the future of citizenship in a globalizing world. Each of these proposals takes issue with a different aspect of birthright entitlement: (1) its nontradability and nonalienability (commodification); (2) its connection to territoriality and statehood (unbundling); (3) the lack of robust alternative entry routes (open-admission policies); and (4) the failure to acknowledge the global distributive consequences of ascriptive membership-transfer regimes (curtailing inheritance). Each proposal pulls in turn in a different normative direction: emphasizing market transactions over political ties; loosening the tie between citizenship and protected rights and benefits; cherishing open borders; and tackling head-on the wealth-preserving aspect of birthright transfers. I evaluate the commodification and unbundling alternatives in the remainder of this chapter. The discussion of open-admission policies and curtailing inheritance is reserved for Chapter 3.

Against Commodifying Citizenship

Unlike more familiar accounts of political membership that treat citizenship as an inalienable legal status, a bundle of rights, or a source of identity and belonging (that is, as capturing core dimensions of our life that deal with our sense of self and place in the world) proponents of the commodifying citizenship approach view citizenship through a very different lens. For them, the market represents a supreme alternative to any limited "range of tired options," as Julian Simon once put it, which informs any other system for identifying preferences and distributing goods.[40] As such, the crux of this approach is that instead of relying on government as the purveyor and grantor of citizenship, access to membership in affluent countries should be sold or auctioned to the highest bidder among qualified applicants; in effect, this would turn political membership into a tradable good like any other. This market-based approach, which represents a Hayekian-like variant of the narrow conception of property, fits into the methodological archetype that Margaret Radin calls "universal commodification"—treating everything that is of value to individuals and communities as translatable or commensurable into a single measure or unit of analysis, here defined as commensurable monetary worth.[41] If everything that we value is ultimately judged according to its price tag (or the willingness of individuals to pay for it), then according to the logic of universal commodification, nothing prohibits the application of this rationale to the terrain of citizenship.[42] This approach thus assumes that nothing is lost when our affiliations and relations with others (here, comembers in self-governance) are stripped down to terms of a sale-and-purchase contract.

Addressing this line of argument, endorsed by leading economists, is important because of its rising popularity in the world around us. It also highlights the dangers of portraying citizenship as a mere tradable good that simply requires sending in a bank wire transfer or delivering a stack of cash in exchange for political membership. But in order to reach this conclusion, we must first examine carefully the positions taken by leading economists who have tried to give flesh to the idea of "commodifying citizenship." The most immediate fact to notice here is that even among those arguing in favor of commodification, there are meaningful disagreements about how precisely to interpret the imperative of selling access to membership. Barry Chiswick, for example, argues that a country like the United States should set a *fixed entry price* to be paid by anyone seeking its membership benefits. Gary Becker suggests that entry permits should be *auctioned off* to the highest bidders. Others suggest a *mixed-admission route,* whereby preference is given to those who are most qualified (according to government-set criteria) and willing to pay the highest bid (the market mechanism) for purchasing their way into the desired polity.[43] Although these approaches represent variations on a theme, it is clear that those who view citizenship as fungible in this way hold an unflagging faith in the market as a fair distributor: in their words, it allows "*anybody* in any part of the world the *same* opportunity to buy an [admission] visa."[44]

Alas, is that really the case? To begin with, the argument in favor of commodifing citizenship appears willfully blind to various information and knowledge asymmetries among the expectant global cliental. For instance, how, by whom, and in what vernacular will information be disseminated worldwide so as to ensure that everyone—including the fragile, the illiterate, the penniless, or the person with no access to the mainstream media or Internet outlets—gains a fair shot under this system? Add to this the very real concern that power relations, gendered trajectories, and economic barriers would almost certainly price out the vast majority of the world's population from the chance of bidding for admission to highly desirable countries. But this line of response, while absolutely valid, already concedes too much; it is confined within the language of economic theory rather than external to it. Within the confines of economic theory, a sophisticated advocate of commodification could respond to criticisms by, for instance, adding third-party private investors or insurers to the picture. On the basis of an individual's future employment prospects, these third parties could grant loans to those without sufficient cash to buy their way into the polity.[45] Or they could argue that it is fair to discriminate on the basis of future productivity or income, because this method of admission rewards those who are more resourceful and entrepreneurial, and thus, according to this world vision, more deserving of the various returns that money can buy—including the ability to purchase citizenship itself. In short, access to membership is seen as a reflection of financial might, or a test to the willingness to spend one's capital on acquiring citizenship titles in the world's more affluent polities.

Although we have become almost oblivious to the manifold ways in which the language of the market now creeps into every corner of our lives, I believe this tendency must be resisted in the realm of citizenship. Indeed, it is difficult to think of any admission method more in contrast with the goal of reducing global disparities of wealth and power. It also drastically breaks course with the self-proclaimed legacies of immigrant nations that historically allowed newcomers from very modest beginnings the opportunity to pull themselves up by their bootstraps (rather than demanding a hefty entry fee before giving them a chance to come in). Those in favor of commodification instead demand the cash upfront. This shuts the metaphoric golden door for everyone but the economically self-assured, leaving outside anyone belonging to the huddled masses yearning to breathe free. As a result, it may only further exacerbate present inequalities in life chances rather than ameliorate them.

Citizenship as we know (at least since Aristotle) is constituted of *political* relations; as such, it is expected to both reflect and generate a notion of participation, co-governance, and a degree of solidarity among those included within the body politick. It is difficult to imagine how these values could be preserved under circumstances in which insiders and outsiders are distinguished merely by the ability to pay a certain price. The objection here is to the notion that everything, including political membership, is indeed commensurable and reducible to a dollar value. To trade in citizenship, then, is not only to violate its core features but also to further institutionalize inequality: it is to grant admission to the political community on nothing but financial might. And those who can afford the economic privileges of citizenship under this system of auctioning entry permits are most likely not the ones most in need of its enabling and leveling up capacities. Rather than to reduce global disparities in rights, goods, and opportunities, to commodify citizenship is to aggravate these inequalities.

Staunch defenders of the commodification approach clearly understand that they are facing a hard sell. As Gary Becker admits, "some people object to the sale of [entry] permits because, as they say, 'citizenship is not to be for sale.'"[46] This moral intuition runs deep; most people express strong reservations against the notion of attaching a monetary tag to citizenship.[47] The reasons are plenty. For one, such a move may erode the inalienabilty of equal entitlement, which in turn may cause irreparable harm to the vision of citizenship as grounded in long-term relations of trust and shared responsibility, thus spelling the ultimate demise of the political into the economic. It may further undermine bonds of co-authorship, cross-subsidization of risk, even sacrifice that might be expected in times of need. Moreover, citizenship currently involves making collective decisions and translating them into binding political commitments that are larger than oneself, extending well beyond the life span of each generation of members. Add to this the concern that turning citizenship into a money-based prize contradicts any Walzerian-like notion of complex equality, which holds that advantage in one sphere (here, wealth) cannot be legitimately transferred to another (in this case, membership).[48] This makes the idea of selling membership unnerving for anyone who objects to the reduction of the political and the ethical into the bare economic, with the latter's imperialistic perception of trades as occupying the full terrain of human value and meaning.[49] Just as I think we should strongly object to hollow membership in the case of the mere nominal heir (the person who has no real and effective link to the political community but accident of birth, as shall be discussed in Chapter 6), I believe we must resist with at least equal force the notion that money can buy "love of country" or secure membership in it.

It is encouraging to recognize that even property theory itself shares this intuition; indeed, it recognizes that some things are not for sale.[50] Although the "free alienability of entitlements" (the lawyer's term for the sellability or tradeability of assets) is a core principle of contemporary property law, there are notable exceptions. In contrast with the commodification logic that calls for "unregulated markets in *everything*,"[51] scholars and jurists have long defined and defended the status of certain kinds of entitlements as "*in*alienable possessions."[52] In its strongest form, *inalienablity* means that certain things or relationships are categorically excluded from the market.[53] Classic examples of inalienability in other contexts include protected religious or cultural artifacts, national-heritage treasures, social security, welfare benefits, and other government-backed entitlements provided by the regulatory state, voting rights, and so on.[54]

Selling such entitlements would, as one scholar eloquently puts it, "diminish the self and by extension, the [political community] to which the person belongs."[55] As a legal matter, these inalienables cannot be sold or traded, in large part because they are perceived as identity-defining for their individual holders or the larger collectivity.[56] Prohibiting the substitution of membership for money is here seen as validating the expression, symbolic or actual, of a distinctive historical and cultural legacy (the national-heritage category) or significant manifestations of one's legal standing as an equal member in a given community's social and political life (voting rights and other government-backed entitlements).

These protections are regarded as priceless: they bear a nonmonetary value that justifies placing them above exchange value and safely outside the realm of the market. As a normative matter, shielding certain goods and relationships from the logic of commodification permits keeping them at bay from what Michael Sandel once dubbed the "degrading effect of market valuation and exchange." The argument here is that the moral importance of the political and civic goods at stake—the very properties that make citizenship a unique interpersonal relationship among members and between them and a representative government—is such that they can only be said to be "diminished or corrupted if bought or sold for money."[57]

In rejecting the narrow conception of property that reduces everything to monetary value, we can begin to see more clearly the implications of the broad conception of membership: citizenship both recognizes and preserves for each member something that goes beyond a mere financial worth; allowing each to bolster certain irrevocable protections and the equality of sharing in the membership and governance of the commonwealth.[58] This relationship not only expresses a particular political affiliation, but also stands for enabling qualities that are nonfungible precisely because they are recognized as bound up with defining the self and facilitating well-being.[59] These include: a sense of belonging; freedom from want; inclusion in the franchise; access to whatever public goods, privileges, and benefits attach to the status of membership—to mention but a few core instantiations. Together, these protections are seen as contributing to one's freedom, security, and well-being. When taken in this larger context, the case against selling citizenship becomes crystal clear: the distinct political and civic qualities of citizenship cannot be reduced to a market price without substantially altering, if not outright dissolving, the bonds of membership itself. The legal fact that citizenship is formally excluded from market exchange or trade (a point to which I return later) can thus be understood not as an oversight, but as a key feature that protects its distinct character and the values it seeks to uphold. The setting aside of citizenship from the market prevents a substantive loss from occurring. To oppose commodification, then, is to guard against devaluing and diminishing the broad conception of citizenship and restricting the rise of its nemesis, the narrow vision of trades.

In the real world, however, the commitment to maintaining citizenship as a noncommodified entitlement is facing mounting pressure. In the world's most desired immigrant-destination countries, including the United States and Canada, and more recently, Germany and the United Kingdom, governments themselves, the public trustees of citizenship, are now offering membership titles "for sale" to those willing to bring significant amounts of cash and investment into the receiving polity. The United States, for instance, has set the bar at US$1 million for a green card under the EB-5 (the relevant visa category), whereas Canada offers a bargain for investors who wish to settle in North America: once they have a business plan that is approved by the government, those with a minimum net worth of CDN $800,000 merely need to invest CDN $400,000 to gain admission. The United Kingdom similarly offers residence permits in exchange for investment of GBP 750,000 in British stocks and the holding of additional funds of at least GBP 250,000, while Germany (until recently a declared nonimmigration country) now charges one million Euros for the privilege of establishing permanent residence within its territory.[60]

These commodified-admission routes, known as the investor categories, currently account for a limited stream or quota of entrants per year. But they are alarming because of the implicit normative message they send: that people should be able to buy their way into the body politick. Given the pressures of globalization and privatization, we may witness greater emphasis on these emerging cash-for-passport admission routes. Although some economists will be quick to note that such programs can create a hefty stream of revenue for governments, this is hardly a strong enough justification to endorse them. The desire to enlarge their coffers may, as a matter of real-life experience, explain why some off-shore economies periodically offer cash-for-passports programs (typically until the moment when these passports becomes devalued in the international mobility market because border control agents in desired countries begin to notice their inflation). However, it threatens to corrupt the very "asset" that is put on sale. The concern is this: what changes when we sell citizenship is not just the *price tag of membership,* but its substantive content as well. In addition, it will likely reshape the *class of beneficiaries* that are likely to enjoy it; reliance upon market mechanism will not only deprive the vast majority of the world's population from even gaining a chance of access to citizenship in well-off polities, but it may also deprive present members (those without sufficient funds to eventually purchase such titles) of their presently inalienable possession and ownership of their secure membership titles.

This is a very drastic, and, as I have suggested, misguided turn. Still, several scholars have taken up the task of imaging how our world might look were the market, in lieu of the state, to govern access to, and the transfer of, political membership. "If we take the basic incidents of citizenship to be protection of members and participation in modes of governance," explains a recent study, "the market for citizenship could form around offer of and demand for these services. Indeed, the offer of broader packages of citizenship services would be the basis for product differentiation."[61] The latter is a euphemism for providing lesser rights and services in exchange for lower fees.[62]

In this commercialized citizenship universe, professional advisors may well be regarded as more suitable for the task of managing membership portfolios than elected representatives. Thus, democratic participation may become the exception rather than the rule in this alternative, for-profit citizenship universe. Instead, we may witness the rapid takeover by technocratic, financial advisors who may recommend rationing access to membership and its accompanying benefits, or more strictly tailoring the provisions for admission in order to reduce the risk of including unproductive members or those who are likely to become a net-drain on the respective citizenship portfolio. With this logic in play, we may eventually see the rise of a stock exchange for trading membership corporations or some futuristic international center for registering such citizenship sales and purchases, perhaps even the creation of a transnational regulatory authority that would provide the required oversight for this new and lucrative market.

Under a pure market system, those with less disposable cash may not even be able to afford purchasing any membership titles. In this scenario, they would loose the ability to make claims for equal voice and participation as well as the safety net provisions that are currently granted to them as part of the state-backed protections that attach to the right not to be excluded. Unlike the optimistic vision of a deterritorialized conception of membership (which I discuss below), in this alternative narrative, where access to citizenship depends on one's wallet size, little will remain of our current understanding of bounded communities. Instead, we will likely see the rise of gated, private-club-like citizenship communities offering competing bundles of purchased services and protections. This is not a utopian vision of greater equality or free movement for all, but rather a darker and more stratified—let alone tightly controlled—world of privatized access to citizenship's goods, reduced into purchasable commodities with differentiation in price and product quality.

This is a frightening future, representing the triumph of economics over politics, changing membership into a marketable commodity with the risk of losing everything that makes citizenship meaningful and worth preserving today: security; identity; belonging; an equal voice in governance; a safety net; a basic public-minded commitment to a long-term time horizon of intergenerational responsibility and continuity, to name but a few. Add to this the very real concerns I have already alluded to about the uncertain, limbo situation of those who fall short of the means to pay the membership mortgage. Once admission to citizenship becomes reliant on an auction or a hefty fixed-entry price, many people may find themselves unable to afford membership rights and services of any kind. Given the long-standing concern of international law and political philosophy with statelessness, it is unclear which institution would bear the responsibility of taking care of the needs and interests of nonmember populations in this brave new world of commodified citizenship. The specter here, as one commenter powerfully asserts, is that of "unconstrained survival-of-the-fittest market relations, with the dispossessed falling helplessly to the wayside."[63] This is a desperately cold and dangerous place to be, as Hannah Arendt and Giorgio Agamben remind us, analyzing, in a different context, the bare and naked life of the state-less, protection-less person.[64]

Commodified citizenship thus offers a radical rewriting (if not erasure) of the logic of *in*alienable membership. In fact, it turns this logic on its head. "Wealth buys membership": the market here becomes the sole and omnipresent purveyor of access to citizenship and its accompanying benefits, ultimately replacing democratic governance and the ability of the affected population to act in concert as lawmakers and guardians for advancing their political communities at large. This is a dystopia, a dangerous development that must be curtailed on pain of dissolving most of the major achievements of the modern history of citizenship.[65] Within the intellectual context of developing the analogy to inherited property, identifying and defending the inalienablity of political membership therefore becomes crucially important for three main reasons.

First, it permits us to resist the imperialist logic of universal commodification (or what Joseph Stiglitz calls the zeal of "market fundamentalism"), which is found in many stripes of the narrow conception. Second, it helps sharpen the distinction between treating citizenship as if it were a complex form of inherited property (the conceptual analogy that I develop throughout this book), and the endorsement of the actual treatment of citizenship as an alienable commodity. The latter position represents the ultimate application of the trades logic of the narrow conception of property to the domain of political citizenship. The former holds that any meaningful expression of political membership cannot be reduced to a pure commodity; the web of social ties and responsibilities that make citizenship meaningful simply cannot survive (without a significant loss and deep mutilation) as a mere tradable good. Third, it allows us, in the spirit of the broad conception, to acknowledge that citizenship inevitably has both a nonpecuniary value (such as its identity-generating and security-enhancing qualities) as well as more quantifiable aspects (such as its significant wealth-preserving properties). This multifaceted feature is familiar from property law and theory's conceptualization of the inalienable; the fact that there are some quantifiable aspects to otherwise nonpecuniary goods should not lead us to erroneously conclude that "behind every property-like categorization, stands alienation."[66] When applied in the context of citizenship, it is imperative to account for these multidimensional and noncommensurable aspects of political membership if we are to find more equitable and justifiable responses to the global distributive inequalities currently sustained through birthright citizenship regimes.

The Unbundling of Citizenship

Is there a brighter alternative to the dystopian future of commodified citizenship? Some believe that the unbundling of citizenship in the new era of de-territorialized politics provides the answer. On this view, familiar notions of political membership will eventually dissolve and lose their significance in our increasingly globalized lives. Instead of endorsing a top-down model that requires the formal abolition of borders or birthright entitlements (as advocated by those who envisage the rise of a central world citizenship model), proponents of post-, de-, and transnational alternatives rely on softer legal changes, emerging from the ground upward.[67]

The specifics of the unbundling metaphor may take one of many different forms. Some commentators emphasize the decoupling of political authority from territory.[68] Others point to the disaggregation of citizenship as a secure bundle of rights and privileges that attaches to membership in a bounded community, highlighting instead the growing prominence of regional and international human rights regimes. Still others suggest that the concept of sovereignty itself is being partly decentered, pointing to the emergence of multiple actors, groups, and institutions that are operating both above and below the state level.[69] The ultimate conclusion of this unbundling theory, as David Jacobson aptly puts it, is that "the 'pact' between state and citizen is *broken*."[70]

The thrust of the argument is that we are already witnessing the disassembling of the holy trinity of modern statehood: the knot that binds together territory, authority, and rights (to borrow from Saskia Sassen's terminology).[71] This is typically accompanied by the claim that, as an alternative to citizenship-based protections, emerging transnational and international human rights discourses are gaining sway as a world-level organizing principle.[72] These emerging instruments are seen as capable of granting protection to a person's basic rights, wherever that person may be, irrespective of his or her formal membership status (or lack thereof) in a given polity. Yasemin Soysal eloquently summarizes the argument: "national citizenship is losing ground to a more universal model of membership, anchored in deterritorialized notions of persons' rights."[73]

Although the unbundling thesis (in its various manifestations) enjoyed a heyday in the closing decades of the twentieth century, it has received some scathing critiques at the dawn of the twenty-first. For one, several scholars have noted that it draws too sharp a contrast between the local and transnational, losing sight of how the latter is often dependent upon, or a product of, the former.[74] Similarly, the notion of a zero-sum game between the national and the international tends to ignore the manifold ways in which one transforms the other (and vice versa), and the reality of more flexible, embedded or overlapping membership affiliations to more than one locus of citizenship.[75]

Furthermore, despite predictions about the demise of old demarcating lines that are based on territory and identity, and the rise of a new postnational model in which "universal personhood replaces nationhood; and universal human rights replace national rights," the protection of individuals, especially nonmembers, still relies heavily on domestic (and increasingly regional) regimes, which have not abolished the distinction between the citizen and the alien.[76] As Linda Bosniak's work meticulously establishes, this distinction often hits hardest when the topic of analysis is the definition of membership boundaries themselves, the regulation of cross-border mobility, and the right to enter and remain.[77] The vision of universal personhood replacing nationhood may become a reality some day, but that day has clearly not yet arrived.

If anything, we are witnessing an unmistakable surge toward an ever tighter and harsher regulation of borders throughout the world.[78] This trend began prior to the events of September 11, and has accelerated dramatically in its aftermath. Add to this the fact that when the unbundling of territory from authority occurs, nothing stops governmental or regional border-enforcement agencies assigned with the task of stopping the admission of "unwanted intruders" from expanding their enforcement mandate beyond territorial borders. In this way, de-territorialization can be used as a license to pursue more aggressively their access-restricting mandate, often far away from the actual, territorial border itself.[79] This new extension of authority permits the detachment of border controls from their traditional location at a country's edges, and further limits the rights of nonmembers trying to get in: the latter are often interdicted en route, long before they reach the promised land of immigration or prosperity.[80] Witness the increase in national border officials stationed overseas at key departure points and this extraterritorial reach of national immigration policies comes starkly into focus (think, for example, of U.S. officials at Caribbean airports or British officials at the Eurostar/Eurotunnel terminals in France). Even the otherwise optimistic story of European citizenship has a less sanguine dimension, which often gets lost in the discussion; the landmark opening of the internal borders in Europe has been consistent with a closing of the external borders to non-EU nationals. This has lead to the construction of a massive union-wide visa and biometric-regulatory virtual-walls system to protect those at the inner core from those who are pounding on Europe's (mostly) closed doors. The external-oriented European Union border-regulation agency known as Frontex, based in Warsaw, is there to assist in this.

In short, the de-territorialization of political authority, which has been hailed in the literature as a sign of the coming of age of human rights instruments and the growing importance of personhood over membership status, has perhaps materialized for those already within a fortress Europe, but has also bred a new form of exclusion around the walls of the fortress. As just mentioned, national and regional regulators have become increasingly bent on adopting policies of interdiction, which permit immigration officials to conduct their gate-keeping mission on foreign soil with the same binding legal effects as if their actions were taken within the jurisdiction.[81] In Europe and beyond, the de-territorialization of political authority is captured by regulatory and enforcement agencies, which have turned it into a hyperrestrictive tool of cross-border regulation and restriction, rather than an inclusive, all-welcoming instrument of human rights.[82]

Governments around the world are further using the concept of de-territorialization to devolve enforcement powers to a host of local and supranational authorities as well as nonstate actors (for example, airline companies that are fined for carrying passengers lacking proper documentation, thus shifting the onus of border control onto private, commercial, and most importantly, nonaccountable agents).[83] Finally, instead of losing control, immigration and enforcement agencies have creatively regained or even expanded their reach. This is evident, for example, in the concentrated effort to reformulate entry and immigration-admission categories, giving preference to highly skilled migration streams over and above family reunification or humanitarian categories in the global race for talent; or the rise of social contract obligations in most European countries, making admission more difficult for those with lesser resources or nonmainstream cultural or religious affiliations. It is also reflected in the trend toward restricting the rights and protections granted to lawful permanent residents (green card holders) in the United States, the deepening of regional and international cooperation among police and immigration enforcement agencies in the efforts to prevent unwanted admission, the use of biometric information, fingerprinting, shared look-out lists and databases, as well as the increased use of smart or virtual borders—all big-brother-like tools designed to more effectively regulate cross-border mobility in the age of conflated national security and global migration pressures.[84]

Finally, with the war on terrorism giving birth to Guantanamo, extraordinary rendition, water-boarding, Abu Ghurayb, undisclosed black-site investigation centers, to mention but a few familiar examples, we are witnessing today the sheer vulnerability that attaches to the deprivation of the property-like bundle of protections traditionally offered by citizenship. International human rights instruments, although promising in principle, have to date provided mostly cold comfort to those detained under the current political atmosphere of heightened national-security alerts.[85] Clearly, the situation may change for the better in the future, but we still need some evidence to support the view that this is merely a temporary drawback in the otherwise onward march toward a new, postnational era.[86]

Some of the early declarations of the ultimate demise of citizenship and regulated borders thus appear to have been premature and overly sanguine;

they systemically ignore the potential for national or transnational regulatory agencies to recover their authority to control membership boundaries and to adjust their reach to new patterns of global mobility. But we are now seeing a readjustment of sorts. This is taking place both in the academic literature, which seeks to relocate citizenship as one among many meaningful sources of identity and affiliation, and in the advocacy world as well, where regional, international, local, and national tools are used interchangeably and often simultaneously to advance the rights and protections of those with less than full membership.[87] Although I fully share these commitments, I believe that the unbundling theme is most productive when treated as a basis for respecting transnational ties and identities as coexisting with (rather than replacing) our belonging to one or more political communities. What I reject is the notion that we must debunk citizenship (rather than attempt to preserve and strengthen its best characteristics) as a precondition for making our world a more just and fair place for its inhabitants. There is, however, no need to be constrained by this artificial zero-sum matrix, as I will attempt to demonstrate in subsequent chapters.

Where "unbundling" of territory, authority and rights proves particularly fruitful, however, is in the realm of political participation. We are witnessing here the generation of creative openings and institutional architectures outside and beyond the traditional framework. This creates a larger space for cross-border and cross-cultural democratic discourse, in which participants can express their interests and needs, regardless of whether or not they have formal citizenship status.[88] This does not require creating a superstate or alter-*demos;* it permits instead multiple levels of governance to flourish. No less significant, this grassroots development aims to push the boundaries of conventional wisdom: instead of focusing on existing structures of membership, it offers an aspirational call to adopt a new ethics that extends the reach of our solidarities and responsibilities beyond the immediate circle of members to which we happen to belong.[89] This transnational variant of the unbundling narrative also encourages fresh responses to the various problems of unaccountability and externalities that require political organization and legal action beyond that taken at the purely national or formal international level. Consider here examples such as the disciplining effect of transnational civil litigation, undertaken by private actors and nongovernmental organizations seeking to hold multinational corporations to account in cases of severe human rights violations, wherever they happen to have occurred, even if that was half the world away from the well-tended headquarters of these multinational corporations.[90] Another promising development is the growing emphasis placed on human security (not just national security) and the creation of new complaint mechanisms that permit individuals to hold their states to account under regional and international law standards. Or consider the establishment of new venues of notification for citizens' intervention in environmental legislation proposed in countries other than their own, such as NAFTA's green protocol, or the emerging significance of direct input from the local level into European Union–wide legislation, both of which provide noteworthy illustrations.[91]

Add to this institutional creativity the burgeoning economic impact of remittances sent by international migrants, expanding patterns of circular migration, and growing knowledge and infrastructure transfers by diaspora communities directed to the betterment of the home country that they left behind, and these transnational patterns begin to mark a set of promising changes in the way in which individuals and communities redirect political participation and economic opportunity in a more globally redistributive fashion. Although these patterns are encouraging, there is still plenty of room for receiving and sending countries, as well as intergovernmental and issue-specific institutions, to improve matters through coordinated actions to allow those affected by policies made outside their territorial jurisdiction to gain meaningful venues of participation alongside more established institutions of citizenship and democratic participation.

Another development to watch for is the mushrooming recognition of dual nationality, which by last count is now accepted in one form or another by more than half of the world's countries. This development roughly coincides with the current wave of economic globalization. Such acceptance represents a drastic break away from the early twentieth-century hostility against multiple national affiliations, as crystallized in the 1930 Hague Convention, whose preamble declares that "it is in the general interest of the international community to secure that all its members should recognise that every person should have a nationality and should have *one* nationality only." In this respect, the relaxing of the territory-authority-rights knot has allowed a greater multiplicity of political-membership affiliations to coexist and flourish, far exceeding what was imagined as possible under the far stricter (one person, one nationality) rule that exemplified the logic of the classic Westphalian model.

The Humpty Dumpty Effect

Without discounting the value of these developments, a final observation about the unbundling narrative remains in order: it has the potential to dangerously interact with the commodified citizenship logic. The major concern here is that by encouraging the dissolution of the bundle of benefits and protections that currently attach to citizenship, proponents of the unbundling vision will also begin to fuel an alternative discourse as well—one that urges the privatization and fragmentation of citizenship, and that implies less collective responsibility for the well-being of members.[92] Once broken up, the collective achievements of citizenship, just like Humpty Dumpty, may never be put together again.

By emphasizing the broken pact between the state and the individual, the unbundling discourse may inadvertently provide ammunition for those supporting the withdrawal of the encroaching state and the rise of an all-encompassing self-regulating market instead. Although issuing from very different ideological premises, this dual-track attack may end up drastically eroding the right-not-to-be-excluded and at the same time shift the right-to-exclude from the political to the economic sphere. If followed, such a trajectory would amount to the further hollowing out of the enabling side of citizenship, whose commitment to a range of public goods, from access to clean water and safe streets to education and health care, as well as cross-subsidization of risk and collective action in the citizenship zone has already sustained serious attack. In this scenario, the devaluation of bounded membership (a cause célèbre by postnationalists) may go hand-in-hand with the thinning out of the content and scope of the right-not-to-be-excluded. It may instead endorse a more laissez-faire, fend-for-yourself conception of membership.[93]

In sum, there is much to be celebrated about the expansion of transnational affiliations and the opening of new, often overlapping venues for expression of political voice and democratic iterations. But nothing in this narrative of a more multifaceted world of cross-border participation (with its emphasis on strengthening and multiplying local, regional, national, or international entry points) justifies the conclusion that we must celebrate the demise of protected membership in a collective political enterprise. Unlike those who celebrate the "broken pact" between the individual and the state, I strongly believe that the invaluable properties of citizenship should not become the price paid for a more flexible regime of international voice and opportunity.

THIS CHAPTER HAS OUTLINED and assessed the competing visions of world citizenship, resurrected borders, commodified membership and unbundled citizenship. It has highlighted the respective merits and shortcomings of each approach. Of the options discussed thus far, the transnational variant of the unbundling narrative is the most attractive because it holds the promise of ameliorating problems of unequal voice across national and regional borderlines through direct and indirect forms of politics and governance that operate both above and below the state level.

A more profound message, however, lies beyond these concrete observations. Instead of treating robust citizenship and global redistribution as having inherent tension with one another, the central message that I take from these recent transformations on the ground is that the national and international can, and must, coexist and may constantly help to reshape and refocus each other.[94] One emergent possibility of such interaction is that of enlarging the moral and legal boundaries of our communities of care and responsibility beyond those of established citizenship. Although some see the solution in emphasizing the importance of voluntary nonterritorial identity affiliations (such as religion, gender, and so forth), there is no reason for us to assume that such overlapping affiliations will offer a panacea to address the deep inequities in life prospects that now attach to bounded membership. To squarely address this concern, and without resorting to the options of either erasing borders altogether or ballooning membership to encompass the world *simplicitier,* it might be better to acknowledge (for some, concede) the enormous social advantages of having stable citizenship regimes. This still doesn't address the problem of unburdened intergenerational transmissions of membership, which grant a world of opportunity to some but denies it to others. What is missing, therefore, is an argument that maintains the best of bounded membership—with its ability to promote internal redistribution and support co-governance—while at the same time confronting the dire global inequalities in life prospects that take cover behind the naturalness of the current birthright citizenship/property transfer regime.

What is hanging in the balance is an attempt to respect certain special relations while also expanding the provision of fair access to voice, wealth, and power globally. The classic analogy to consider here is that of *inherited* property: while permitting the intergenerational transfer to occur, it is not without responsibility or liability toward those who do not share similar bounty. This has potentially far-reaching implication, especially for the development of new remedies to overcome some of the shortcomings of the options currently on offer. Consider the fact that it was none other than the forefather of modern economic theory, Adam Smith, who famously argued that once the recipients of bequests, to use the language of the Roman law, "are said to be emancipated" (by having received their portion from the estate), inheritance tax duties can be imposed. Across the Atlantic, in America, some of that country's most famous millionaires became the most vocal advocates in favor of curtailing the intergenerational transfer of large fortunes. Andrew Carengie, for example, declared himself in favor of an inheritance tax based explicitly on a diffusion of wealth argument. The core rationale that I wish to export from the province of inheritance debates to the citizenship realm is that instead of altogether cutting the intergenerational transfer, taking action (here, through inheritance levies and related measures) geared toward the ends of achieving greater social equality is legitimate, indeed required, in order to justify the transfer itself.

By extension, in a world of deep inequality like our own, hereditary membership in well-off polities may continue to exist, but if and only if state (or transnational) action is introduced for the benefit of the larger community of those left outside the membership; for instance, by placing what in the next chapter I call the "birthright privilege levy" on automatic recipients of title so as to ensure that everyone, regardless of where or to whom they were born, must receive basic protections to permit them to live above a threshold, ensuring (at minimum) an acceptable level of subsistence and basic goods. This is compatible with a vision that holds that more robust obligations, or enabling commitments, are reserved for co-members of a shared political unit. This position can be coherently defended from different starting points, including need-based, rights-focused, or outcome-centered approaches. The citizenship-as-inherited property perspective creates an additional basis for defending and discharging the transnational distributive transfers that are likely to be required in order to fulfill the threshold obligation, and thus begin to dismantle the disparities that currently attach to birthright citizenship without demanding the abolishment of bounded membership per se.

Nothing in this vision of a more just world order requires that we give up the commitment to a robust conception of enabling citizenship, which, as we have already seen, invokes significant co-obligations among members. Equally, it does not imply that we owe nothing to those who remain outside our circle of members due to birth-based circumstances beyond their control. It is the entail-like inheritance of membership through strict intergenerational transfer, as codified in our current citizenship laws, that places a burden on the beneficiaries of birthright to share in their windfall political estates. This can be done either through the redistribution of membership titles (open-admission policies) or by finding alternative remedial mechanisms to help diffuse wealth and power concentrations (curtailing inheritance). Fleshing out the institutional implications of these ideas is the task to which I now turn.

CHAPTER THREE

A New Basis for Global Redistribution: The Birthright Privilege Levy

> Give a man fish; you have fed him today. Teach a man to fish; and you have fed him for a lifetime.
>
> OLD CHINESE PROVERB

IN THE PREVIOUS CHAPTER I rejected the diametrically opposed abolition versus resurrection-of-boundaries options. The discussion also cautioned against the commodification and unbundling visions of citizenship. Here, I wish to explore a more promising line of resolution: holding that bounded communities may continue to exist so long as their members recognize that they must address and redress the profound global consequences of the property-like birthright regimes that maintain their privilege. This permits upholding the collective good of membership in a jointly governed polity, as well as protecting its core enabling function. At the same time, this approach opens the door for imposing legal obligations on the well-off as a means for greater redistribution of opportunity globally. The key move here is to target the weakest moral link in the present allocation system: the transfer of citizenship according to birthright.[1]

Given that we live in a world marked by massive inequalities, if the beneficiaries of bounded membership wish to sustain their public inheritance, as I assume they do, they are duty-bound to mitigate its unfair consequences on those who are restricted from their circle of membership solely because of where or to whom they were born. Once we accept this baseline commitment, we can envision creative measures for mitigating the dire opportunity inequities that are currently attached to birthright citizenship. In the following pages, I discuss two main possibilities for discharging this obligation: one is to focus on reallocating membership titles, for instance, by removing barriers to the free movement of people or redrawing jurisdictional boundaries. The other option is to redistribute opportunity by imposing restrictions on the perpetual (and presently untaxed) birthright transfer of citizenship and its immense wealth-preserving consequences.[2] This latter allows for the curtailing of the automatic transfer of swollen fortunes to the heirs of well-off polities, with the added value of generating a stable transnational base for funding subsistence services (health, education, and the like) to improve the situation of those adversely affected by the current connection between birth and citizenship.

My discussion is divided into two parts. I begin by exploring the more familiar idea of reallocating membership titles through open-admission policies. I explain the main rationales behind this kind of policy and also justify some of its core normative commitments. However, I ultimately weigh in against it as the sole or best answer to the problem at hand, largely due to its structural shortcomings. This then sets the stage for my presentation of a different solution in response to the puzzle of birthright citizenship in an unequal world: one that focuses on redistributing opportunity. I argue that this approach has the advantage of improving the situation of people wherever they reside, rather than forcing them to relocate as their main choice for improving their life chances. Specifically, in the chapter's second part, I sketch the contours of the birthright privilege levy, a creative proposal informed by the analogy to inheritance, which aims to tackle the global effects of the intergenerational-wealth-transfer aspect of citizenship, without demanding the abandonment of the collective good of membership as the price for achieving greater opportunity for those who need it most.[3] But first, let us consider the case for open-admission policies.

Reallocating Membership Titles by Reducing Free-Movement Constraints

To place in context the calls for open-admission policies, we must acquaint ourselves with the actual practices of immigration regulation in the real world. At present, all well-off countries impose serious restrictions on entry into their territories, and more so, into their membership communities.[4] In order to be granted admission into a receiving country with the accompanying prospect of applying for citizenship in due course, a would-be immigrant lacking birthright entitlement must pass through what Tomas Hammar elegantly describes as a cumulative series of entry gates: first, lawful admission (receiving an entry visa and crossing the border at a recognized port of entry or by the permission of an authorized immigration official); next, regulation of permanent residence (fitting into a specific admission category or stream of migration that secures permanent residence); and, finally, qualifying for naturalization (fulfilling the requirements set by the admitting state for receiving full membership status).[5]

Each of these entry gates is tightly regulated; indeed, it is becoming ever more difficult for residents of low-income or politically-unstable countries to even gain a temporary visitor visa, let alone to access a permanent residence permit. Given that in the vast majority of cases there are more applicants than visas available to be issued, not everyone who qualifies will get in. No country relieves its incoming migrants from going through a strict review process, and none has unlimited family-based, employment, or humanitarian admission streams.[6] In fact, the reverse is true. Even the classic immigrant-receiving countries (the United States, Canada, and Australia) set limits on the number of immigrant visas that they will issue annually per category, often breaking down the allocation according to a complex calculation of the maximum quotas per admission stream, as well as setting restrictions on the maximum number of entrants per country (in the case of high application rates).[7]

Proponents of open-admission policies wish to change all of this. In an ideal and transaction-free world, they argue, "there would be few migration barriers and little unwanted migration."[8] On this account, a good immigration policy would be to have none at all. In this ideal-world vision, bounded communities may continue to exist but the boundaries between them would no longer form obstacles to mobility. One's spectrum of choice and opportunity would therefore no longer be constrained by, or dependant upon, which side of the border one is born.[9] Plainly put, this is the argument in favor of open-admission. Support for this vision comes from two different camps: free-marketers and moral egalitarians.

The Free-Market Defense of Open Borders

For the free-marketer who is informed by a global welfare perspective, restrictive immigration policies appear as a form of tariff or protectionism: these form a barrier that needs to be removed.[10] The main complaint here is that it is preferable (from an efficiency-oriented vantage point), to "encourage the transfer of 'surplus' people from poorer to richer nations."[11] Such international mobility, it is theorized, would eventually promote convergence in wages and opportunities between sending and receiving areas, through increased competition, specialization, and the economies of scale. The international mobility of persons is here treated as advancing aggregate levels of prosperity worldwide and as a core factor of production; as such, it is often lumped together with advocacy favoring the reduction of barriers to the free movement of goods, services, and capital across borders.[12] On this account, it is predicted that global migration pressures will only subside when the marginal return of moving is no greater than staying put in one's country of residence. No one seriously doubts that any real-life march toward such an equilibrium, if aggressively launched, might (at least in the short run) end up leading to dangerous overcrowding, social instability, perhaps even a severe political backlash. Even pro-open-admission economists admit that the effects of migration are hard to predict or model, in part because there is little agreement on how precisely to define and count the benefits and costs, or what unit of analysis to place at center stage (global or national welfare, the results for sending or receiving countries, immigrant or native populations, individual or group effects, and so on).

While acknowledging these difficulties, it is important not to lose sight of the bigger picture. For its avid defenders, the case for removing barriers to migration from an international economics perspective fits well with an endorsement of a neoclassical theory of free trade, which ultimately cherishes free exit and entry of capital and labor in order to increase allocative efficiency.[13]

The Moral-Egalitarian Argument in Favor of Free Mobility of Persons

For the moral-egalitarian philosopher, however, the defense of open-admission policies relies on very different grounds. Instead of highlighting efficiency gains, the argument in favor of open borders relies on three interrelated premises: egalitarianism, universalism, and impartiality. The combined effects of these principles of equal liberties, the inherent moral worth of each person, and the concern for impartiality leads proponents of open-admission policies to demand that individuals be granted *un*limited freedom of mobility across international borders.[14] This defense then gains further refinement: first, it advances the claim that freedom of mobility is an important human right and should be defended as such (the freedom argument). Second, it suggests that open-admission policies are worthwhile because they serve as an indirect tool for reducing poverty (the equality argument) by providing the background conditions that will permit, or at least increase, the prospects for individuals to change their membership affiliation if they so wish.[15]

As Veit Bader rightly observes, the first strategy of presenting freedom of movement as a basic human right treats it as an important liberty in itself; it therefore holds independently of problems of real-world inequalities.[16]

Although clearly valuable in its own right, the freedom argument per se is less interesting for the purpose of our discussion, especially given that hardly anyone suggests that freedom of mobility is absolute. It may be overridden by other liberties, and, at least in principle, be restricted by special moral and legal obligations to fellow members or by compelling manifestations of democratic self-determination.[17] The second claim, which combines freedom with equality reasoning, is more relevant. It creates a connection between the obligation of wealthy nations to admit nonmembers and the failure to guarantee a threshold level of human functioning and well-being to those outside our bounded communities. Robert Goodin lucidly explains this last point, suggesting that open admission can be interpreted as a second-best mechanism for global redistribution: "if we cannot move enough money [or infrastructure support] to where the needy people are, then we will have to count on moving as many of the needy people as possible to where the money is."[18]

If the case is so simple, then why have only "very few political theorists propose[d] to open immediately and completely all borders"?[19] Part of the answer, explains Will Kymlicka, is that the call for removal of obstacles to international mobility remains unrelated to peoples' existing convictions; it simply strikes people as too remote from the political reality in which both domestic and international law permits such regulation and the way in which many democratic countries routinely exercise their power to enforce border-control provisions. The vision of open borders represents so "radical [a] departure from the actual practice of liberal democracies . . . [that] apart from a few academic philosophers, no one takes it seriously."[20] Although this may be a fair assessment of the present state of affairs, it is not by itself (as Kymlicka himself suggests) a good enough reason to shelve the argument for open admission; many of the ideas that we now hold dear were deemed widely utopian before they transformed our world. This includes some of the very foundational concepts that we take for granted today: extending the franchise serves as an illustrative example. It was without doubt a fundamentally radical thesis when it was first introduced, challenging hierarchies that were then thought to be natural and immutable.[21] To provide just one testament to the depth of this conviction, consider the fact that in *The Canterbury Tales* we find that the franchise was treated as coming from "goodes of body"—a *physical* trait of the beholder, rather than a political right bestowed upon the person by a community of equals, as we regard it today.[22]

Although it is tempting to assume that the problem lies with our limited foresight, there are more serious shortcomings that ultimately explain why the open-admission argument has gained limited traction. Some reasons are prudential and contingent: in the world around us, we find countries struggling to manage their already carefully tailored migration streams. Indeed, many jurisdictions have embarked in recent years on the path of further tightening admission in light of globalization pressures, making it harder for newcomers to get it. There seems to be little political appetite for adopting more open-admission policies any time soon.

Another set of reasons is more principled: control over admission is still seen as an important prerogative of sovereign authority and democratic self-governance. These much vaunted qualities are an expression of each polity's ethos, geopolitical concerns, economic needs, historical ties, and moral responsibilities toward nonmembers. Therefore, under a policy of tightly regulated borders (the prevailing situation), a receiving polity is permitted to set its own levels and priorities of admission. Each country is, however, expected to set nondiscriminatory criteria for each migration stream, and then select immigrants from a pool of self-identified applicants from abroad.[23] Yet this situation does not satisfy the open-border advocate; she rightly insists that there is much to be said for permitting people to leave at will the country into which they happen to have been born, and allowing them to enter and eventually acquire full membership status in the new political community into which they have chosen to emigrate.[24] There is much to commend in this vision, but it is equally not trouble free. Part of the concern with this picture is that it is framed on the basis of an assumption that international migration processes necessarily reflect choice and agency. Another problem is that too little attention is paid to the various identity, gendered (and related) costs of human displacement and unrootedness. The issue here is whether asking people to move out of their communities and homes to overcome want is indeed the king's road to enhancing freedom and equality worldwide, or whether it should be supplemented by a vigorous commitment to reducing disparities in life prospects wherever they reside, in order to ensure that no one is forced to leave because no other alternative is on offer to them.[25] What remains undisputed, however, is that in contrast with the ascription of status by birth, any degree of increased opportunity and human mobility across borders is preferable to none at all. Such mobility, in an unequal world, also bears a marked redistributive quality: most migrants move from poorer to richer countries.[26]

The latest data on global migration trends show that approximately sixty percent of the world's migrants have settled in advanced industrial countries, with a growing concentration of international migrants in Europe and North America.[27] The remaining forty percent have moved primarily from poorer to richer developing countries, such as from Bangladesh to India or Belize to Mexico, thus complying with the general trend of movement toward greater opportunity.[28] Many of these migrants send remittances back home, at an astonishingly high dollar value. Recent World Bank estimations peg annual remittances at US$250 billion a year (the total amount may actually be higher, given that these estimates do not include transfers through unofficial channels).[29] The vast majority of these remittances are received annually by residents of developing countries. Within those countries, these remittances are typically used directly by low- and middle-income families, rather than channeled through governmental or international agencies. To get a sense of the full extent of this injection of funds, consider the fact that these remittances are almost as large as foreign direct investment, and more than twice as large as the total sum of official foreign-aid assistance given by richer nations to promote development.[30] Remittances are also celebrated as a powerful tool of self-aid: it is the emigrant's own effort that is the source of their family or community's financial advancement. In this way, sending money home contributes to redistributing the world's income without the various strings and conditions that usually attach to international loans by the World Bank or infusions of money from private, commercial, or development-focused financial institutions.[31]

Economists who take a global welfare perspective further submit that even a "marginal liberalization of the international labor flows would create [significant] gains for the world economy."[32] These gains are estimated to raise the worldwide real income at a significant rate, leading researchers such as Bob Hamilton and John Walley to assert that removing restrictions to mobility across borders could more than double real income worldwide.[33] As Philip Martin observes, most economists would welcome the introduction of more open-admission policies because, as mentioned earlier, it "increases allocative efficiency, allowing the world to make the most efficient use of available resources and thus maximize production."[34] This argument promoting freer movement is based upon an aggregate welfare perspective that treats the entire world as the relevant unit of cost-benefit analysis. It is far less concerned with whether the gains are maximized at the expense of exacerbating (rather than reducing) the gaps between winners and losers in the new global economy.

Add to this the very real problem that immigration is not always voluntary, nor is it equally open to all. To begin with, it requires sufficient funds to sponsor the necessary transportation, access to visa or immigration services (in the case of lawful admission), or resort to increasingly pricy (let alone dangerous) clandestine routes of unauthorized migration. It further requires sufficient knowledge of where to move in order to improve one's economic prospects and to gain greater political freedom, in addition to basic linguistic and occupational skills, the willingness and ability to leave family members and a familiar cultural context behind, and related factors that deeply, and often unequally, shape the potential mobility of men and women in international patterns of migration.[35] That is, there is a problem of gender, resource, and information asymmetries, which could potentially create a bias against those who may be most in need of the redistributive (and arguably also the liberating) dimension of global migration. Another concern is that migration is not always based on free choice. Movement across borders may be the end result of domestic or regional policies of ethnic discrimination, dislocation, or outright violence, systemic deprivation by a central government, natural disaster, hunger, disease—to list but a few of the more familiar factors that push people to flee their homes and seek refuge in neighboring regions or faraway countries.[36]

Despite (or perhaps because of) these mounting pressures, we find that many host countries are increasingly placing strict and stringent screening and admission requirements, effectively imposing insurmountable barriers for a good proportion of the world's in potentia migrants. These barriers include factors such as the prohibitive costs of even launching the application process for lawful admission, the need to undergo an interview in a foreign consulate or embassy that may be located hundreds of miles away from home, and so on.[37] The imposition of these barriers is anything but accidental; as John Tropey bluntly observes, "limiting ingress into the territory is the best way for states to avoid entering into potentially costly obligations to nonnationals. Passports and visa controls are crucial mechanisms for this purpose, the 'first line of defense' against the entry of undesirables."[38]

Efforts to take active and preventive steps to control first entry have further intensified in recent years. To curb unwanted migration, those traveling without proper documentation or visa papers are often interdicted outside the boundaries of wealthier polities; that is, their cross-border journey is stopped before they manage to enter the desired immigration-country's territory. For instance, Canadian immigration officials are now regularly stationed at international airports where they have the authority to refuse any person from boarding a flight to Canada if that person lacks proper documentation or admission papers. Immigration officials from Australia and the United Kingdom are also similarly stationed in major transportation hubs, and the United States too has recently adopted similar overseas-interdiction policies. Add to this the fact that certain regulatory responsibilities have been downloaded to nonstate actors (such as commercial airline or cruise companies), which must verify that those boarding their vessels have valid travel and admission visas or risk the sanction of heavy financial penalties imposed by the admitting state. To provide just one example, the American government now requires that airline companies electronically submit passenger lists to U.S. authorities before departure as part of the effort to create virtual walls that extend far beyond the territory itself.[39] In the same vein, the European Union is fast becoming the world's leader in biometric regulation of cross-border mobility, while at the same time creating a more harmonized control regime by the Member States. This involves measures such as enforcing common admission restrictions and introducing a unified list of countries whose passport holders must be issued a visa in order to enter the external boundaries of the European Union.[40] In 2001, that list included no less than 132 countries, almost three-quarters of the world's polities, exempting only the citizens of relatively affluent and stable countries from this requirement of preclearance. Such selective admission, concludes a recent study, creates a pattern of growing "inequality in access to foreign spaces, reinforcing existing inequalities between rich and poor nations."[41] These combined visa restrictions and border controls make it much harder for most residents of low-income, unstable, or culturally "foreign" countries to lawfully reach the shores of the promised land of immigration.[42] Thus, even if perfectly implemented the adoption of more relaxed admission policies would prove helpful only to some, but certainly not all, of those who may wish to emigrate to freer and more prosperous societies.

From the perspective of citizenship as a repository of collective identity, a robust policy of open borders may be seen as a crude mechanism for addressing the problems of global inequality of voice and opportunity. Members of bounded polities may wish to endorse a particular vision of the common good through the enterprise of shared citizenship (for example, by prioritizing the separation of state from religion; endorsing liberal democratic values; supporting a relatively robust welfare system; or preserving a distinct culture or way of life). One need not be a communitarian to appreciate the weight of these collective identity arguments. Even Joseph Carens, the scholar perhaps most closely associated with the argument in favor of open-admission policies, has identified legitimate grounds for restricting international mobility, especially if such limits "promote liberty and equality in the long run or because they are necessary to preserve a distinct culture or way of life."[43] For Carens, some legitimate reasons to restrict free movement include the prevention of harm (there is no duty to accept a person who poses a serious threat to national security), the maintenance of liberal institutions (a state is permitted to restrict the admission of those who would threaten the liberal character of its regime), and the preservation of public order (a polity can set limits on the number of newcomers it admits in order to avoid chaos or the breakdown of law and order, which "makes everyone worse off in terms of both liberty and welfare").[44] These arguments are clearly not culturally neutral, nor are they presented as such. They favor the preservation of a distinct manifestation of collective identity in established liberal-democratic polities: a fighting creed in a world of increased schisms, as some may perceive it today.[45]

Importantly, the upshot of the collective identity claim is not to advise against *any* immigration. Rather, it affirms that some control may legitimately remain in the hands of each admitting community (or any number of them in concert) so long as basic international human rights standards (such as *nonrefoulment* in the case of refugees and asylum seekers, or the prohibition against sending a person back to a country where they may face torture) are upheld. Once this concession to bounded membership is made, however, we are no longer in the ideal realm of open borders as the free marketers or moral universalists envision. Instead, we find ourselves facing regulated, semiclosed borders, a familiar feature in today's political reality. The likely fallouts are also all too familiar: debates over how many people to accept per annum, on what criteria, and according to what selection procedure. As I explain below, once we look at the limited levels of admission slots offered by the world's industrialized countries, recourse to regulated international mobility (as opposed to open borders) proves itself to be even more stratified and exclusionary than it is typically represented as being. This only underscores the basic question of why some people naturally belong to well-off polities because of accidents of birth while others are barred—by barbed wire and guarded borders—from joining in.

Notwithstanding the tendency to emphasize the liberatory or emancipatory value of immigration, there are (from the emigrant's perspective) significant personal costs to international mobility as well. Although immigration often bears great promise, it also usually involves significant expense, including a deep sense of loss for what is left behind (*The Namesake* is one of the many haunting artistic expressions that explore this narrative).[46] Whether temporary or permanent, emigration is still a hardship: it involves being torn from familiar settings, homes, languages, histories, traditions, and even close family members. For unskilled migrants in particular, such a move may in practice involve taking "dirty, difficult, demeaning and dangerous" (the so-called "4-D") jobs that place them at the bottom end of the socioeconomic ladder in the new country.[47] They may further face structural obstacles or outright discrimination, especially if they belong to marginalized or racialized minorities. If they lack legal status, these labor migrants often become vulnerable to economic and other forms of exploitation as well. The threat of deportation in particular drives undocumented migrants into a shadowy world of invisible existence in which avoiding contact with official or governmental agencies must be achieved at almost any cost for fear that their unlawful immigration status will be revealed.

To add further complexity, under the current political environment immigration, whether legal or illegal, is increasingly perceived by many residents of well-off polities as a threat and a burden. There are persistent calls to erect impenetrable, high-tech, and virtual borders to protect the integrity of the territory from these unwanted intruders, as we have seen in the previous chapters. Growing disagreement about the economic impact of global migration on the local workforce has also become a hot political topic, which intersects with recent debates over the degree of cultural and linguistic integration that can be expected (and demanded) of newcomers.[48] These tensions are not entirely new, but they have become more pronounced and urgent in the post-9/11 era. In the European Union, the suggestion that immigrants sign a social contract as a condition for inclusion shows the deep suspicion with which many countries now view even lawfully admitted immigrants, let alone unauthorized entrants.[49]

These tensions are likely to further intensify with the growing concentration of migration pressures: more than ever before, a relatively small number of advanced industrial countries host the bulk of the world's international migrants. In 1990, thirty countries with the largest migrant populations accounted for 75 percent of all migration; in 2005, only twenty-eight countries constituted that proportion.[50] But these figures do not tell the whole story. By 1990, almost 15 percent of all migrants worldwide had settled in a single country: the United States. Over the last fifteen years, that percentage has grown steadily. In 2005, the United States hosted almost 20 percent of the total number of migrants worldwide (the actual percentage is probably higher, as these figures do not include the estimated 10 to 12 million undocumented migrants residing in the United States). Of these immigrants many have arrived from poorer and less stable countries, making the United States a major global redistributor of opportunity, at least for those who have reached its shores.[51] It is no surprise, then, that immigration has become such a controversial and heated topic in recent American politics. Similar debates over immigration policy and its impacts on the welfare and security of the domestic population have, in different tones and with different results, raged in other well-off countries in which migrants comprise a high percentage of the overall population, including Australia, France, the United Kingdom, and Spain.[52]

Another set of concerns relates to the failure to establish greater international coordination or a global regulatory regime of cross-border movements of people. This lack of coordination means that crucial policy decisions, concerning who to admit, why, and for what length of time, are typically made unilaterally by the receiving country; sending countries have little formal say in these matters.[53] A very different path of growing international cooperation has been chosen in regards to open trade (relating to the mobility of capital and goods), which is facilitated by the proliferation of bilateral, regional and international instruments, most notably the always-expanding World Trade Organization (WTO). Yet when it comes to people, the trend has been toward "unilateral, reactive, and essentially restrictive migration policy."[54]

Part of the problem derives from the receiving countries' perception of immigration as a tool to advance their own respective needs, commitments, and interests, rather than a collaborative effort to be coordinated with sending countries or a redistributive measure to alleviate the world's inequality problems.[55] To provide just one illustration, Canada's Immigration Act explicitly pronounces that it is designed "to permit Canada to pursue the maximum social, cultural, and economic benefits of immigration."[56] This national welfare perspective is still the *sine qua non* of immigration; attempts to change it by creating new regional and international agencies have been slow to arrive.[57] The main exception here is the undertaking to provide temporary or permanent resettlement for those whose basic safety is at stake, including refugees, asylum seekers, victims of trafficking, and other protected persons. These humanitarian-stream admissions remain, however, a small part of the overall flow in all admitting countries. If anything, irregular migrants are now ever-more restricted in their international travel, making it harder for genuine refugees to reach these safe havens in wealthier nations given the amplified law-and-order mandate of most border-control agencies.[58] One such example is the procedure of expedited removal, introduced into U.S. immigration law in 1996, which now permits low-level officers at any port of entry to conclusively turn back a person who arrives without the required documentation or admission papers based on mere administrative discretion. This stands in sharp contrast to the standard requirement that a judicial hearing be made before removal, the process that applies to anyone already within the territorial boundaries.[59]

The final, and likely most significant, shortcoming of open-admission solutions ultimately lies with the numbers. Even if all the concerns mentioned above could be addressed, there would remain an upper limit to the institutional capacity of well-off polities to admit newcomers. While there is no agreement on what the "absorption limit" of each country might be, or how best to calculate it (as a relative percentage of the total population, an absolute or annual ceiling, and so on), the fact remains that, in practice, immigrants do not constitute more than 10 percent of the population in almost two-thirds of the countries that permit regulated migration. Among the countries where the percentage of international migrants is higher, only thirty-five have a population of at least one million; that is, these are countries with a relatively low absorption capacity in the first place.[60] Even in the world's major countries of immigration, such as the United States, Canada, and Australia, the percentage of the foreign-born population has never much exceeded 10 to 20 percent of the total population, and these figures refer to the crests of high waves of international migration. We are currently in the midst of one such historical crest. Today's foreign-born population in the United States accounts for 12.9 percent of the population, 18.9 percent in Canada, and 20.3 percent in Australia. Of these newcomers, most are in fact long-term residents who have already been naturalized in their adoptive countries.[61] This is important: the absorption capacity of these particular countries may be greater than others precisely because they have had a relatively steady and stable stream of admission and well-established processes of naturalization. The absorption capacity may be even lower if admission by many is sought in a short period of time; for instance, in response to circumstances that exceed the control of any single polity, such as geopolitical instabilities, environmental catastrophes, economic crises, or armed conflicts.

Even if we do not factor these potential disasters into the equation, the basic problem does not dry up: assuming a world with diverging political regimes and marked economic disparities, we can safely assume that a far greater number of people may wish to enter if provided with a safe and legitimate path in order to do so. The latest available statistics show that approximately 1.75 million immigrants are admitted annually by leading Organization for Economic Co-Operation and Development (OECD) countries.[62] The population residing in the world's poorer and less stable regions amounts to roughly 4.5 billion people. This leads to a ratio of 1:1500 (0.00065 percent) between those granted admission and those who may wish it. Such figures provide just one means by which to measure the tremendous gap between the potential volume of international migration and the current levels of regulated admission. And recall that these numbers do not account for unauthorized entries. Nor do they capture the huge number of people who may desire to move to another country but for whatever reason (personal, financial, familial, political, and so forth) have not actually made any official immigration inquiries.

A similarly revealing insight is captured by looking into the diversity-immigration category in the United States, which offers an annual draw for 50,000 immigration visas, open to nationals of countries deemed underrepresented in U.S. admissions. Individuals applying for these diversity visas must meet certain basic requirements in order to qualify for selection (for example, they must have a high school diploma or equivalent and must have at least two years of experience in an occupation that requires at least two years of training). These requirements, which emphasize education and employability, already narrow the field significantly, but despite very slim chances for selection, about 8.7 million applications were received in 2003; the numbers climbed to more than 10 million registered participants in 2008. Most of these applicants, harboring dreams of a winning entry to the United States, were from developing countries in Asia and Africa: Bangladesh led the pack (more than 1.7 million applicants) followed by Nigeria (684,735).[63] These figures are staggering, but they may well represent only the tip of the iceberg.[64] If permissible admission routes were open to them, many more people, including those now discouraged by legal restrictions or the risks of unlawful crossing, might choose to improve their situation through immigration so long as conditions remain dire in their home countries. Under ideal conditions, it may be true that "most human beings do not love to move," and they may well prefer to remain in the places and communities to which they feel attached, even if a better life could perhaps be sought elsewhere.[65] Yet in a world of severe inequalities, people are unmistakably voting with their feet: they are taking increasingly dangerous routes in order to enter the territories of well-off countries, often putting their lives at risk, just like the stowaways whose tragic story I recounted in the introductory chapter. Others have come to rely on "coyote"-assisted clandestine crossings under the burning sun of the Arizona desert or the dangerous crossing of the Iberian sea, to name but two of the more familiar unauthorized-entry routes that have come to the forefront of public debate.[66]

As Philip Cole keenly observes, well-intentioned arguments in favor of open-admission policies (as advanced by moral universalists) have generated their own problem of exclusion: "if we accept the legitimacy of any of the arguments which impose an upper limit on the number who can be admitted as new members, the challenge is not so much how to arrive at that number, but to decide who will be included within it."[67] Instead of distinguishing between members and nonmembers, observes Cole, "the crucial boundary now runs between non-members who will be included and those [who] will remain excluded."[68] In short, proponents of greater permeability have paid too little attention to the structural limits of the proposed remedy and the depth of the disparities at issue, which call for a more direct resolution to the problem of perpetuating the unequal life opportunities that currently attach to birthright citizenship—rather than merely relying on indirect measures, such as advocacy for open-admission policies.

But let us not despair. The articulation of the problems with international mobility is not intended to belittle the significance of this option. For those without birthright privilege in an affluent democracy, immigration provides a possible way to attain the precious and globally scarce good of citizenship in a stable and well-off polity. It thus opens the gate that typically remains tightly sealed by birthright entails. Once admitted, individuals and families gain the right not to be excluded, with all the security and opportunity that attaches to such status. In this respect, regulated migration represents a lifeline, substantively transforming the universe of those who lack inherited title. While fully acknowledging this crucial feature of the international migration process, I still believe that we must also recognize its Achilles' heel. As a tool of global redistribution, international migration provides extremely generous returns to a limited group of recipients: and largely to those individuals whose employment skills or family ties provide them more swift admission through existing immigration categories in receiving states. Regulated migration also offers hope to those admitted under the various humanitarian categories, though as mentioned earlier, such admissions typically represent only a small percentage of the overall annual intakes.[69]

Although "saving one life, is saving the world" (as the Talmudic saying goes), it is still difficult to ignore the fact that any form of international migration can ultimately assist only a limited number of people. I mentioned earlier that there are roughly 2.7 billion people living on less than $2 per day, and more than 4.5 billion altogether in the world's "less developed" and "least developed" countries (to use the bureaucratic terminology of the United Nations). Suppose we set out to address the charge that rich nations should open their borders more fully, on the grounds that it is deeply unjust for morally arbitrary factors to determine people's life chance. Imagine if we then increased levels of admission by a margin of 100 percent, or even 500 percent. Even this drastic move would not alter the fundamental problem we face; the majority of the world's destitute would still see little opportunity to gain (lawful) entry into desired destination states.[70] In most cases, the international migrants that manage to reach the wealthy countries are not drawn from the ranks of those living on less than $2 a day. Consequently, as a global redistribution tool, migration fails to reach those at the bottom of the distributional matrix.[71] In light of this analysis, it becomes clear that the demand for immigration may prove far greater than the limited supply on offer. In the larger scheme of things, this redistribution is only a drop in the ocean. And it is a complicated drop at that: moving people across borders and offering them resettlement in a new country is a difficult process for all involved, even under the best of circumstances. At present, it is rendered even more complex by the growing political resistance to immigration among members of well-off polities who feel that their own security, identity, and relative advantage are at stake.

Taking these considerations into account does not necessarily discount the argument in favor of greater mobility as an expression of human liberty and freedom. But it does demonstrate that if opening our borders offers only the second-best option for alleviating disparities in a drastically unequal world it may be time to return to the metaphorical drawing board and search for more direct ways to respond to the connection between birth, citizenship, and unequal opportunity. We have just seen that even in a best-case scenario, international migration would only provide the answer for a small fraction of those in need globally; this approach also fails to address the dire conditions that cause people to want to leave their home countries in the first place.

Having identified some of the shortcomings of increased global mobility as an ultimate solution, I now turn to the alternative of *redistributing opportunity*. This approach aims to provide a more far-reaching solution and to improve the situation of all people wherever they happen to have been born. On this alternative, the focus is shifted from ownership and possession of membership entitlement per se to its derivative benefits, which are more easily distributed.[72] Redistribution of this kind allows us to tap the vast accumulation of wealth and opportunity that has been sustained by the current birthright system of entailed citizenship, and draw on it as a steadfast source of revenue for funding redistributive programs wherever they are needed most. This solution is of course fully compatible with a call for greater mobility across borders, whether in the near or more distant future.

Curtailed Inheritance: Taxing Birthright Recipients of Membership Title

The challenge for us is to target the injustice of a birthright-transmission system that permits morally arbitrary circumstances of birth to dramatically shape people's life chances while at the same time preserving the collective good of citizenship. Also contemplated is the expansion of the very definition of access to membership beyond birthright entitlement, as articulated in Chapter 6. As I argued in Chapter 1, once we reconceptualize membership status in an affluent society as a complex type of inherited property, the distributive implications of hereditary citizenship become more immediately visible: they can no longer hide behind the naturalizing veil of birthright. What remains to be seen, however, is whether the valuable aspects of bounded membership (including its identity, security, and enabling dimensions) can be sustained, while at the same time addressing the presently inequality-perpetuating *transfer* mechanism of citizenship: the transmission of birthright. I shall argue here that to treat citizenship as if it were a special kind of property is to invite parallels from core insights in inheritance theory to the arena of birthright citizenship. This analogy gives rise to a novel solution: given the limitations on the redistribution of citizenship titles per se, greater promise lies in imposing justifiable restrictions on the inheritance of membership entitlement in ways that target the perpetuities aspect of birthright citizenship.

What we must do, then, is tackle head-on the perpetual and unrestricted transfer of membership. This automatic transfer constitutes a morally weak link, inviting legal intervention. I discussed previously the long-established tradition of thinking critically about the perpetual intergenerational transmission of wealth and power in the context of property theory. It is useful for us to revisit here some of these theoretical foundations, as they may provide a starting point for the development of related ideas and techniques in the realm of birthright citizenship. Rather than contemplate the extremes of either trivializing notions of political membership or refortifying borders with renewed vigor, the way forward is to think creatively about new ways to reduce the correlation between birthright citizenship and inequality of actual life opportunities.

The curtailing inheritance approach that I put forward in the following pages provides an important missing link in this regard. It introduces a new argument for rewriting the property-like dimension of citizenship, establishing a threshold duty to legitimize an otherwise unjust transfer system by ensuring that the basic life prospects of those denied membership are fulfilled. This redistributive duty effectively acts as a direct corollary to the right of members to enjoy the privilege of their inherited entitlement. Such an approach takes seriously the special relationships encapsulated in the broad conception of membership, while at the same time attending to the impact of birthright transfer on those locked outside the enclosed circle of members. It introduces the option of taxing the more fungible (or wealth-related) aspects of recipients' inherited membership titles without intruding into the more identity-laden dimensions of bounded membership. I will label this redistributive remedy the *birthright privilege levy.*

This framework of analysis permits overcoming the (misguided) perception that to maintain the valuable properties of bounded membership, we must accept as inevitable its pernicious distributive consequences for much of the world. The answer fortunately, does not force an either/or solution. We can both defend the best of citizenship's enabling qualities and at the same time challenge its worst gate-keeping effects. Recognition of the dramatic and unjust effects of birthright membership regimes is the first step. What follows is an effort to mitigate the harmful effects of the lottery that distinguishes "us" from "them." This effort may take the form of requesting recipients of inherited titles, namely those with a vested interest in preserving the existing legal regime, to improve the life prospects of those who have arbitrarily been denied similar opportunities. As a final step, the details of program development must be worked out to address the critical concerns of health, education, access to clean water, shelter, and the like, so that at least certain minimum standards are guaranteed to all who are affected by the birthright lottery.

Acknowledging the ethical imperative for remediation only takes us so far. Significant challenges remain. Since ours is a world of guarded borders, citizenship in an affluent and stable polity remains both immensely valuable and beyond the reach of the vast majority of the global population. The suggestion to toll the privilege of citizenship inheritance fully acknowledges this reality. It is informed by a relational and institutional approach to global justice that demands accountability for the fact that the very same birthright citizenship laws that grant membership in well-off polities to some inevitably interact with others to whom access is denied.

In the closing section of this chapter, I elaborate upon the institutional means for enabling initiatives. But first, I turn to the role of estate taxation in the context of property and inheritance theory as supplying the foundations of the logic of the birthright-levy.

Borrowing from Inheritance in Property Theory

Most theories of justice and property allow for unequal accumulation of wealth and other resources. A quick guide to the perplexed is still called for, however, in order to articulate the considerable amount of thought devoted to providing justificatory grounds for defending such inequity in the distribution of holdings. More important still for the purposes of our discussion is the recognition that all modern theories of property and justice impose significant restrictions on the social institutions that generate inequality. This is precisely what is missing in the prevailing framework of birthright citizenship. Here, we find very few (if any) obligations imposed on the beneficiaries of hereditary title to contribute to the redistribution of opportunity or equalization of fortune through the reduction of social inequality of those having a less privileged starting point. Instead, it upholds and reinforces the outdated structures of entailed ownership—the dead hand controlling the unequal distribution of opportunity with dramatic effects on the living—to which all modern property theories take issue.

The basic dilemma is this: inheritance violates the ideal of equality of starting points; wealth is opportunity and inheritance distributes it very unevenly.[73] The solution, for most thinkers, is to impose restrictions against the unrestrained inheritance of swollen fortunes. As one account nicely puts it, "justice demands a constant erosion of accumulated fortunes to limit this influence."[74] It is intuitively clear that in an unequal world, inheritance of the "property" of citizenship distributes opportunity very unevenly. As we have already seen, birthright citizenship in a well-off polity carries with it not only important identity and security values but also significant opportunity-enhancing implications for the recipient. In spite of this, the mainstream literature on the topic of citizenship has paid very little attention to these dramatic distributive aspects of bounded membership on a global scale. This, in turn, serves to camouflage the significance of the legal regime of transmitting citizenship primarily through ascriptive mechanisms, making access to membership a distributor of highly unequal life prospects. It is possible, however, to overcome this stalemate by expanding our analysis of citizenship beyond its familiar identity-bonding dimension to include the wealth-preserving aspect, too. This can be achieved by drawing upon the manifold critiques of unfettered inheritance that are elaborated in the realm of property.

Virtually all the giants of social and economic thought have paid close attention to the question of the intergenerational transfer of wealth and its implications on equality of opportunity. Competing philosophical accounts of property and inheritance are offered by almost all the major schools: classic liberal thinkers, utopian socialists, analytical marxists, contemporary liberal egalitarians, and libertarians.[75] Although I can recount only a handful of these arguments here, the crucial point is this: all agree that a relevant distinction exists between the initial acquisition of property and its transfer by inheritance; the notion that far more extensive restrictions can be placed on the latter than the former is also widely shared.[76]

Inheritance poses a number of challenges for jurists and philosophers: it does not sit well with the major bases for acquisition of property (effort, merit, distribution according to productivity, need, and so on); it may lead to an inefficient allocation of resources; it limits the freedom of those who are excluded due to predetermined circumstances surrounding their birth; and, most importantly for our discussion, it violates the principle of equal opportunity. To paraphrase William Blake, some are born to sweet delight; others to endless night. Importantly, this is not some genetic or innate endowment that we cannot control; rather it is a human-made regime of legal entitlement that our citizenship laws perpetuate and then disguise under the cloak of a natural given. In the march of history, we have many times before seen the privileged attempt to give a sort of social sanction to their landed or inherited property, whether through claims of a divine order in older times or in more recent times through the instrumentality of laws imposed by themselves. In the case of citizenship, as with property, these laws are coercive; their effect is felt not only by their beneficiaries, but also by those excluded from access. In the realm of hereditary membership, it leads to an unbalanced concentration of power and wealth in the hands of heirs of certain body politicks, while preventing others from entering these membership systems or enjoying their benefits on fair and open terms. The reason is simple: "the influence of the institution of inheritance highlight[s] the effects of all other inequalities, by determining the vantage-ground upon which different groups and individuals shall stand, [and] the range of opportunities which shall be open to them."[77]

In their writing on economics, many classic liberal political and legal theorists (including Jeremy Bentham, William Blackstone, Adam Smith, Immanuel Kant, and John Stuart Mill) have argued that the right of inheritance may be upheld, but only if significant restrictions are imposed upon it. These thinkers flatly reject the Lockean view of property and its succession as natural rights. Rather, they treat rights such as inheritance as *created* and *regulated* by law in civil society.[78] There is no sound reason why this view cannot be extended (based on the analysis offered here) to the realm of citizenship, also. As such, both are subject to regulation and limitations, including the instrument of taxation. In *Commentaries on the Laws of England* (1766), Blackstone famously notes, inheritance is "clearly a political establishment; [it is] not *natural,* but merely a *civil* right . . . [W]ills, therefore, and testaments, rights of inheritance and successions, are all of them creatures of the civil or municipal laws, and accordingly are in all respects *regulated* by them."[79] Thomas Jefferson echoes this notion imbuing it with radical redistributive implications when stating that the "portion [of the earth] occupied by any individual ceases to be his when he himself ceases to be, and reverts to society."[80] We shall later see that many other iconic thinkers share this intuition; the debates among them focus on what precisely reverts to the society—the whole estate, part thereof, the reminder after fulfilling certain justified expectations, to name but a few possible resolutions. The crucial point here is that any of these options is preferable over the current citizenship status quo of unburdened intergenerational transmissions of prized membership titles.

In their writings, neither Bentham nor Mill regard succession by collateral heirs as a right at all and recommend its abolition. Even inheritance by direct descendants may be limited to a reasonable degree. In his *Supply without Burthen or Escheat vice Taxation* (1795), Bentham launches a vigorous attack on the ethical justifications of the institution of inheritance and insists upon the "unburthensomeness" of levying heavy taxes on it. Whereas the abolition of inheritance would promote indifference and create a disincentive to accumulate wealth, limited inheritance, as Bentham proposed, would not "preclude a man from changing his estate, from changing the nature of it, or from giving or spending it in his lifetime." In *Theory of Legislation,* Bentham outlines his proposal for limitations on intergeneration transfer of wealth. "When property by death of the proprietor ceases to have an owner, the law can interfere in its distribution, either by limiting in certain respects the testamentary power in order to prevent too great an accumulation of wealth in the hands of an individual, or by regulating the succession in favor of equality in cases where the deceased has left no consort, nor relation in the direct line, and has made no will. The question then relates to new acquirers who have formed no expectations; here, equality may do what is best for all without disappointing any."[81] Bentham went on to propose a regulation of inheritance according to the following principles: "1st, Provision for the subsistence of the rising generation; 2nd, Prevention of disappointment; 3rd, The equalization of fortunes."[82] It is this latter restriction that currently remains unfulfilled in a world where birthright principles both determine the boundaries of membership and reify them as a natural allocation of entitlement that is *not* subject to consideration of equalization of fortunes. According to Bentham's contemporary, Adam Smith, it would be both expedient and just to reduce the fortunes of certain individuals (after they received what he calls "their portion") if the well-being of the majority could thereby be enhanced. Inheritance as the product of impersonal market forces could be regulated by taxation of heirs if it resulted in overenrichment of the few.

John Stuart Mill agrees. Unlimited succession and inheritance do not make sense from a macroutilitarian standpoint. Unearned advantages that stem from inherited wealth and the consequent distribution of benefits and opportunities in an inverse ratio to labor must be limited.[83] Mill's position was, in fact, more far-reaching than Bentham; "he adopted the substance of Bentham's proposal to collateral inheritance, but he went farther and wished to limit inheritance in the direct line also."[84] Restrictions, he argued, must be put on the estates that people should be permitted to obtain by inheritance or bequest. Specifically, Mill advocates two such core restrictions: first, "a limitation of the *sum* which any person may acquire by gift or inheritance to the amount sufficient to constitute a moderate independence";[85] second, a *progressive tax upon all inheritance above a certain minimum,* set at a rate to produce the greatest revenue without inducing evasion or concealment of property.[86]

These are powerful ideas. Applying them to the realm of hereditary citizenship may, literally, change our world. Just imagine the potentially striking ramifications of imposing a limitation on the public inheritance (or "sum" in Mill's terminology) presently passed down (without any redistributive justice obligation) through birthright citizenship to the recipients of title—yet without abolishing their secured enjoyment of the enabling dimension of membership, or, to follow Mill, its "nourishment of independence." This alternative structure of citizenship transfer permits freeing up the *remainder* to progressive taxation, with proceeds to be directed toward improving the life prospects of those who are not so fortunate.[87] The beauty of this model is that it does not deprive the birthright beneficiaries of their citizenship entitlement; instead, it distributes the social benefits that derive from membership in well-off polities across borders to those who are left outside for no reason other than their station of birth. It also responds to the urgent need to provide such infusion of resources to fund "global public goods" (like the environment, poverty reduction, and so on) and contributing toward the goal of improving the enabling function everywhere, thus reducing the correlation between birthright citizenship and global disparities of voice and opportunity.

This borrowing from property theory thus justifies imposing a limitation on the presently unburdened citizenship inheritance that is bestowed upon windfall recipients. It permits us also to revolt against the injustice of this present situation, according to which birthright heirs are released from any legal responsibility for the betterment of the lives of those who are coercively excluded by no fault or responsibility of their own, but instead by the legal regime that underpins the lottery of birthright.

The writing on the wall is clear: the present entail-like regime of transfer must not be permitted to continue unchecked, especially once we adopt the citizenship-as-inherited-property analogy and take account of birthright's significance in shaping life prospects in an unequal world. The children of well-off polities have done nothing to merit more opportunities in life than the children of poorer nations, yet the current property/membership system grants the former ample privileges without imposing any corresponding obligations upon them to break down the concentration of wealth, security, and freedom that they have done nothing to earn.

Unlike the other proposals on offer (which we saw in this and the previous chapters) the birthright levy does not embrace the devaluation of citizenship's enabling function or the special relations that generate such a heightened obligation among members; instead, it seeks to mitigate the external distributive implications of birthright's gate-keeping operation. Returning to the analogy to property and inheritance, it is notable that Mill asserted that those with special relations (here, children) have a legitimate expectation of the provision of "such education, and such appliances and means, as will enable them to start with a fair chance of achieving their own exertion of a successful life. To this every child has a claim." But he also added an important caveat: "I cannot admit, that as a child, he has a claim to more."[88] This last point is important. Beneficiaries of *jus soli* and *jus sanguinis* may well have a legitimate claim to expect fulfillment by their political community of "a fair chance of achieving their own exertion of a successful life." But this does not automatically confer on them a more expansive right to the whole estate. Rather, once "thus much has been done," in Mill's words, the children's interests and expectations are in no way violated if "the remainder of the parent's fortune is devoted to public uses."[89] Again, we fail to find any similar restriction in the current world of birthright citizenship, where the heirs of well-off political communities are automatically and uncritically assumed to deserve entitlement to the "whole estate." This argument is particularly powerful with regard to those aspects of citizenship's inheritance that are more clearly the workings of fortune passed down to us by distant forebears than any form of value-additive activities of the present generation.

Another compelling idea in this context is the notion of a "declining intergenerational entitlement" structure that resembles an innovative proposal developed by Eugenio Rignano in the early twentieth century as part of the effort to curtail the inequality that attaches to intergenerational transfers of wealth.[90] Rignano was searching for a way to restrict inheritance without destroying the incentives that motivate individuals to work and save; his proposed solution to this dilemma was "to differentiate the right of bequest according to the 'origin' or 'age' of the property to be bequeathed."[91] In a nutshell, his schema differentiated between the property that a person created or saved during his or her lifetime and that which was inherited. "Earned" property was classified as "0 transfer" property, and carried with it an irrefutable claim to ownership. At each stage that the property passed down the generations, the transfer value increased: "1 transfer," "2 transfer," and so on. The greater the transfer number, the weaker the claim to inheritance became—each "level" attracting a graduated higher rate of taxation. The importance of the Rignano principle to the current discussion is reflected in its reference to the intergenerational transmission mechanism: as the distance in time increases, the claim diminishes. The "Rignano principle," as it came to be known, stipulates that the higher the number of transfers, the weaker the entitlement of the heir; this in turn permits a steeper rate of taxation on the iterated intergenerational transfer. In other words, the greater the generational distance from the original title holder, the weaker the recipient's claim for unlimited and uninterrupted transfer of the bequest. (I explore the declining entitlement principle's implications for citizenship in Chapter 6.)

In contrast with the creativity and riches of these insights (developed in the realm of property and inheritance), the current state of the theory and practice of birthright citizenship leaves much to be desired; we have not developed even the basic vocabulary and analytical categories to begin to address some of the fundamental inequalities inherent in the present system. For example, we are unable to draw similar restrictions in the citizenship context against an unlimited and perpetual transfer of entitlement as we have succeeded in doing in the realm of property law. Nor are we yet able to draw a line between what is rightly owed to children and the remainder that can legitimately be devoted to public uses. Equally, we have yet to even consider seriously the introduction of birthright privilege levies (the subject of my discussion in the following section) or declining membership entitlements (discussed in Chapter 6) that are gaining credence in current times. These are merely a few concrete and promising lines of inquiry that the analogy to inherited property allows us to ponder, and which I address in this and subsequent chapters. Searching for the appropriate balance between protecting the interests of heirs and taxing their inheritance is anything but new in the realm of property; however, an analogous discussion has yet to begin in the realm of citizenship. Although many details need to be addressed as to how to design and enforce these changes, the most important point I wish to stress here is that it represents an important way to reduce the wealth and power concentration that currently remain shielded behind entail-like membership transmission lines and to tackle the consequent disparities in the estate (or opportunity) granted to children according to nothing but their station of birth.

Treating birthright citizenship as a special kind of inherited property thus allows us to import these core insights. It provides us with a rich new vocabulary for generating fresh answers to old questions about how best to mediate the demands of special relations and universal commitments, inheritance and redistribution, citizenship and justice—especially those dealing with ownership, selection, and allocation. More importantly still, I believe this reconceptualization enables us to understand the need to amend the present system of birthright attribution of political membership so as to establish transnational redistributive requirements that will curtail its present contribution to the unequal distribution of voice and opportunity on a global scale.

Applying this compelling logic to the contemporary world provides ample reason for imposing some method of global redistribution on the "remainder" component of the inherited social and other derivative benefits attached to birthright citizenship. Just as progressive inheritance taxation is imposed in order to diffuse the perpetual accumulation of swollen fortunes within the domestic realm, restrictions on the wealth-preserving aspects of birthright citizenship are justified on the grounds of limiting and reducing the continual accumulation of power and affluence in certain body politicks and their cascading generations. If the parallel holds, we find an elegant and intuitive solution to the puzzle of birthright citizenship with which we began.

The obligation to have the remainder devoted to public uses can be interpreted narrowly or broadly, and this is an issue that must be resolved through reiterated deliberations within and across political boundaries. Whatever the standard chosen, there can be no doubt that any acknowledgment along these lines would surely surpass the current absence of obligation. By tying the right to enjoy the transfer of membership by birthright to the imposition of restrictions upon this transfer, we move from the realm of *moral charity* in aiding those outside our borders to that of a *legal duty* to reduce the disparities in life prospects that attach to this system of title transfer in our world of persistent inequalities. To fail to do so is to lose any shred of legitimacy of the existing property/membership inheritance system. By following through on this duty, however, we can begin to undo some the worst effects of the current intergenerational transmission of unequal opportunity on account of the entrenched connection between fortuitous circumstances of birth and entitlement to political membership. The main point here is to recognize that by drawing the analogy of inherited citizenship to intergenerational transfer of wealth and property, a new space is opened up for developing precisely such a platform for change.

Not surprisingly, the dilemmas and tensions provoked by the topic of property inheritance have not escaped the attention of contemporary political and legal theorists. I turn to the core observations of John Rawls, Ronald Dworkin, Robert Nozick, and Brian Barry as a representative sample. The Rawlsian position is, in a nutshell, to offer a synthesis of respecting property rights, individual freedoms, and a commitment to social justice. Rawls thus accepts certain intergenerational transfers of wealth as long as they satisfy the difference principle—that is, inheritance is permitted, provided that the resulting inequalities are to the advantage of the least privileged members of society and are compatible with liberty and fair equality of opportunity.[92] This leads to an endorsement of progressive inheritance taxes to "encourage the wide dispersal of property which is a necessary condition, it seems, if the fair value of the equal liberties is to be maintained."[93]

Ronald Dworkin offers a more comprehensive take on the subject. Dworkin emphasizes the distinction between the consequences of arbitrary brute luck and the consequences of people's own choices.[94] Granted, it is often difficult to differentiate between the two in real life (not least because the former may lead to a situation in which the latter is more likely, and vice versa). In principle, however, justice requires the compensation of individuals for those circumstances beyond their control or for which they cannot be held responsible. A distribution of resources that compensates people for aspects of their situation determined by luck is therefore warranted. Property and wealth inheritance, especially as they relate to vesting estates in persons in some remote time in the future (and by extension birthright citizenship laws) seem appropriate contexts for applying Dworkin's intuitive compensatory matrix. Because the automatic bequest of citizenship bestows unearned advantages and opportunities on some people while excluding others not as a consequence of their actions and choices, but through accidents of birth, it systemically disadvantages those born on the other side of the border of prosperity and security. The special advantages gained by the former may therefore be burdened (or "taxed") to compensate the latter for their arbitrary adversity. There is no real question that an entitlement pattern in which a small subset of the global population is immensely enriched by repeated transfers of birthright-like entails creates an unfair advantage while generating power relations that inhibit the freedom and opportunity of the rest.

Even the ultralibertarian Robert Nozick, who admits fewer restrictions on the acquisition and transfer of property than most other entitlement theorists, specifies as a central tenet of his "unpatterned" theory of justice the requirement that unequal distribution should result from just transfers of justly acquired holdings.[95] Applied to the context of citizenship, it is yet again hard to see how the transfer of property/membership according to birthright fulfills the cardinal requirements of fairness and openness. If anything, from a libertarian perspective, such fixed and repetitive intergenerational transmissions of wealth (and power) through life estates must be seen as problematic; they limit the freedom of each generation to alienate, restrict efficient use, and bar new entrants simply because of the lack of fair and open procedure in obtaining the holding. It is this perpetuity aspect of the transfer that must concern the libertarian, just as an entail structure of property transmission distorts both risk and opportunity (for many of the reasons already articulated in Blackstone's *Commentaries*, as we saw in earlier chapters). This discomfort is clearly marked in Nozick's work as well. As he puts it, "bequests that are received [by those close to the deceased] sometimes then [get] passed on for generations, . . . producing continued inequalities of wealth and position. . . . If it seems appropriate for [the original earner] to pass on what she has earned to those she cherishes and chooses, we are far less certain it is appropriate when these others do the same. The resulting inequalities seem *unfair*."[96] In *The Examined Life*, Nozick specifically addresses the topic of perpetual inheritance, holding that while an original property owner has a right to bestow his fortune upon his or her children or grandchildren, the bequest can only be transferred once. (This is a crude variant of Rignano's principle of "distant in time, weaker in entitlement.") The recipients of bequests can convey any amount that they themselves have earned, but are prohibited from passing on their own inherited wealth; this avoids situations where unearned fortunes "cascade down the generations."[97]

From the other side of the ideological spectrum, liberal egalitarians such as Brian Barry also support a closely related conclusion, holding that the claims of heirs to the special advantages derived from the efforts of their ancestors are quite limited. In *Democracy, Power, and Justice,* Barry argues, much like Nozick though with greater redistributional consequences, that "although the present generation might legitimately derive some special advantages from the efforts of the preceding one, and perhaps the one before that, the part of what they passed on that was in turn inherited from their predecessors should be regarded as by now forming part of the common heritage of mankind."[98]

Birthright Privilege and the Citizenship Levy

These insights lead me to develop a potentially far-reaching idea: namely, placing a birthright privilege levy on the *transfer* of political membership to address the global distributive consequences of birthright citizenship. Tapping into the remainder portion of the unearned advantage of citizenship inheritance could help rectify the coercive and unjust effects of this regime and fund worldwide redistribution of opportunity; the goal here would be to strengthen the enabling function of membership everywhere. The idea is that revenues generated by the privilege levy on inherited citizenship in an affluent polity would be devoted to specific projects designed to improve the life circumstances of children who are most adversely affected by the legal connection drawn between circumstances of birth and citizenship. We can envision these revenues being used, for example, to create a worldwide safety net with the task of ensuring that no child, no matter where or to whom she is born, is left without access to basic goods, such as clean water, food, shelter, education, health care, and so on.[99] In a world where almost a billion people are struggling just to survive, ensuring freedom from want is no small improvement; establishing a more equitable sharing of the spoils of automatic transfers would surely represent a giant leap. This vision of redistributing opportunity globally by placing a tax-like burden on the automatic membership-entitlement transfer locally is, in a nutshell, the core idea behind the birthright privilege levy.

Although novel in its application to the intergenerational transfer of citizenship, the notion of leveling opportunity through burdening inheritance is quite familiar in property theory, as we have just seen. Many of the giants of social and political thought have supported and defended this path, and they have done so from different premises and while holding different ideological stances. Placing such a levy on birthright citizenship for the advancement of global redistributive goals thus holds a tremendous potential: unlike the other alternatives on offer, it offers a defensible formula that allows the continued existence of the special bonds of membership in a polity, while acknowledging as binding a set of external obligations toward those left outside our bounty. In this way, moral commitments to global distributive justice are meaningfully transformed into binding legal obligations.

By taxing the privilege of transmitting membership in this way (rather than taking away ownership from those who were bestowed citizenship at birth), the assumption that such disparities cannot continue to exist in an unequal world without restriction or remedy is met with a concrete legal response. As a policy tool, putting levies on bequests at the moment when wealth is transferred from one generation to another has always been employed to enhance progressivity.[100] In the context of citizenship, the relevant transmission occurs when the public title of citizenship is bestowed upon a birthright-membership heir in a well-off polity.

Building on these notions, the global birthright levy is intended to redistribute resources (or valuable infrastructure, services, or transfers-in-kind) from those who have disproportionately benefited from the intergenerational transfer of the property of citizenship to those who have not. It combines "privilege-accession" taxation with expenditure programs that, in Anne Alstott's words, "level-up opportunity."[101] In this way, it establishes a new basis for tackling the problem of birthright citizenship and global (in)justice, without calling for an outright abolition of bounded membership as a precondition for responding to the claims of those who are not recipients of the property itself. By tying the redistributive obligation to the very legitimacy of the system of transfer, the levy offers a solid and continuing source of funding for improving the life prospects of those adversely affected by the birthright system of membership allocation.

As I mentioned earlier, under the influence of Ronald Dworkin's work, it is now commonplace to distinguish between unequal outcomes that result from people's choices and efforts, and those that result from a windfall. The former are seen as permissible (with some restrictions under specific circumstances), while the latter are typically considered morally weak bases for enrichment. This leads to the stipulation that recipients of unearned fortune should transfer some of their chance gains to those who suffer from equally undeserved misfortune. Heirs who gain birthright citizenship—often from parents who have themselves inherited membership—have in no way "earned" their wealth and entitlement as a result of relevant choices or efforts. It is for this reason that tapping a portion of the remainder of citizenship inheritance is entirely consistent with the notion that the effects of predetermined circumstances on a person's life opportunities should be minimized, as much as possible, without violating other relevant values and interests.

Constraints on windfall benefits may still be consistent with the expectation that all children born in wealthier polities are entitled to enjoy "such education, and such appliances and means, as will enable them to start with a fair chance of achieving their own exertion of a successful life." Birthright citizenship may still ensure a priority claim to life's essentials. What is unfounded is any claim to the whole estate as of right. Instead, the remainder may be put to common, transnational benefits. In this way the inequity of accidents of birth with respect to citizenship entitlement may no longer hide behind a veil of naturalness.

Beyond its potential to offer tangible assistance to those who need it most, placing a levy on inherited privilege also has a powerful symbolic or signaling effect.[102] Consider these other well-known examples: we tax polluters or other property holders when their behavior is seen as socially irresponsible or harmful to others. Such taxation imposes visible costs and highlighting disapproval of the failure to consider an action's consequences.[103] The same logic applies here as well. A birthright privilege levy on citizenship signals to the beneficiaries in well-off polities that they cannot continue to enjoy inherited accumulated wealth and power without restraint. This is especially so in a world like our own in which many want for even basic safety and other life necessities. Similar arguments were advanced in the past in favor of imposing domestic liability to curtail the intergenerational transfers of "swollen fortunes" (as Theodore Roosevelt memorably put it). For instance, advocates of the federal estate tax in the United States, which was adopted in 1916, were well aware of its signaling effects. Indeed, most accounts suggest that they saw the estate tax (applied at progressively graduated rates) as a way to highlight socioeconomic matters rather than focus on its purely fiscal effects.[104] The point was to find a legal policy that responded to the moral outrage expressed by many at the time against the staggering wealth that had been accumulated and passed down the generational line by a very small number of American family dynasties. This transmission of wealth was seen to grant an unfair head-start: an advantage that made even orthodox economists uncomfortable "with the transmission of rewards so totally unrelated to the recipient's own contribution."[105]

To import these ideas from the world of property theory to the domain of citizenship and global justice requires several modifications. For one, given that citizenship is a multilayered concept, the global redistribution levy can be undertaken in many different ways, all of which target the wealth-preserving aspects of intergenerational transfers rather than the identity-bonding and other nonquantifiable characteristics of citizenship. The birthright levy may involve the familiar route of resource transfers (calculated as some proportion of the worth of the entitlement of inherited citizenship, as described below). Just like any estate or inheritance taxation, the birthright privilege levy would be owed just once in a lifetime; discharging the obligation may take the form of a lump sum or lifetime annuity, depending on each polity's own practices and principles.[106] The duty owed (or service in lieu, as discussed below) should ideally be partly subsidized by each member of the political community in fulfilling this collective obligation that arises out of the good of membership.[107] For, according to the broad conception, each enjoys the same right not-to-be excluded from whatever enabling opportunities and decision-making mechanisms are attached to the prized citizenship entitlement. However, given the reality of internal inequities within every society, raising revenue to fulfill a polity's transnational contribution to the birthright privilege levy fund will inevitably involve (just as with any other discussion about progressive inheritance taxation) complex decisions about where to peg a threshold for exemptions and how best to define justifiable deductions. Without delving into too technical a discussion, it is enough at this stage to state the overarching principle: once a country's redistributive duty is set, the birthright privilege liability should apply to everyone within the well-off political community who enjoys its enabling functions, subject to familiar need-based, gender-sensitive, minimal-income thresholds and related exemptions and deductions.[108] This rule-plus-exemption structure is significant in ensuring that global transfers do not worsen intranational distribution of opportunity.

The privilege levy could equally well, or perhaps preferably, be paid in the form of public service. Here, again, each member shall contribute according to her ability. For example, as a birthright heir you might be expected to make some use of your privilege to do good in the world; if you did not, your political community would have to compensate for your failure to act by making a financial contribution to, or an investment in, infrastructure in a less advantaged polity.[109] Given the scope of the problem of global disparities, we must, as Abhijit Vinayak Banerjee recently put it, "reject counsels of despair about the futility of [global] development aid" and try instead to find sensible ideas that actually work.[110] In our context, the most sensible ideas refer to improving the basic life conditions that put millions of innocent children at severe risk: malnutrition, lack of access to safe water or the absence of medical treatment, to mention just a few major culprits. Although a range of answers have been proposed to respond to the mega challenge of making poverty history (the familiar slogan referring to the United Nation's Millennium Development Goals to which the world committed itself in 2000), the birthright privilege levy can make its mark by "saving lives and educating minds" while responding to the different voices and demands raised by the relevant populations in need. This active, do-good commitment may be implemented in various imaginative ways. Consider just a few illustrative examples: the public-service component of the levy can be fulfilled by the creation of a Global Teaching Fellows Program, the Midwives International Volunteer Corps, or the Society of Engineers for a Safer World. In each of these examples, citizens-of-privilege are transformed into foot soldiers in the fight to eradicate the staggering consequences of the injustice of birthright citizenship in today's world.[111]

By going beyond the tired reliance on impersonal and often cumbersome foreign aid programs (which have had a troubled history of being misapplied or not fully utilized to assist those in dire need), birthright privilege levy makes concrete the struggle against global deprivation. It invites those enjoying the privilege of birthright to appreciate the bounty of their inherited property and bear its accompanying moral responsibility toward those not so fortune. Bringing this message back home can be achieved, for example, by providing infrastructure and doing groundwork in villages where pregnant mothers currently have no access to pre- and post-natal care; in cities where children enter the workforce before they ever reach the age of primary school; and in towns where sewage-treatment systems remain a pipe dream and where people of all ages continue to consume dangerously contaminated water. In each of these, and many related examples, contributors to the global safety net (and their local counterparts) can make a significant difference for the better. Opening these redistributive and participatory routes, along with greater options for migration, development, and good governance reforms, permits overcoming past mistakes, focusing instead on real and tangible improvements in the lives of those most adversely affected by the lottery of birthright. Building roads, power lines, schools, and clinics is surely better than allowing unearned fortunes to swell and cascade down the generational lines without restriction. In this way, the global birthright levy also contributes to another, and more immediate, task of making visible (through the signaling effect) what is now taken for granted; namely, the natural entitlement through membership at birth to profoundly unequal life prospects and potential for well being.[112]

Although there is a long-standing tradition that urges members of wealthier nations to contribute to bettering the lives of those who are less fortunate, the birthright-levy proposal shifts such redistribution from the realm of charity or morality to that of *legal* obligation, one that grows coherently from the analogy to inherited property. It also emphasizes empowerment, local organization, and skills and infrastructure transfers over and above any righteous (and corruption-prone) cash donations; these sentiments are shared by many engaged in "making aid work" on the ground. The familiar rationales for making transborder contributions from wealthier to developing countries can be quickly (and all too simply) summarized as following: (1) the moral imperative/humanitarian grounds (for instance, treating extreme poverty as an injustice that shocks the conscience and requires the rest of the world to bail out those facing premature death from hunger or near-absolute deprivation);[113] (2) some form of restorative justice (for example, compensating countries or peoples for past wrongs or unjust enrichment often due to a history of colonization or occupation);[114] (3) a utilitarian diminishing-returns argument (for example, an additional dollar goes much further in Mozambique than it does, say, in Canada);[115] (4) reputation benefits for contributing and cooperative nations (this includes gains in international reputation and credibility for the countries participating in such international efforts); and (5) direct or indirect promotion in concert of the self-interest of the donor and recipient states (for instance, development funds used to address acute problems with significant cross-border externalities, such as health pandemics, nonstate terrorism, ecological disasters, geopolitical instabilities producing large numbers of displaced persons, and so forth).

Although all of the above justifications have been discussed extensively in the literature and bear significant merit, it is only when we view citizenship as an arbitrary advantage obtained through the accident of birth and codified in existing citizenship laws that it makes sense to view the global levy on the immense opportunities that attach to inherited membership in terms of legal obligation. It is in this context that I present the proposal to establish a levy on the privilege of gaining birth-based entitlement to membership in a well-off polity: a proposal that is designed to supplement rather than replace the existing bases for reducing global disparities.

Institutional Design Options for the Citizenship Tax

What would a birthright privilege scheme look like? I briefly sketch here a number of different methods for financing the birthright privilege levy; these possibilities are raised here in order to generate discussion rather than to provide an exhaustive list of options for implementation. As Brian Barry once observed, "economists and accountants [and we might add, lawyers and development experts] would no doubt have a field day arguing about the details."[116] Defining different possibilities for institutional design is undoubtedly a serious and sensitive business, but the process begins first and foremost with a compelling and creative idea. In what follows, the several possible forms that this proposal might take are considered in order to encourage serious debate about the possibility of taxing birthright privilege.

There are two different issues here: determining who must pay and how much (the revenue-raising side), and ensuring that the funds raised are used to extend basic opportunities to all in the best possible way (the expenditure side). The wealth of development literature and experience over the last decades clearly shows that the design and implementation of global redistributive programs must be informed heavily by contextual decision making and local consultation. I treat these as accepted ground rules for the birthright privilege levy. But before contemplating whether governments, NGOs, national, local, regional or international agencies (or a combination thereof) are best suited to providing a particular service or whether we should set up a new infrastructure program, we must first explore how to establish a system of contributions that is able to support a constant and stable stream of global transfers destined for enhancing opportunity.

When we contemplate the possibilities for calculating the contribution of each government, we can envisage a formula based upon its annual birth rate (typically calculated as the number of live births for every 1,000 people), multiplied by a fixed dollar base, representing a onetime payment per child that would offset the advantage gained from inheriting citizenship in a well-off polity in the context of an unequal world. These revenues would be used strictly for infrastructure programs directed at enhancing the situation of children in the recipient countries (for example, eradicating malnutrition, providing clean water, investing in health, education, and so forth). The goal here would be to distribute opportunity more fairly, weakening the current correlation between birth-based membership attribution laws and the unequal distribution of starting points in life.

We can further imagine a division of the world into ranked groupings, such as the familiar UN categorization that distinguishes between "more developed regions" (comprising all regions in Western Europe plus North America, Australia, New Zealand, and Japan; in other words, the more prosperous and democratic countries of the world) and "less" and "least developed regions" that would define which countries would be asked to collect the levy for the birthright fund and which would benefit from it.[117] Such a mechanism would clearly represent an improvement on the status quo, where the heirs of entailed citizenship are subject to zero taxation for their privilege (just like so many generations of aristocratic dynasties under the landed estates regime). This division of states also carries with it a pragmatic advantage in that these worldwide categorizations already form part of an institutional structure and could therefore facilitate a swifter implementation of the privilege levy. The main disadvantage, however, is that this division into the "haves" and "have-nots" might be too crude to account for the potentially vast differences in gross domestic product (GDP) and per capita income among the more developed countries, and the ever-greater variation in the needs of children in the less and least developed countries.

A more nuanced variation is to move from a fixed categorization mechanism to a more flexible system, in which the birthright privilege levy is funded by annual contributions calculated in reference to size of citizenry, actual birth rate, and a given country's ranking on an internationally recognized matrix, such as the UN Human Development Index. The idea here is that the proceeds (or equivalent contributions through in-kind transfers) would be distributed on a parallel basis but in reverse order. Assume, for example, a matrix with 200 countries. The country occupying the first spot represents the most-well-off polity in terms of human development, while the country ranked two-hundredth is the most disadvantaged. On this matrix, the country ranked number one will be obliged to make transfers to the residents of country 200, calculated, for example, at a set rate of say $1,000 per capita (multiplied by that country's newborn population per year). The country ranked number two will make transfers to country 199 at a declining rate of $990 per capita. Country three will contribute its proceeds to country 198 at the rate of $980 per capita and so forth. (Each country's precise level of contribution would be periodically revisited.) The advantage of this institutional design is that it accounts for the relative advantage gained by birthright citizenship in different polities and aims to ensure that the heaviest obligations are imposed on the governments whose citizens are the greatest beneficiaries of the present property/membership regime.

Another creative possibility that can be built into these various proposals is to implement a tax discount or substitution scheme. For instance, the wealthier grouping of countries (or a single member thereof) could qualify for such a discount by either (a) operating extended immigration admission routes or larger overall allowances of entry permits for migrants from the poorer ranked countries, or (b) establishing public service options for its citizens, in conjunction and consultation with local or national authorities, to create a transnational pool of birthright-levy volunteer corps, whose task would be to transfer skills, knowledge, technology, education, health, and so on.[118] Such a system would provide a quantifiable contribution on the ground, avoid the endless hazards of corruption and meddling of various intermediaries that often attach to monetary donations, and create an expanded social and global awareness of those participating in these international exchange programs—potentially sowing the seeds for lasting bonds that would reach beyond any such formal public service period.[119]

Just as we can imagine a situation of a tax discount, well-off countries may be subject to a levy "multiplier" as well. Consider a scenario where an advanced industrial country chooses to implement a policy that resembles the commodification approach (discussed in Chapter 2) by admitting as immigrants only those who can pay a hefty entry price and closing the door to anyone else. This is a step backward in terms of global redistribution of opportunity, which in the account offered here needs to be reflected in the imposition of a heavier levy liability.

Obviously, there are many details that must be ironed out before the birthright levy, in any of its variants, could begin to funnel infrastructure funds (or service-in-kind) from the heirs of entail in well-off polities to those disadvantaged by the very same laws of birthright allocation in pursuit of a global redistribution of opportunity. Assuming that the proposed birthright privilege levy scheme gained international momentum, it could offer a viable way forward from the current system in which no moral or legal obligation is acknowledged with respect to the dramatic disparities in advantage that are transmitted by birth. Surely it is time to move beyond the status quo in which ascriptive membership regimes have been condoned, and even actively supported.

To sum up, the birthright privilege levy, as conceived here, is designed to generate a viable and reliable source of revenue to ensure that no child falls below a certain threshold of life-expectancy and well-being. A variety of creative institutional methods could allow us to reach this objective, which itself is uncontroversial. Indeed, the world has already committed to it as one of the global millennium goals. The more charged question is how to identify this obligation as a demand of justice and a duty of the privileged that goes beyond charity. Moving beyond the familiar set of pleas for global justice that appeal to our shared humanity, the discussion above has uncovered a deep analytical basis for transferring wealth in the form of the birthright levy. If well-off polities wish to legitimize their membership boundaries, they must redress the global distributional effects of their entail-like citizenship transfer laws. In this way, the birthright privilege levy provides a concrete legal response to an unjust situation in which inherited title to membership both disrupts the equality of starting points and perpetuates a structure of "unearned advantage" (as Mill so famously put it).

In formulating my proposal for the birthright privilege levy, I must stress again that I have taken the world as we find it as my starting point. The present context dictates that states remain the key players. But there is no inherent reason why the levy could not, at least in theory, be extended to supra or subnational entities in the future, especially if they gain some degree of power to define membership. Moreover, the regulative principle for determining how much redistribution ought to take place is open to a range of interpretations. I favor a more expansive reading according to which the birthright levy's ultimate goal is to improve the enabling function of citizenship everywhere, thus providing real opportunity for everyone and reducing the presently unacceptable disparities in life prospects that attach to birthright membership. This is, without a doubt, an ambitious undertaking. It could significantly transform our world, making birthright citizenship a less significant distributor of well-being.[120] But this may take time. A more immediate task is to eliminate the risk of absolute deprivation from the face of the earth. This goal is indeed within reach.[121] The creation of a steady revenue source through the birthright privilege levy and a matching opportunity-increasing expenditure program (under the auspices of the worldwide safety net) represent an important step in that direction. The global disparities of opportunity are so steep that even relatively modest transfers (of skills, knowledge, investment) can make a significant difference.

Whatever interpretation is chosen, any workable plan is preferable to the status quo. As matters currently stand, the lives of a quarter of all children under the age of five are, in the world's poorest countries, at risk due to severe malnutrition as documented by UNICEF's most recent reports. Consider the following facts: malnutrition contributes to more than half of all child deaths around the globe. The total stands at an incomprehensible 5.6 *million* children per year.[122] At this rate, "out of every 100 children born in 2000, 30 will most likely suffer from malnutrition in their first five years of life, 26 will not be immunized against the basic childhood diseases, 19 will lack access to safe drinking water and 40 to adequate sanitation, and 17 will never go to school."[123] It is a gross understatement to suggest that the world is failing these innocent children. Holding recipients of membership titles in the world's affluent countries to account for their unearned advantages—namely, the significant public inheritance that they enjoy in the form of birthright-citizenship entitlement—represents a crucial step toward establishing an enforceable obligation on windfall heirs to improve the basic quality of life of others who have not been so fortunate.

Another advantage to consider is that, unlike international migration, which offers high returns to only a relatively small group of beneficiaries, the birthright privilege levy distributes benefits more widely. It thus has the potential to reach those who are most in need globally—like the malnourished children described above. In a world of increasingly resurrected borders, these children and others like them have only the slimmest prospect of ever enjoying the benefits of lawful and authorized cross-border mobility. The birthright levy possesses yet another salient feature: it relies neither on charity nor on the good-heartedness of the hereditary recipients of citizenship. Instead, once the inherited property-like dimension of citizenship is brought fully into view, those who benefit disproportionately from this system (the recipients of birthright citizenship in well-off polities) may come to recognize that providing some redistributive benefits to those who remain outside of their world is a worthy cause not only for the sake of ameliorating global injustice but also from the self-interest aspect. The system we currently have of stringent immigration controls and border checks has not managed to make those protected by these increasingly mounting walls feel less threatened and more secure—despite the political rhetoric to the contrary.[124] Improving the situation of those pounding to get in is the morally responsible, practically implementable, and viably sustainable alternative.

Finally, it is important to stress that the birthright privilege levy that I have sketched here has not been developed in a vacuum. It fits within the wider tradition of envisioning new instruments and methods to secure funding for international development projects, addressing structural inequalities, and creating conditions under which people are more likely to find security and opportunity wherever they are born. Securing the means to pay for such visionary projects is a topic very much in vogue among academics and policymakers alike since the launch of the Millennium Development Goals. Whenever these goals are discussed these days, it is hard to avoid the set of thought-provoking and increasingly influential ideas that ensue and that set out to capture the imagination of many—and hopefully, the attention of the politicians and other policymakers as well. These include: Hillel Steiner's defense of a "global fund" (a fiscal mechanism to be used to pool all land values worldwide and distribute them universally in the form of unconditional individual entitlements); Thomas Pogge's "global redistributive dividend" (a dividend to be extracted from natural resources, set at a fixed rate, with the primary goal of relieving global poverty and the secondary aim of promoting environmental protection); and Jagdish Baghwati's "brain-drain tax" (placing a legal obligation on highly skilled, high earning migrants who have moved to wealthier polities to pay a tariff whose revenue will be directed to poorer countries, if they wish to retain their home countries' citizenship as well as benefit from the advantages reaped in their adoptive countries as well). Perhaps the most familiar and prominent of all these trailblazers is, however, Noble laureate James Tobin's "currency-exchange transaction tax," often simply referred to as the "Tobin Tax." As some will recall, more than a quarter of a century ago Tobin argued in favor of imposing a small transaction tax on the massive daily exchanges in the currency markets, in order to decrease the volatility of prices caused by speculative trading. His original proposal can be interpreted "as a way of throwing sands in the wheels of international finance," and combating market volatility by imposing a penalty on short-term speculation in currency trade across borders.[125]

As might be expected, Tobin's proposal received significant attention; it involved both endorsement by supporters and criticism by naysayers. The latter group highlighted concerns about the administration of the proposed tax and potential coordination problems, neither of which represent trivial concerns. (The same is inevitably true for any transnational levy, including the birthright privilege levy.) In the context of the Tobin Tax, the sheer volume of daily clearing and netting activities in the currency markets makes the task of acting in concert a complicated one, with multiple deals taking place in multiple dealing sites and representing a daily turnover estimated at some 1.2 billion dollars in 2001. Although a currency transaction tax can in theory be implemented by a single country (an option that informed the United Kingdom's discussion of the "Sterling stamp duty"), it most likely requires a significant degree of multilevel cooperation or international management so as to avoid the migration of foreign exchange markets to tax-free jurisdictions.

Despite these concerns, and although it has not been implemented to date, the Tobin Tax has enjoyed a remarkable revival in recent years. It is now being explored by various governments, global and local activists, and international institutions as part of the search for new methods to bridge the development financing gap that has opened up as states try to find ways to fulfill their obligations under the Millennium Development Goals. It is in this spirit and context that the birthright privilege levy is proposed, with the hope of generating similar discussion and galvanizing momentum for action.

However, it is also important to highlight the marked distinctions between these proposals. Tobin, as a free marketer, suggested imposing a transaction tax in foreign exchange markets as a market-correcting instrument (creating a disincentive to engage in speculative exchange rate trading), rather than as a global redistributive scheme. The privilege levy, for its part, is motivated by the plight of an unjust system of distribution of membership titles that systemically and severely restricts opportunities for the vast majority of the world's population. It takes the vital concern of moral universalists to secure basic equality in a stratified world as its guiding light, and from that starting point seeks to build a global redistributive framework as a general duty, over and above which co-members of bounded communities bear the special ties and heightened obligations of citizenship. The Tobin Tax and the birthright privilege levy thus spring from different intellectual traditions; what they do share in common is the ability to provide a secure revenue stream for financing projects to improve the world.

The conceptual analogy to property theory and practice that has guided my analysis here leads to the conclusion that if birthright recipients wish to continue to enjoy the immensely disproportionate wealth and power that they have inherited under the current property/membership system, they must also—in our increasingly interdependent global environment—attend to the world around them. This involves contributing to the improvement of the life prospects and well-being of those whom they presently choose to keep at bay. The levy establishes a duty to provide a level of subsistence to those denied access, but does not categorically forbid the birthright recipients' right to maintain their inherited citizenship privileges—if they follow through on their corollary redistributive duty. As such, it places a legitimate constraint on these intergenerational transfers of membership titles, and offers a promising and concrete path toward a more just distribution of opportunity globally.

PART TWO

FROM GLOBAL TO LOCAL: OVERINCLUSION, UNDERINCLUSION, AND DEMOCRATIC LEGITIMACY

CHAPTER FOUR

Blood and Soil: Birthright Citizenship in the Domestic Arena

> Another country was a country that belonged to other people. We had to accept the fact that the things we were using would never belong to us, and that this country, this other land, would never belong to us, either.
>
> ORHAN PAMUK, *My First Passport* (2007)

PREVIOUS CHAPTERS have explored the implications of birthright citizenship on global inequality, but what about its effects in the domestic arena?

The second part of this book will move from the global to the local in its questioning of birthright citizenship, looking at "in-state" problems of birthright citizenship in the bounded membership arena. In a world of perfect stability and zero mobility (like that envisioned in the introductory chapter), we might expect that all those people residing in the territory or descending from a parent member were immediately given citizenship and its enabling properties. But we do not live in such a world. Instead, in the messy reality of our time, we continue to rely to a surprising extent on the legal allocation of individuals to membership units on the basis of ascription. Beyond the concerns this regime raises in the global context, which we have already explored, the domestic arena is not immune from legal inequalities either. The situation often arises in which descendants of families who have long left the country may still acquire automatic membership by birth, whereas the children of immigrants who permanently reside in the polity may remain excluded from citizenship.

In confronting these concerns, I first chart and critically assess the reality we find on the ground. This methodology helps identify the consequent problems of over- and underinclusion that arise from birthright citizenship regimes. These issues create serious mismatches between actual membership in the polity and the legal definition of inclusion that still relies far too heavily on ascriptive criteria. This, in turn, leads to a considerable gap in democratic legitimacy. From the perspective of underinclusion, we are faced with a situation where not all those who are permanently subject to the full force of the laws of a state are included in its citizenry, lacking not only the political right to participate and express their voice, but also the basic dignity and security that attaches to equal membership status. With respect to overinclusion, we find those who have never set foot in the country and who may bear little, if any, genuine ties to it (such as descendants of an ancestor who has long ago left the birthright polity) are recipients of inherited title and are thereby automatically granted the privileges and protections of citizenship. This leads to an asymmetry between the power to make decisions and the actual responsibility of living through their consequences. Such an asymmetry violates the basic idea of democratic self-governance as sharing in a political community of equals.[1]

My account of over- and underinclusiveness arising from birthright citizenship intentionally highlights the centrality of legal institutions in shaping and enforcing membership as an inherited entitlement. Focusing on the actual building-blocks of citizenship as a creation of the law permits us to consider the differing interpretations given to birthright principles and to arrive at alternative membership definitions developed in the local and international contexts.[2] This process yields refreshing insights into how we might redefine access to citizenship at the national level as well. To this task I devote the closing chapter of the book.

If we assume that birthright citizenship laws are intended to serve as a proxy for future involvement in the country, then the use of both *jus soli* and *jus sanguinis* will include those with no substantial ties, while excluding many who do have such ties. This leads to a situation in which those who remain outside the ascriptive definition of the *demos,* despite sharing in its society and economy, are denied the basic security and dignity that is associated with membership. But this need not be the case. I shall argue (in the following chapters) that the failure to establish a nexus between right and duty can be addressed by reducing the weight of birthright in allocating citizenship titles and adopting instead a new membership criterion, *jus nexi.* Here, the basis for assigning citizenship is neither *jus soli* (birth in the territory) nor *jus sanguinis* (descent from a member parent), but rather a more grounded connection that stems from being a participant in the relevant bounded membership community. This approach emphasizes the significance of actual membership or the social fact of attachment over and above any privilege of inherited entitlement.

But before we turn to the task of reconstruction (in Chapter 6), it is imperative to gain a full view of the problems at hand. My discussion in this chapter proceeds in three parts. I begin by providing a brief account of the historical origins and contemporary effects of *jus soli* (territoriality) and *jus sanguinis* (parentage)—the two birthright principles that govern the automatic attribution of membership entitlement. My inquiry takes place in the context of real examples drawn primarily from the experiences of the United States and Canada (as representatives of the *jus soli* tradition), and Germany and Israel (as illustrative of *jus sanguinis*). This selection of countries represents a range of approaches to the territorial and parentage birthright principles.

Next, I reevaluate the prevailing belief that "civic" and "ethnic" nations are fundamentally distinct in their approach to the allocation of membership to their citizenry. If this were the case, one could reasonably expect to find substantially different criteria of allocation in each type of polity. Instead, I show that the ostensible contrast between the principles of *jus soli* (generally associated with civic nationalism) and *jus sanguinis* (often described as a manifestation of ethnic nationalism) does not stand up to scrutiny. Like their ethnic counterparts, civic polities tend to reserve a privileged place for the criteria of *blood and soil*—as opposed to consent and choice—in the attribution of political membership.

Finally, I say a few words about naturalization, which is the only legal method for acquiring political membership after birth. Although gaining much attention in the public debate, this route of admission accounts for a relatively small percentage of the citizenship acquisitions worldwide: as we saw earlier, the population of international migrants accounts for less than 3 percent of the total global population. Everyone else gets sorted into their membership community at the point of birth.

The Birth Circumstances that Count: Territory and Descent

How did we come to rely on birth as the determinative characteristic in the attribution of political membership? What is the historical background to the dominant birthright legal principles through which citizenship is currently acquired and transferred in the world? The following pages step back in time in order to provide a brief exploration of the origins of the major legal principles that govern citizenship-attribution rules in the world today: *jus soli* and *jus sanguinis*.

Jus soli: *The Territoriality Principle*

The *jus soli* principle, which is part of the common-law tradition, implies a territorial understanding of birthright citizenship. It recognizes the right of each person born in the physical jurisdiction of a given state to acquire full and equal membership within that polity. The *jus soli* principle finds its historical roots in the feudal system of medieval England, in which "ligeance" and "true and faithful obedience" to the sovereign were owed by a subject from birth: "for as soon as he is born he oweth by birth-right ligeance and obedience to his Sovereign."[3] In the landmark *Calvin's Case,* decided in 1608, Lord Coke employed the concept of ligeance to explain the unmediated relationship that is created for life between the monarch and all subjects born within the monarch's dominion.[4] According to Coke, this relationship between king and subject was defined by reciprocal duties of allegiance and protection and part of an immutable hierarchical natural order.[5] The resulting implication was clear: once a subject of the king, always a subject.[6] All persons born within the King's dominion were under his protection; in return, they owed him allegiance. In the common-law tradition, *place of birth* thus became all-important to the allegiance between ruler and subject, establishing lifelong rights and obligations on both sides. This connection is recited, many years later, by the High Court of Australia in *Pochi* v. *Macphee* (1982): "natural-born subjects are such as are born within the dominions of the crown . . . ; that is, within the ligeance, or as it is generally called, the allegiance of the king."[7]

It is widely recognized that *Calvin's Case* is the earliest, most influential theoretical articulation by an English court of what came to be known as the common-law *jus soli* principle, according to which a person's membership status was vested at birth and was based on place of birth.[8] Involving all the important English judges of the day, *Calvin's Case* was, as the judges put it in their decision, "the longest and weightiest that ever was argued in any Court, . . . the longest in substance . . . the weightiest for the consequent, both for the present, and for all posterity."[9] This case involved a young Scottish child, Robert Calvin, and the question of whether he could succeed a landed estate in London. The answer depended on the classification of the child's membership status: if classified as "alien born," he would have been unable to bring any real or personal action for lands within the realm of England. The Court decided in Calvin's favor, holding that young Robert was not an alien given the fact that by the time he was born, the King's sovereignty already extended to Scotland. As a child born *within* the King's realm, he was an English subject, and as such, he was entitled to inherit land in the King's dominion.[10] As Lord Coke summarily put it: "Calvin was born under the King's power or protection; *ergo* he is no alien."[11] This intimate connection between birth and membership status emerged in a feudal system in which land was the main source of political power. In that system, it seemed natural that an individual's position within the social order and his political allegiance were both assigned by the circumstances of birth. But this, we are repeatedly told, is not the approach favored in our modern world of free and autonomous individuals who can direct their own life and realize their potential, if they so choose. Why, then, do we maintain a system of allocation of citizenship according to the circumstances of birth?

In its modern guise, *jus soli* no longer refers to the connection between a monarch and his or her subjects. Instead, it refers to the political relationship between governments and their citizens. Despite this significant change, the legal mechanism for transferring entitlement to membership has remained largely the same: it continues to emphasize place of birth as the definitive criterion for automatically allocating or withholding citizenship. In its purest form, *jus soli* is blind to any considerations *but* birthplace. Accordingly, any child born under the jurisdiction of a given polity must automatically acquire citizenship regardless of the circumstances under which her parents entered the country, her parents' residence status, her length of stay in the state, effective ties to the polity, and so on. The only relevant factor is whether the child was born *within* the territory over which the state maintains (or in certain cases has maintained or wishes to extend) its sovereignty.[12]

As observed by Christian Joppke, the current reality of cross-border mobility entails not only greater immigration, but also increased emigration. In other words, it cuts both ways: nonmembers enter and members leave.[13] The main advantage of birthplace citizenship, which is an unintended consequence of the common law's feudal emphasis on the territorial connection at birth between subject and monarch, is that it provides an attributive mechanism to incorporate the children of newly arrived immigrants into the polity in which they are born.[14] In this modern manifestation of *jus soli,* it is often seen as democratic and inclusive: children born to noncitizen parents (even if the latter are themselves barred from legalization and naturalization) are given a fresh start.[15]

In the United States, this is the precedent set by the seminal case of *Wong Kim Ark* (1898). In that decision, the U.S. Supreme Court held that children born in the United States are entitled to obtain citizenship irrespective of the membership status of their parents.[16] To reach this inclusive interpretation of the Fourteenth Amendment's "subject to the jurisdiction thereof" provision of the Citizenship Clause, the Court adapted the ancient common law's notion of allegiance to fit America's constitutional reality, holding that

> every citizen or subject of another country, while domiciled here, is within the allegiance and the protection, and consequently subject to the jurisdiction, of the United States. His allegiance to the United States is direct and immediate, and, although but local and temporary, continuing only so long as he remains

within our territory, is yet, in the words of Lord Coke, in *Calvin's Case* "strong enough to make a natural subject, for if he hath issue here, that issue is a natural-born subject."[17]

Such a comprehensive application of *jus soli* is rare today; the United States and Canada are among a handful of countries that still adhere to it. Even England, the birthplace of the territoriality principle, has abandoned its unconditional application.[18] In 1981, with the passage of the British Nationality Act, the territory-centered conception of political membership that dated back to the 1608 *Calvin's Case* was modified. A new component of *descent* was added, such that automatic citizenship is now only conferred upon children born in the territory to at least one parent who is a citizen or permanent resident. Children born in the territory to unauthorized migrants are no longer automatically granted the privilege of citizenship. Instead, they can acquire full membership status on the basis of a combination of birthplace and residence if they have fulfilled the requirement of ten years of habitual residency in the country.[19] Similar changes have taken root in other common-law countries, including Australia, Ireland, and most recently, New Zealand.[20]

If we assume that the rationale for the attribution of citizenship on the basis of territoriality is that birth in a given country serves as a proxy for future residence, the unconditional *jus soli* principle may prove to be overinclusive. It may grant automatic membership to people who have little substantive connection to the polity aside from birth within its jurisdiction. This situation may occur, for example, when a child is born to visitors or short-term visa holders who have no intention whatsoever of establishing permanent residence in their child's country of birth. In this scenario, the "precious good of life-long citizenship [is bestowed] on mere transients and passers-by."[21] This randomly acquired citizenship is hardly ever limited, let alone revoked, even if its bearer has never revisited the country and/or has not established any substantive ties to it at any point during her life. This lack-of-substantive-ties scenario is clearly distinguishable from the case of children who are born in the territory to noncitizen parents for whom that polity has effectively become the permanent place of residence. In the latter case (as I will explain in Chapter 6) there is a web of connecting factors that makes the local-resident's membership in the polity a substantive and meaningful source of the rights and privileges of citizenship.

These distinctions are not merely academic; they matter greatly in shaping public opinion and legal policy as well. For example, in recent U.S. debates, we find a failure to acknowledge that the majority of children born in the United States to noncitizen parents have deep and lasting ties to that polity (in contrast with the overinclusion of children born to short-term visitors who have established little if any substantive connection to the polity). Yet the present American anti-immigrant rhetoric is dominated by a pejorative image of "anchor babies" and "opportunistic mothers." The latter are alleged to cross the border without legal permission just as they are about to give birth so that the child will be born on American soil. This secures for the child the advantages of being born a U.S. citizen.[22] The mother might continue to reside in the United States or alternatively return to her home community, but that does not change the fact that the child is *already* entitled to full membership in the U.S. polity. This is the case because the American constitutional framework elevates the fact of birthplace to an absolute norm. If the event of birth occurs *within* the territory, then that child is "one of us"; if not, she is a total stranger, an outsider, a noncitizen.[23] Under these conditions, "who could blame the Mexican mothers for what they do? . . . They seek to improve the life chances of their children," often at considerable cost and risk to themselves.[24] In practice, there is little empirical evidence to support the idea that clandestine border crossing by pregnant women is at all prevalent. Instead, this serves as a smoke screen behind which the more profound questions are obscured. This is a matter I return to in Chapter 6 when I discuss the *jus nexi.*

In contrast, the most glaring example of the underinclusion problem occurs in the case of minors who lawfully enter the country with their immigrant parents at a young age. Because of the U.S. territorial-based rule of citizenship attribution these children, who were born outside the territory, are not automatically entitled to citizenship—even if they arrive in their earliest infancy and subsequently spend the rest of their lives in the United States. Instead these children bear the alien mark by sheer accident of birthplace. Since they were not born on American soil, they are not guaranteed the crucial right to remain in the country, as this right is reserved for citizens alone. This situation puts these children in a potentially dangerous citizenship limbo: many families mistakenly believe that once they have established legal residency in the new home country, their foreign-born children are on an equal footing with their native-born siblings. But this is not the case. Foreign-born children, unlike any siblings who are natural-born citizens, are subject to potential removal, exclusion, and expulsion. Both Canada and the United States, two of the world's most inclusive *jus soli* countries, do not grant children who have arrived in these countries at a young age the basic security and protection that attaches to citizenship: the right to indefinitely remain in the country.[25] Instead, their birth outside the territory makes these individuals legally excludable and vulnerable, under certain conditions, to deportation from the only country that they have ever known as their home. (As discussed below, *jus sanguinis* countries have been more accommodating, allowing similarly situated children to stay despite their birth outside the state's territory.)[26]

The case of *Romans* v. *Canada* (2004) demonstrates some of the more disturbing aspects of the birthplace principle for this class of children.[27] Romans arrived in Canada from Jamaica as an eighteenth-month-old infant in the company of his parents. Five years after their arrival, his parents became citizens. However, they did not realize that they had to separately file for naturalization on behalf of their child. Romans thus remained a lawful permanent resident of Canada, but never became a citizen. As a teenager, Romans began to display symptoms of schizophrenia. Following conviction for several criminal offenses, he was ordered deported from Canada.

Romans challenged the deportation order issued against him. In the many stages of his appeal, it became clear that beyond his own complex situation there was a more general issue to be addressed: is it justifiable to deport a person who has lawfully resided in Canada since early childhood, and has no substantive membership connections outside of this political community, on the alleged ground that he has violated the conditions of his initial admission (presumably undertaken at the age of eighteenth months)? Currently, courts in Canada (as well as in the United States) hold long-term permanent residents who arrived as young children to the same standards as adult immigrants. Hiroshi Motomura calls this the "immigration-as-contract" model.[28] In this strict account, admission to the country by lawful newcomers (including permanent residents) is "just a temporary grant of permission that the government can revoke at any time."[29] This view, as Motomura explains, conflicts with more contemporary views of contract as involving a set of social obligations that may evolve over time well beyond the parties' original expectations and understandings. The immigration-as-contract model, which is problematic even in reference to adults precisely because it does not permit later adjustment to changed circumstances, is simply implausible in regard to the situation of children who, like Romans, were brought into the country in their infancy. Technically, however, since Romans did not hold the precious property of citizenship, he did not gain protection from being excluded from the only country he knew as home. The domestic and international authorities who heard the case acknowledged that the *Romans*-type situation presents an extremely heart-wrenching human drama, but this sorry state of affairs is not sufficient to quash the deportation order; legally, only citizens have an absolute right to remain in the country.[30]

An even more extreme illustration of the problem at hand is found in the American case of *Ortiz-Martinez* (2007).[31] Here, a child who arrived as a legal permanent resident (green card holder) in the United States ten days after his birth, lived in the country all his life with his two U.S.-born siblings, went to school there, and supported his ailing and disabled mother was nevertheless ordered deported to Mexico at the age of twenty-one because of minor criminal conduct at the age of eighteen. He had never resided in his "home" country nor had any family or other ties to it. It is hard to find a case in which the arbitrariness of the lottery of birthright is more pronounced: had Ortiz Martinez' mother, who had lawful permission to enter the country, arrived in the United States just before his birth, he would have been a full member, and as such would have enjoyed the inalienable properties of citizenship, including the right not-to-be-excluded from membership itself. Instead, he is stripped of his actual membership ties and forced by a coercive removal order to return to a country that is foreign to him. The genuine links here clearly point to the country of immigration and permanent residence (the United States), the only political community that has been his actual and permanent home for effectively all of his life. The larger lesson to be drawn here, beyond Ortiz-Martinez' own sad story, is that the strict and formalistic emphasis on defining the circle of membership based on territorial presence at time of birth has a dark, exclusionary side to it.

Another glaring manifestation of the underinclusion problem prevailed until recently in the United States in the case of foreign-born adoptees who were brought into the country by their adoptive American parents, much like Ortiz-Martinez, only days or weeks after birth. Because of the U.S. territorial-based rule of citizenship attribution, these foreign-born adopted children were not legally recognized as members of the American polity even if they spent the rest of their lives in the United States. To overcome some of the more troubling effects of the birthright-territoriality principle, the U.S. Congress enacted the Child Citizenship Act in 2000.[32] This new Act confers U.S. citizenship automatically and retroactively on certain foreign-born children adopted abroad by citizens of the United States.[33] In other words, the United States now attributes automatic citizenship to foreign-born adopted children as if they were born to American parents abroad. This creates a legal fiction that erases the distinction between biological and adopted children by inserting a parentage component *(jus sanguinis)* into the United States' otherwise *jus-soli*-dominated regime of citizenship attribution.[34]

Although the U.S. Congress addressed the problem of foreign-born adoptees of U.S. parents, no similar relief has been offered to immigrant children who have arrived in the county at a tender age and may, under certain conditions, still face the *Ortiz-Martinez* or *Romans*-like predicament of being deported by virtue of a government order to remove them.[35] Although they are for all practical purposes full members of the community, these foreign-born children are nevertheless vulnerable to the severe sanction of removal because they are legally categorized as noncitizens. No amount of time, cultural emersion, or effective ties to the polity appears to remedy their initial lack of "ligeance" to the territory. As authors of a leading comparative study of citizenship law and policy observe, membership "rules that require birth in the state make citizenship (other than by way of naturalization) impossible for this class of children."[36] Contrast this situation with children born on American soil, but who have never lived there. The latter are guaranteed full membership for life, while the former are not given the right to remain in the only country they know as home. Akin to *jus sanguinis,* which I shall discuss next, *jus soli* generates serious problems of over- and underinclusiveness in the body politick. And unlike its popular portrayal, *jus soli* is not fully reflective of consent or choice.

Jus Sanguinis: *The Parentage Principle*

Complex demarcation patterns also inform the parentage principle of birthright attribution of membership: *jus sanguinis.* Unlike *jus soli, jus sanguinis* does not elevate the territorial connection at birth to a guiding principle of citizenship attribution. Instead, it confers political membership on the basis of descent and pedigree. The children of present members of the polity, regardless of place of birth, are automatically defined as citizens of their parents' political community.[37] Whereas *jus soli* is traditionally followed in common-law countries, *jus sanguinis* is the main principle associated with citizenship attribution in the Roman-law tradition and is followed today in continental Europe and other civil-law jurisdictions worldwide.

The modern manifestation of *jus sanguinis* arose out of the post-French Revolution Civil Code of 1803, which departed from the principle of territoriality. The French Civil Code held that as citizens, parents (specifically, fathers) had the right to transfer their status of political membership to their offspring at birth, regardless of whether the child was born in the country or abroad. During the Napoleonic period, the concept of membership attribution on the basis of descent was considered fresh and radically egalitarian. Departing from the feudal tradition of *jus soli,* which linked subjects to a particular land and to the lord who owned the land, *jus sanguinis* linked citizens to each other and to their joint political enterprise through membership in the nation state.[38] Together, they constituted "a class of persons enjoying common rights, bounded by common obligations, formally equal before the law."[39]

During the nineteenth century many other countries, including Austria, Belgium, Greece, Spain, Prussia, Italy, Russia, the Netherlands, Norway, and Sweden followed suit and adopted a *jus sanguinis* approach.[40] Colonial expansion assisted the spread of the principle overseas. Some of the countries that adopted the *jus sanguinis* model in this fashion, most notably Japan, still strictly rely upon the descent-based attribution of citizenship despite the fact that many of the countries in which the principle originated, for example France and Germany, have since reformed and moderated their own strict domestic application of the descent principle.[41]

Under any version of the *jus sanguinis* principle, the crucial question to determine is who gains the right to transmit membership to as-yet-unborn generations. Most countries have resolved this constitutive dilemma by adopting what Rainer Ohliger calls the "zero option," whereby all persons residing in the territory of the newly established country on a particular day (usually declared soon after independence) are automatically granted citizenship.[42] In principle, this permits the creation of a heterogeneous and inclusive community to be "reproduced": when citizens procreate, the diversity of composition is transmitted to future generations through the parentage-based birthright principle. In this respect, there is nothing intrinsically ethnocultural about the idea of a community of descent, so long as people from different backgrounds gain full citizenship upon the establishment of the polity or through the subsequent naturalization of immigrants from different parts of the world.[43]

In practice, however, the reliance on descent in the transmission of citizenship has gained exclusionary overtones often associated with ethnic and national favoritism, especially when there are few (if any) mechanisms for nonnational newcomers to gain access to full membership. This places them and their children in a particularly precarious state due to their lack of inclusion in the political community. This problem of underinclusion is further aggravated by the fact that many *jus sangunis* countries permit favorable membership-admission routes abroad to those deemed (on national, ethnic, religious, or linguistic grounds) as the nation's scattered sons and daughters whose return the home country patiently awaits.[44] Although permitting a perpetual transfer of title with respect to children born outside the territory to parents of the "appropriate" stock, *jus sanguinis* does not provide similar access to citizenship for the children who were born within the polity's territory to parents who do not have a share in the "bloodline." The main concern here is that a strict interpretation of *jus sanguinis* perpetuates the exclusion of certain segments of the permanent population of a given polity by denying them full access to the rights and benefits of citizenship, based on the criterion of ancestry that they can neither choose nor change. Under such conditions, *jus sanguinis* constitutes a deeply objectionable system of legalized ascriptive hierarchy.

Perhaps the most familiar example of the perpetual intergenerational exclusion of permanent residents from full membership in the polity on the basis of *jus sanguinis* can be seen in German citizenship law prior to its reform in 2000. Historically, German citizenship law attributed membership based exclusively upon parentage entitlement. Noncitizens (and their children) were precluded by blood from becoming citizens. Naturalization was considered exceptional, granted only when the applicant was considered to be culturally integrated into German society. Even then, it was contingent upon the condition of furthering the public interest.[45] Thus, even long-term permanent residents born and bred on German soil had no legal right to become full members of the body politick in the absence of the appropriate heritage. This noncitizen status would thus be propagated from generation to generation: once the parents were excluded from membership, neither they nor their children could alter this designation through residency, consent, or voluntary action. This policy created a class of second- and third-generation descendants whose ancestry flatly prevented them from obtaining citizenship, no matter their level of self-identification with the country or the fact that they had resided in it for their whole lives. Forever doomed to remain noncitizens, these children, and especially those belonging to ethnic and religious minorities, were thus left legally vulnerable without the added layer of property-like protection that full membership grants to its holders.

When the long-awaited change in German citizenship law took effect in 2000, children born to long-term permanent residents finally gained the right to acquire citizenship upon the basis of birth in the territory—regardless of the membership status (or lack thereof) of their parents. As with the introduction of the Child Citizenship Act in the United States, which added a component of *jus sanguinis* into the American *jus soli* regime, the new German citizenship law represents a retreat from a pure model. In this case, the model of *jus sanguinis* is modified by a *jus soli* component.[46]

The application of *jus sanguinis,* just like *jus soli,* generates significant mismatches between birthright citizenship and actual membership. For instance, in a system in which membership is transmitted primarily on the basis of descent, the offspring of an emigrant parent gains automatic citizenship in the parent's country of origin, even where the family has severed all effective ties to the society that they have left behind. Depending on each country's specific citizenship laws, membership may be transmitted down through the generations either for a limited period of time or in perpetuity. *Jus sanguinis* can therefore lead to a situation of overinclusiveness: individuals may enjoy the advantages of membership in a polity without sharing any of its obligations.

A recent illustration of this problem can be found in the *Sheinbein* case (1999), which involved an American adolescent who held dual citizenship by birth (American/Israeli) and was accused of a brutal murder in a Washington, D.C. suburb.[47] Sheinbein had lived his entire life in the United States and had no apparent ties to Israel. However, having been named a suspect in the murder case, he immediately fled to Israel, whose citizenship he held by virtue of *jus sanguinis* (Sheinbein's father was an Israeli citizen) and whose laws do not permit the death penalty for convicted criminal offenders.[48] The United States requested Sheinbein's extradition. However, according to Israeli law (which follows the Continental tradition in these circumstances) an Israeli citizen may neither be extradited nor even stand trial for crimes he is alleged to have committed in another country unless a special quorum of the Israeli Supreme Court approves such extradition. Sheinbein's lawyers argued before the Israeli Supreme Court that the immunity from extradition provided by Israeli law was absolute because it was status-based: it required no proof of real or effective ties to the state once birthright citizenship is established.[49] By a narrow margin of three to two, the Court accepted Sheinbein's position. However, the Chief Justice Aharon Barak, in a minority opinion reasoned that the rights and protections associated with citizenship "can be claimed only by a citizen for whom 'Israel is the center of his or her life and who participates in its life and joins his or her destiny to that of the country.'"[50] In other words, the chief justice sought to introduce an element of genuine, meaningful membership in the polity into the legal understanding of status-based entitlement to the right of citizenship. The *Sheinbein* saga thus illustrates perfectly the potential for overinclusiveness that is inherent in *jus sanguinis*. Here, a person who had only a tenuous connection with a society was entitled to membership solely on the basis of descent and then abused this connection to avoid standing trial in the country to which he formally and substantively belonged.

Consent versus Ascription in the Birthright Citizenship Game

Another way to illuminate the shortcomings of both the *jus soli* and *jus sanguinis* principles is to question the well-established distinction between civic and ethnic nationalism.[51] Civic nationalism, it is often argued, refers to a political community of equals that is created by the free consent of the governed.[52] Accordingly, inclusion in the state rests upon the individual's choice to become a member of the polity. Those who are governed must have equal access to political participation and an equal right to determine how sovereign power is exercised.[53] Ethnic nationalism, on the other hand, reflects an understanding of the citizenry body as a community formed through ethnic or national ancestry, which often predates the creation of the "depository" state itself. Accordingly, a citizen's attachment to a specific political community is inherited, not chosen. This attachment provides the ties that connect the past to the future, permitting the community to preserve its distinct cultural, linguistic, or ethnonational character. Citizenship, by this account, establishes a legal mechanism for a society to achieve regeneration—passing down a legacy from one generation to another indefinitely, while asserting a link back into time immemorial.[54]

With this typology in mind, we might expect to find two very different legal procedures for establishing membership in these distinct kinds of political communities. In a civic nation, we might expect choice and consent to play a key role in the acquisition of membership. In an ethnic nation, on the other hand, we might expect intergenerational continuity to figure prominently in the reproduction of the collective. Here, ascriptive membership-attribution rules that express the idea of citizenship as an inherited status are to be expected. These rules reflect a logically consistent manifestation of a diachronic dimension of nationhood, which privileges the children of current members while excluding all others by automatically entitling them to participate in the political enterprise of their forefathers.

Clearly, the idea of allocating political membership on the basis of *ascription* is at odds with the foundations of civic nationalism, which stresses the value of choice by the governed. Unlike consent, merit, achievement, residency, compensation, or need, the acquisition of automatic (birthright) membership in the polity is, arguably, the least defensible basis for distributing access to citizenship because it allocates rights and opportunities according to aspects of our situation that result from unchosen circumstances that are fully beyond our control.[55] This runs counter to the core principles of liberal and democratic theory. Unlike what this account might lead us to predict, the experience in countries that are widely viewed as archetypes of the civic model (think of the United States or Canada in this regard) shows that even they fail to establish choice and consent as the guiding principles for their citizenship laws. Recall the proclamation of the American Constitution's Fourteenth Amendment: "all persons *born* or naturalized in the United States, and subject to the jurisdiction thereof, are citizens of the United States." In the same vein, the Canadian Citizenship Act provides that citizenship is bestowed on those "born in Canada." That is, birth on Canadian soil is a necessary and sufficient condition for acquisition of full membership.[56]

In addition, neither Canada nor the United States distribute the lifelong good of political membership solely (or even primarily) according to anyone's willingness (regardless of where or to whom they were born) to consent to the authority of their democratic governments. Nor do they admit as members all those from outside their territories who identify with their political ideals of freedom and liberty. Instead, just like ethnic nations, they acquire the bulk of their population through inherited membership entitlement rather than by individual choice or active consent.

Furthermore, several *jus sanguinis* polities have proven better able than the classic *jus soli* countries of North America to address the scenario of a young child entering a country with her migrant parents. Whereas reliance on the strict territorial-dimension of citizenship transforms these children into a class of outsiders potentially subject to deportation, a growing number of parentage-based membership countries now permit children born *outside* the territory but raised *within* it to acquire citizenship by way of a simplified declaration following a predefined period of permanent residence.[57]

It is precisely the lack of emphasis on birthplace that makes such a solution possible in *jus sanguinis* countries. The result is that children who would otherwise straddle the line between inclusion and exclusion are granted the security and equality that comes with full membership.[58] In practice, then, *jus sanguinis* countries display a healthy dose of practical wisdom in their implementation of the bloodline principle, allowing for greater innovation and experimentation than is suggested by most political and legal theorists.

Still, it might be argued that birth is a relevant criterion (even in a world fraught with deep inequality) so long as it serves as a tool to predict who might *potentially* be entitled to full membership in the polity. But if that were the rationale for existing birthplace-centered rules, then we would expect to find the widespread use of supplementary measures such as residency or "center of life" requirements to define who *actually* belongs to the political community rather than sheer reliance on the arbitrary event of birth in the territory. However, in practice civic nations do not require any measure of implied consent from those who are automatically ascribed membership at birth. In fact, the reverse is true.[59] Even if a natural-born citizen has left the country and no longer has any effective ties to the polity, there is no corresponding loss of the rights and benefits of citizenship. This is surprising: it is yet another example of the relative importance of legal conscription, as opposed to choice and consent, where membership status is concerned.

The absence of an affirmation requirement is all the more glaring when we compare the natural-born citizen with the naturalized immigrant. The latter gains access to full political membership in the state only after passing through an elaborate series of gates and rites of passage and by proving, through the actions of migration and the willingness to resettle in the admitting country, that he or she has rightly earned the precious property of citizenship. Acquisition of postbirth citizenship through naturalization demands not only the screening of the would-be citizen's background and qualifications by the relevant governmental agencies, but also the exercise of agency and participation (for example, applying for citizenship and swearing allegiance) on the part of the immigrant.[60] Furthermore, we find explicit consent requirements in the immigration laws of *jus soli* states while there are none with regard to citizenship. This fact further undermines the claim that the consent of the governed can be tacitly attributed.

According to the tacit-consent theory, choice for the natural-born citizen is de facto reduced to a matter of nonmobility across borders: a manifestation of free will is (presumably) implied by nonaction, that is, by remaining put in the country. This assumes that international mobility is purely a matter of individual choice and agency, as if we were already living in a world of open borders. Another concern with the tacit consent theory is, as already mentioned, the selective scope of application: if it applies to those who have never taken the risk of emigrating, why doesn't the same theory apply to others? For example, should this tacit consent not apply to lawful immigrants who have already demonstrated their commitment to stay through the action of departing their country of origin (whether by force or choice) and then resettling in the admitting state? Clearly, these individuals and families made a serious commitment to the new home country by submitting themselves to the authority of its laws, in certain cases at the risk of losing their affiliation to their respective birthright membership communities. If anything, their implied consent seems to be stronger than that of the natural-born citizen who has never made any life-transforming decisions about where to live and under what government. Yet it is only the immigrant who, at the end of a long and arduous process of review and approval, is permitted access to the body politick through a ceremonial oath and related rites of passage where they must declare their intent for seeking full membership. The natural-born citizen, in contrast, automatically receives the inherited entitlement as a matter of (legal) course.

So we see that the only place where consent theory can apply coherently is in explaining the rules that govern immigration policy (rather than citizenship allotment), where the individual must come forward and express her willingness to accept the host country's political norms, often under oath. Increasingly, "applicants for citizenship are expected to pass a test to prove that they are *more* knowledgeable about the society they want to join than its current citizens."[61] For those who have successfully passed the citizenship test, the ceremony of naturalization concludes the pact based on the mutual consent of the individual and the political community: the state must approve her candidacy and she must pledge allegiance to her new home country, its constitution, and governing political principles. No similar act of explicit consent or rite of passage is ever demanded of individuals who happened to be born into the political community.

A defender of birthright attribution of citizenship in civic nations might, however, assert that choice is indeed present in the system: a natural-born citizen may renounce his or her citizenship. (This process usually requires submission of a formal expatriation request to an authorized government agency.)[62] Unlike the standard defense, choice and consent are not considered here to be conditions for admission into political membership. Rather, they protect the right to exit the community (with the important caveat that a citizen is not expected in the typical course of events to renounce citizenship merely for the sake of evading taxes, escaping military service, or avoiding the reach of the law; again reflecting the basic idea of a nexus between the rights and duties of membership).

Finally, to define consent as tacit (that is, through "nonexit") might serve as a convincing argument if assessed merely from the domestic angle. The argument loses much of its force, however, from the global perspective. This is particularly true when tacit consent is presented as proof to the claim that those residing in the world's less stable countries, or in failed states, have presumably agreed to stay—and the proof, so goes the argument, is "in the pudding"—they have not left. This might seem persuasive in a world with minimal differences in life chances across political units, but this is definitely not the world in which we really live. With disparities between countries so great that about half of the population of the world lives, according to the World Bank, "without freedom of action and choice that the better-off take for granted," it seems disingenuous to suggest that nonexit for those who lack minimal freedom of action and choice can suffice as expression of consent.[63] Even where members of less well-off polities manage to depart their home communities in search of a better future somewhere else, no other country has an obligation under international law to provide them with the right of entry (unless they are refugees seeking asylum from persecution). This is because, according to the current world system of birthright membership laws, such admission is reserved exclusively for those who already belong; typically those who are born in the territory or to parents who are themselves members.[64]

Thus—rhetoric to the contrary notwithstanding—in both *jus soli* and *jus sanguinis* countries it is blood and soil, not choice and consent, that play a decisive role in establishing entitlement to the specific political membership that the individual possesses. Both parentage and territorial principles rely upon circumstances of birth as the main criteria for distinguishing insiders from outsiders. In other words, both membership-transfer principles are ascriptive in nature; they remain caught in the territory/blood trap, despite their very different narratives of nationhood and statehood.[65]

In the maze of citizenship laws, we clearly need to keep track of each country's distinct rules and procedures. But it is just as important to recognize that consent and choice are not automatically associated with the territorial model. If anything, it appears that the choice to commit oneself to citizenship is more commonly developed in *jus sanguinis* countries, at least as far as the determination of membership status for children born on native soil to foreign parents is concerned.[66] Although we may still find differences in the membership-attribution laws of *jus soli* and *jus sanguinis* countries (and also among countries that share the "civic" or "ethnic" traditions), the basic claim that such distinctions can be explained on the basis of the dichotomy between consent versus ascription is, by and large, not borne out by the legal reality.

Naturalization

As the U.S. Supreme Court memorably pronounced in *Wong Kim Ark,* there are "two sources of citizenship, and only two: birth and naturalization."[67] The latter represents the only legal avenue for the acquisition of political membership after birth. Interestingly, the very term *naturalization* reflects the iconography of lineage, as well as its etymological roots. The word derives from *nasci* (Latin), which means "to be born"; the term *natur*alization therefore suggests that the postbirth admission to citizenship is a symbolic and political rebirth into the new membership community.

This postnatal path to membership, at the end of which stands the ultimate prize of citizenship in the country of immigration, is long and arduous. As we have witnessed in previous chapters, to become eligible for naturalization, a person must first be legally admitted as a long-term resident; before that, he or she must have gained a valid entry visa to the country. In a world of regulated borders, this is not easy, especially when the individual is seeking entry to one of the world's more prosperous nations. Each year, only a minuscule percentage of the global population is granted a coveted immigrant visa and is permitted to enter through the "golden door" and into one the world's richest countries (here defined as OECD members); the latest data stands at a *total* of 1.75 *million* per year.[68] In a world of more than six billion people, many of which live in abject poverty, the actual admission rate represents only a very small percentage of those who may wish to leave, were they to be granted a lawful and safe path by which to do so.[69] Global inequality patterns also make their mark here: citizens coming from countries perceived to be poor and unstable must typically satisfy more stringent visa requirements upon admission to affluent countries than those seeking transfer from one OECD country to another. This difference applies not just to applications for permanent residence, but also to requests for temporary entrance.[70]

Where the individual in question follows the route of initial lawful entrance, followed by a specified period of residence, a family connection can be helpful. If the individual is married to a citizen, the permanent residency requirement is usually reduced in length.[71] Those who seek to naturalize in the absence of a family connection are subject to stricter requirements. First, the applicant must pass a process of screening and approval by the pertinent state authority. This includes the provision of detailed personal information to the host country about finances, education, employment history, family, and so on. Also required are both police clearance and a medical examination, which take place prior to entry into the jurisdiction of the destination country; the finger-printing and police clearance are formally designed to verify that those with criminal records are not granted entry, while the medical examination serves to block admission of those newcomers with infectious diseases or other socially stigmatized ailments. Furthermore, most applicants must now undergo a comprehensive face-to-face interview prior to obtaining an immigration visa. Even then, the final decision concerning acceptance or rejection of one's admission petition occurs at the point of entry, the border itself.

But this is not the end of the governmental review or monitoring process of the credentials and behavior of those-not-born-here. As the U.S. Supreme Court once put it, without mincing its words, "an alien seeking initial admission to the United States requests a privilege and has no constitutional rights regarding his application, for the power to admit or exclude aliens is a sovereign prerogative."[72] When applying for naturalization (that is, many years after gaining initial admission) the nonmember is recognized as having already transferred herself and her allegiances to the political community. This growing affiliation is acknowledged by the current legal framework governing postnatal access to citizenship: "once the alien gains admission to our country and begins to develop ties that go with permanent residence, his [or her] constitutional status changes accordingly."[73] Still, when seeking full inclusion as a member, those who have already become part of society's fabric are reminded that without inherited title they are not yet equal; certain limitations on permanent residents' freedom of association, privacy, and expression are permitted, although similar limitations would not routinely be imposed on those already within the innermost circle of membership.[74] In order to reach that innermost circle, those seeking postbirth citizenship must further consent to reveal in the process "all facts which in the opinion of the [immigration authority] may be material to the applicant's naturalization."[75] This is yet another legal reminder of the distinctions that remain between those who are naturally entitled to citizenship and those who must comply with the admitting state's immigration contract.[76] If they wish to gain a chance to overcome what they have not acquired at birth, namely, a blood-based or territorial link to the well-off polity, they must adhere to the terms set by the admitting state.

This nonnegotiable contract is pretty elaborate: in Canada and the United States, for example, following admission into the country, the applicant must remain physically present there for a predefined legal residency requirement period, in addition to demonstrating basic knowledge of their new home country's language, political system, and forms of government.[77] Most European countries have adopted an even stricter approach to naturalization and in recent years initial admission as well. Typically, immigrants must satisfy longer residency requirements, meet a higher degree of language competency, prove economic self-sufficiency, in most cases demonstrate a deeper level of integration into the host society, as well as sign various social contract agreements. Another key requirement present across the spectrum of admitting countries is that any would-be citizen must not have any criminal record.[78] Even minor offenses may bar a person from gaining citizenship; in fact, they typically lead to the deportation of the lawfully admitted immigrant, sending him back (as in the examples of *Romans* and *Ortiz-Martinez*) to a country where he knows no one, or, depending on the jurisdiction, placing him in a no-man's-land of near indefinite exclusion or prolonged detention.[79] For those permitted to complete the transition process toward postbirth citizenship, the naturalization process usually culminates in a symbolic public ceremony in which applicants pledge allegiance and loyalty to their new home country, sing its anthem, and salute its flag.[80] In certain polities, the newly naturalized must also renounce their previous citizenship. Taken together, these acts are designed to mark the immigrant's rebirth into a new political community. The classic path of naturalization thus represents the culmination of a process of graduated transformation, in which formal citizenship is the ultimate prize.[81]

With the marked increase in dual nationality, we do, however, find declining attention being paid to the requirement that those acquiring a new citizenship abandon the old; people are permitted to hold multiple affiliations. This means that in our world, some will be in possession of more diversified bundles or shares in several membership "corporations," whereas others will own merely a single citizenship parcel (or none at all, for those who are stateless), further deepening concerns about stratification and unequal opportunity. Interestingly, in the new era of global competitiveness and increased commodification, recruiting countries are fast recognizing that gaining greater flexibility (through holding more than one passport) might be very attractive for those who can afford it. In this vein, governments are now willing to proactively use their control over allocating membership resources as part of their economic or development strategy to attract highly skilled migrants and wealthy individuals whose admission is seen as a net gain for the polity.[82]

Breaking away from the romantic emphasis on citizenship as imbued primarily with notions of collective identity and belonging, we increasingly find that national (as well as supranational) policymakers and regulators are becoming far more shrewd in treating membership entitlement itself as a potential added value to attract desired newcomers: for instance, by promising to skilled migrants and other privileged entrants access to citizenship in a well-off polity, recognizing its security and prosperity value for the recipient. This new policy is reflected, for example, in the tailoring of incentive packages that contain the promise of putting certain migrants on the fast track toward acquisition of full membership.[83] This represents a marked policy shift away from the assumptions underscoring the guest worker visa (referring primarily to low-skilled or unskilled labor), whereby it was assumed that migrants who came for the purpose of work wanted, eventually, to return home. The desire to stay is thus guided and incentivized as much by states themselves as by individual immigrants. This pattern of change touches upon the most delicate and contentious issues of citizenship: defining who may gain access to membership in the political community, and on what basis. Recognizing that skilled migrants moving from poorer and less stable countries place a higher premium on citizenship in an affluent and democratic country, advanced industrial countries are utilizing their control over the allocation of these precious membership titles as an important tool to attract and retain those they regard as the world's "best and brightest."[84]

In this context, governments themselves are recognizing the value of citizenship as a scarce and high-demand property over which they have exclusive control to allocate. The permission to treat membership resources as a prize for attracting highly skilled migrants allows governments to regain control over some aspects of their admission policies, but it must also be seen as part of a larger, and more worrisome, trend toward the commodification of membership acquisition that I identified earlier in the book.

Related reconfigurations of citizenship are simultaneously occurring in emigrant-sending countries. Whereas in the past skilled migrants were regarded as lost causes who had betrayed the home national community, these individuals are now courted as long-lost sons and daughters of the home nation, whose "literal 'worth' to the state is invoked, conjuring a vision of citizenship-by-economic contribution."[85] We are thus witnessing a process of change whereby both sending and receiving countries are adopting more flexible approaches to dual nationality, allowing successful migrants to maintain legal ties with their original home countries as well as the political communities in which they have settled.[86]

If we think of immigration as a reflection of the acquisition (rather than inheritance) of the property of citizenship—that is, a process in which a newcomer gradually attains membership by blending his sweat, talent, creativity, and hard work with the soil and people of the admitting country—then it fits with a classic Lockean labor/desert narrative: those born outside the membership "earn" their rightful place or "title" within it. In this account, the process of postbirth admission might be viewed as an ideal facilitator of human mobility and choice, overcoming many of the problems inherent in birthright citizenship. Yet we have just seen how charged and selective this process is in practice, and how value-laden it inevitably becomes. A strict Lockean perception of immigration is also deeply gendered, prioritizing labor-market participation over domestic and often unpaid work for example. It takes no account, as Jacqueline Bhabba rightly observes, of the disparities between men and women in gaining access to "formal and informal structures that facilitate migration (state agencies, travel agents, smugglers, family funding), together with dependent family status, resources inadequacy, personal history and social positioning."[87]

In addition, unlike a natural-born citizen, the naturalized immigrant is carefully monitored at every milestone to the point of actually acquiring the precious entitlement to citizenship. Moreover, those most in need in global terms of unequal opportunity are not the ones in a position to jump-start the process of international migration (again, in part, due to the gendered distribution of poverty worldwide and the fact that women are much more likely to be accompanied by children). And I have not yet even mentioned the actual hardships that undocumented or irregular migrants (both male and female) face once they manage to cross the border, often after paying excessive premiums to people-smugglers and labor-contractors to get them in.[88]

Finally, we saw in the discussion of open-admission policies (Chapter 3) that, despite the massive attention paid to immigration, roughly only 3 percent of the world's population lives in a country other than the one in which they were born. This is a relatively small subset of the global population.[89] Everyone else—namely the bulk stock of the world's population, amounting to some 97 percent—will remain firmly rooted in the countries in which they were born, receiving their citizenship affiliation either by virtue of *jus soli* or *jus sanguinis*. For better or worse, they will experience life according to those opportunities available in the polity into which the arbitrary circumstance of birth cast them.

THIS CHAPTER RECOUNTS the manifold shortcomings of existing birthright principles in defining access to membership within the domestic realm. Tracing the historical roots of present-day *jus soli* and *jus sanguinis* practices reveals the counterintuitive origins and often ironic twists of their contemporary implementation. A consideration of the comparable problems of over- and underinclusion that are found in both civic and ethnic countries challenges the widespread belief that birthright problems are simply a matter of ethnic nationalism (and its bloodline transmission), as opposed to civic nationalism, with its respective territorial emphasis. Despite the centrality of choice and consent as the root of legitimate government in liberal and democratic theory, we find little trace of these ideals in the actual birthright transmission mechanisms of citizenship that are codified in law books and enforced everywhere. In practice, then, both civic and ethnic nations rely primarily on blood and soil in shaping and sustaining the gate-keeping function of citizenship.

Finally, I explored here whether we can find solace in yet another pervasive belief: that immigration and naturalization play a core role in the overall schema of membership allocation. Although clearly important from the vantage point of each polity's population and the welfare of the migrants themselves, this stream of postbirth admission still plays a far more limited role than station of birth in sculpting the body politick. Although this balance may change if birthrates continue to decline as they are doing in most OECD countries, at least for now the stream of migration remains complementary to the king's road of admission via ascription. As such, it does not serve as a magic bullet in the face of persistent problems of birthright-attribution in the world today.

Is there a better way, then, to allocate membership that does not rely so heavily on predetermined circumstances? Is it possible for the legal bond of citizenship to become less of a reflection of our inheritance than a product of our actual, grounded experience of participation in the social life of a particular political community? I believe the answer can be yes; the solution I put forward can be found in the rationale for adopting a more functional and context-specific genuine-connection membership principle, which I call *"jus nexi."* But before I discuss this new principle and how it may represent an improvement on the present situation, we must consider those arguments that oppose any major revision of the connection between birth and political membership.

CHAPTER FIVE

Popular Defenses of Birthright Citizenship and Their Limitations

We are all something, but none of us are everything.

BLAISE PASCAL (1623–1662)

IN THIS CHAPTER, I examine whether the principles of *jus soli* and *jus sanguinis* can be defended on a theoretical level as justifiable mechanisms for providing selective access to a bounded system of membership. I pose this question within the context of both civic and ethnic nations. I provide several arguments that, *prima facie,* supply the strongest justifications for the right of each country to define and enforce its membership boundaries according to birthright rules. These arguments generally fall into six main categories: (1) democratic self-government; (2) administrative convenience; (3) arbitrariness-as-fairness; (4) respect for distinct cultural and national identities; (5) recognition of constitutive ties, and (6) intergenerational bargains. I will evaluate the persuasiveness of each of these arguments in turn. I also point to possible amendments or innovations that might better reflect their underlying motivation. Ultimately, however, I find that prevalent defenses fail to provide justifiable grounds for upholding birthright membership criteria without remediation. To put the point differently: the arguments offered in defense of birthright citizenship are not nearly strong enough to offset the weight of its real-life consequences in terms of the allocation of political voice and opportunity in an unequal world.

Even the most plausible defenses of birthright, which I address here, take as their starting point the domestic or internal structures of a single state. They do not address cross-border or global effects. Nor do they provide convincing answers as to why an entitlement regime that relies on accidents of birth in conferring the good of membership should escape scrutiny given its dramatic effect on starting points in life. Contrary to Michael Walzer's assertion that "we don't distribute it [the good of membership] among ourselves; it is *already* ours," birthright principles, as codified in current citizenship laws, fulfill just such a boundary-drawing function.[1] These laws articulate who may claim that membership is "already theirs," and on what basis. As we have already seen, for the vast majority of the world's population, gaining access to a particular political community is a result of accidental birth-based circumstances. The transmission of the "priceless benefits" of citizenship (as the U.S. Supreme Court memorably put it) on this basis has far-reaching implications both in terms of *who* is defined as a full member and *what* benefits are attached to such entitlement. This dual quality of citizenship—demarcating access and guaranteeing a significant set of protections to those who count as insiders—speaks to the multidimensional implications of enjoying birthright citizenship in an affluent and democratic polity. It further calls attention to the crucial (yet often neglected) distributive consequences of hereditary membership regimes. Once the property-like dimension of citizenship comes fully into view (as we saw in previous chapters), it becomes possible to begin a conversation about what type of principled constraints and practical remedies are required in order to make this allocation system more legitimate without necessarily requiring the wholesale abolition of bounded membership per se. This is the ultimate conclusion that I draw from the defenses of birthright citizenship considered below.

Democratic Self-Governance

To justify birthright membership on the basis of democratic self-governance is to speak to the idea that the laws of a polity ought to serve and reflect the interests of all those who regularly reside within its territory and are subject to its authority[2]—a commitment that I fully share and believe must be reflected in any revised membership principle, such as the *jus nexi* discussed in Chapter 6. However, to rely merely on circumstances of birth in defining the *demos* is to assume a stable and nonmobile populace, a proposition that simply does not hold in today's world. It is this gap between theory and reality that makes the current justification of birthright in the name of democratic self-governance vulnerable to serious criticism, as I will explain below. Another dimension of the democratic self-governance argument is to emphasize the power vested in the people to define the membership boundaries of their communal political enterprise as a core expression of their collectivity, or self-determination. Such definitions of boundaries are usually codified domestically in legal and constitutional documents at the moment a country is founded, or soon after independence. International law has traditionally refrained from intervening in the sovereign prerogative of states to define their citizenship laws, including their decision to rely upon particular birthright principles in the transmission of membership.[3] The contemporary understanding of the self-government argument goes, however, beyond a notion of exercising control over membership boundaries to include equal participation of all those residing on the territory as a substantive element of democracy. This creates a strong presumption in favor of including all long-term residents in the innermost circle of membership. It is here that reliance on birthright alone becomes difficult to defend in a world in which we cannot expect all long-term residents to have acquired ascriptive membership in the *demos.* The following pages articulate several possible variants of the democratic self-government argument in favor of birthright citizenship, although I argue shortly thereafter that these defenses are ultimately untenable.

First, assuming a stable and sedentary population, it might be argued that birth is a relevant admission criterion (even in a world fraught with deep inequality) so long as it serves as a tool to predict who is likely to be affected by the laws of that polity and, as such, who will be entitled to full membership and the incumbent benefits.[4] By dovetailing with the event of birth, citizenship laws, it is argued, provide political voice to the relevant population: that is, those who collectively determine and subsequently bear the consequences of the democratic decision-making process of which they are a part.[5] In practice, however, this formula risks leaving anyone who was not born into the *demos* without access to membership or the corresponding right to vote.[6]

The reality of increased cross-border mobility in today's world can and often does lead to a situation where certain segments of the population that ordinarily reside in the polity have no say in shaping the manner in which sovereign power is exercised.[7] Despite sharing in the polity's economic and social life, they lack official membership status. To put the point more bluntly, long-term "resident stakeholders" (as we might call them following Rainer Bauböck's terminology) are subject to the state's coercive power and binding jurisdiction, yet remain outside the reach of its blood-and-soil membership definition.[8] As such, they are excluded from having equal voice and are denied a seat at the (figurative) table where decisions that deeply affect their lives are deliberated.[9] This democratic legitimacy gap, as illustrated by the situation whereby a country bars some of its permanent residents from gaining citizenship and participating fully in the political process, presents itself in some of the world's most well-established democracies. A prime example is the German treatment of so-called guest workers *(Gastarbeiter)* and their offspring who gained a right to stay but not to become citizens or voters that plagued the country for years until the reform of Germany's citizenship law in 2000.[10] Such exclusion of those who are regularly subject to the polity's coercive power runs counter to the ideal of democratic self-governance as co-authorship of the polity's laws by those who are subject to its rule.[11] As Chris Eisgruber notes, this ideal holds that "the exercise of sovereign power over a person is legitimate *only if* that person shares in the political enterprise. More precisely, the interests of all those living in a polity ought to be taken into account in the making, interpretation, and application of its laws."[12]

Yet in order to reach a situation where all those living in a polity are in fact taken into account in the creation, interpretation, and application of its laws, we cannot simply rely on birthright in allocating membership titles. At a minimum, we would expect to find a range of supplementary measures (residency or other genuine-connection requirements, for example) in use to define who shall acquire membership in the political community, over and above reliance on the arbitrary event of birth. As I have shown in Chapter 4, strict reliance on birth in attributing citizenship may lead to the situation where persons with only minimal ties with the polity are granted all the rights and benefits of membership (overinclusiveness), whereas others who participate in its daily economic and social life are excluded from similar entitlement (underinclusiveness). But if the *demos* is not to be defined captiously, some proximity must be established between full membership in the state and a share in its rights and obligations. For Robert Dahl, the implications of such delineation are potentially far-reaching: "[t]he citizen body in a democratically governed state," he argues, "must include all people subject to the laws of that state except transients."[13] This definition of political membership is, without a doubt, far broader than that described by current birthright citizenship and naturalization laws.

Despite Dahl's intervention, other proponents of the democratic self-governance argument who have based their edifice on the coercive power of the state may still hold that membership boundaries—even those that rely on arbitrary circumstances of birth and bear profound global distributive consequences (as between members and nonmembers outside their jurisdiction)—are justified because only those within the jurisdiction bear the full coercive authority of the laws that they helped create. Michael Blake offers an elegant exposition of this argument, illustrating it by highlighting the importance of the franchise as a sign of full inclusion in the state. For example, he observes that "the denial of the vote in an American election to an American citizen . . . would be objectionable both through the symbolic insult and stigmatization it involves, and also through the lack of autonomy inherent in facing coercive laws one cannot help create."[14] Blake contrasts this with the "denial of the right to vote in American elections to a French citizen living in France . . . [which] has neither of these morally problematic effects."[15] Although Blake is of course correct to point out that in this particular example the boundaries of membership are relevant for delimiting political voice, his account does not resolve the more basic ethical question of boundary making: are birthright citizenship laws themselves, which determine at the outset whether one is an American or French citizen, legitimate and just? How can reliance on a morally arbitrary circumstance, that none of us can control (birth) be transformed into solid democratic grounds for exclusion when those who may want to get in and subject themselves to the coercive authority of the democratic state are denied such access (on the basis of ascription, not choice) long before they can experience the sphere of the state's influence or gain a hand in shaping its citizenship laws?

The issue is this: citizenship laws, which mark the literal delineation between insider and outsider, member and nonmember, have coercive effects that are felt by those on *both* sides of this boundary. On both the literal and metaphorical planes, membership-defining principles represent a category of laws that simply cannot be categorized as having effects borne only, or even primarily, by their beneficiaries; their coercive authority is also felt with major force by those whom they exclude. Even if one adopts a contextual position, as advanced by David Miller, which holds that defining the relevant distribution principle depends on "what is being distributed, by whom, and among whom: especially on the *kind of relationship* that exists between the people among whom the distribution is occurring,"[16] the larger point about the coercive effects of citizenship laws on nonmembers holds. If anything, the contextual focus may lend support to the argument that those closer to the proximity of the territorial border or those with stronger historical ties (through colonialism and conquest, for example) have a stronger claim to gain a say in the decision making itself or in tackling the unjust fallouts of these cross-border coercive effects. If we think of the birthright privilege levy as an infrastructure for reducing inequalities, we can also imagine that certain countries from different groupings which share tighter historical, economic, linguistic, or geopolitical ties may negotiate extended exchange or tax-substitution programs to reflect their contextual interrelationships. Such programs could reflect their interdependence and special relationship over and above the basic birthright levy scheme of redistribution once it is operational on a global scale.[17]

It would also appear that a liberal defense like Blake's should more plausibly lead one to justify a consent or choice-based policy of admission into the polity rather than birthright. Here, the governed would need to explicitly accept the coercive authority of the state. In this case, power will be exercised legitimately only under conditions where fellow citizens partake in making decisions in compliance with a democratic process in which each has an equal voice. But this construction does little to explain why we should make admission decisions based on ascriptive citizenship; if anything, it seems to militate strongly against it. Put differently, the coercion argument does not establish unequivocally that reliance on accidents of birth is preferable to other possible formulas. The central difficulty remains that of defining who precisely fits in the definition of the governed. Is it merely the pool of those who were initially born into the polity, or may anyone join in? The basic problem here, as Fredrick Whelan eloquently summarizes it, is that we face a "logically prior and in some ways more foundational question of the appropriate constitution of the *people* or unit within which democratic governance is to be practiced."[18] Simply pointing out that some people are subject to the coercive power of the state and have partaken in the decision-making process for legitimizing this power is surely better than a situation of full exclusion, and may offer a practical solution to some. But it still falls short of providing a sufficient answer to the principled question of whether reliance upon birth in the assignment of full membership status is justifiable and worth preserving on democratic grounds in today's world.

A final strand of the argument from the democratic *self*-governance school focuses on the idea that the "self" in *self*-determination and self-governance must be defined by the people themselves. In this account, it is legitimate for members of the democratic polity to collectively decide that they wish to delimit the boundaries of their communal political enterprise by adopting the legal principles of birthright transmission of citizenship. The problem with this argument is that it presupposes precisely what is at issue here: namely, the existence of an already legitimately defined political community whose members can then justly determine to whom to distribute membership entitlements in the future. This introduces, as Hillel Steiner points out, a "damaging circularity" into the argument: it does not follow that members of the political community who now wish to transfer citizenship by birth to their offspring are, in the first place, in a position to determine legitimately who should be able to hold such membership, and therefore pass it on to their progeny.[19] In other words, we must have some criterion that is independent of the *demos* available to determine whether the distribution of citizenship titles was just at the initial point of grant or acquisition. Even classic social-contract theories do not resolve this difficulty because they do not ask whose consent is required in order to win the requisite approval. Yet this step is logically prior to deciding whether the transmission of membership entitlement, according to birth or any other selection criterion, is itself legitimate.

In sum, the argument from democratic self-governance (in all its variants) does not prove particularly helpful in addressing the core boundary-making dilemma that is present in defining the scope of inclusion in the polity according to birthright. As Ian Shapiro and Casiano Hacker-Cordon pointedly observe: "[a]n enduring embarrassment of democratic theory is that it seems impotent when faced with questions about its own scope . . . A chicken-and-egg problem thus lurks at democracy's core. Questions relating to boundaries and membership seem in an important sense prior to democratic decision making, yet paradoxically they cry out for democratic resolution."[20] This difficulty in defining the membership of the citizenry body has led some theorists to go so far as to argue that the "demos of democratic theory is in principle *un*bounded."[21] For Arash Abizadeh, this suggests that any regime of bounded membership "must consequently be democratically justified to foreigners as well as to citizens."[22] An even more robust conclusion is reached by Robert Goodin, who, from a premise that all those affected by a political regime are owed a democratic justification, reaches the ultimate conclusion that "*everyone* everywhere [should be given] a vote on virtually everything decided anywhere."[23] This expansive definition would surely enfranchise all those affected, whether members or not, in the decision of whether and how to draw the line that delimits citizenship in a "this or that" specific country. Setting aside obvious implementation problems, there is a more immediate challenge: clearly, this is not the premise on which existing birthright citizenship laws rest. In the actual world, these laws formally reflect only the voices of those included within the walls of the membership community—walls which these very citizenship regimes erected in the first place and now seek to protect.

Administrative Convenience

Bureaucratic efficiency offers another possible line of defense for citizenship ascription on the basis of either territory or parentage. The argument here is that the determination of membership according to birthplace or family lineage offers a clear and reliable international filing system, according to which people are automatically sorted into specific political units.[24] Since birth is usually a publicly recorded event, it provides a relatively non-controversial method for assigning individuals to states.[25] Moreover, this international filing system (if properly managed) can ensure that every child acquires membership within some polity at the moment of joining the larger family of humanity. In theory, an ideal global birthright-attribution system should leave no one in the vulnerable position of statelessness; in practice, however, the combined operation of *jus soli* and *jus sanguinis* has never guaranteed this outcome in a world fraught with political instability and human mobility.

In addition, given that freedom of movement is tightly regulated in the current interstate system, each country is compelled to define its membership boundaries in ways that unambiguously define who belongs and who does not, who may enter and stay—and who may not. Citizenship attribution at birth and the manifestation of this status through documents such as passports and identity cards render these distinctions both easily identifiable and enforceable in the eyes of immigration officials, customs agents, police officers, and so on.[26] Administrative convenience may therefore explain the prevalence of birthright citizenship principles, but it does not justify them. Furthermore, administrative convenience is often perceived in law not as an end in itself but as subservient to other goals and values, such as ensuring fair access to goods or protecting the dignity of the person. In the context of birthright citizenship, the argument of administrative convenience should therefore hold only limited sway: the issue at stake is too crucial to our identity, security, and life prospects to be determined according to the mere administrative convenience of governmental mechanisms.

What is more, there is plenty of evidence to show that administrative convenience has not deterred polities from making changes to their birthright citizenship laws, whether they moved in a more expansive or restrictive direction. For instance, in several European countries that have long followed the *jus sanguinis* birthright attribution principle governments have in recent years been willing to take the additional administrative burden of recording birth and verifying the lawful permanent resident status of the parents as a way to ensure that second and third generation immigrant children gain full membership status. This dual approach guards against the problem of perpetual exclusion by descent, as seen in Germany until 2000.[27] In these instances, placing an added administrative burden on state agencies protects the interests of children who might have otherwise been barred from citizenship.[28]

But just as administrative convenience may have prevented legitimate candidates from gaining their lawful due of citizenship in the past, a move away from this approach may have the effect of restricting access to membership. Take the classic examples of the United Kingdom and Australia. Both countries strictly followed the common-law tradition of *jus soli* until the 1980s. They then revised their respective citizenship laws by adding mandatory residency requirements that supplement the public recording of birth, before granting citizenship to children of undocumented or transient residents. Section 10 of the amended Australian Citizenship Act, for example, holds that a child born to parents who are neither citizens nor permanent residents of Australia can secure citizenship in that country only if the child ordinarily resides there for a period of ten years, commencing on the day on which the child was born. Once this residency requirement is met, the child will acquire Australian citizenship by operation of law on her tenth birthday, irrespective of the immigration status of her parents.[29] This structure of a delayed grant clearly decreases the administrative convenience of assigning membership at the moment of birth, if the child was born in the territory. This additional administrative burden was not, however, perceived as prohibitive when the decision was made to recalibrate and tighten the scope of automatic territorial-based membership under Australia's citizenship law. Along the same lines, the United Kingdom has also narrowed its implementation of the territorial birthright principle. Until the adoption of the British Nationality Act [BNA] in 1981, birth in the United Kingdom was sufficient in itself to confer British nationality on a child. Following the enactment of this legislation, the United Kingdom (the country that invented the common-law tradition of pure reliance on birthplace in assigning membership titles) revised its citizenship-attribution provisions by adding the requirement that a child born to nonsettled parents must fulfill a ten-year residency requirement before gaining entitlement to register as a British citizen.[30] This new procedure is clearly less efficient from an administrative-convenience point of view. However, these additional bureaucratic costs were seen as negligible in relation to the consequences (and costs) of not imposing them.[31] This is plainly stated in the White Paper issued by the British government prior to the enactment of the BNA, which explicitly addressed the consideration of bureaucratic efficiency, acknowledging that "some administrative and practical difficulties" may accompany this change of law.[32] These additional strains (recording birth and continued residence by the child) were not seen, however, as overshadowing the "good case" (to use the British government's terminology) for tightening up the requirements for acquisition of citizenship by birthright.[33]

More recently, Ireland and New Zealand (among the last bastions of unlimited *jus soli* in the world) have also decided to narrow their birthright citizenship provisions. Both countries abandoned their unconditional reliance on birthplace in the early 2000s in favor of a more qualified approach that takes into account residency and the parents' immigration status before entitlement to membership is conferred upon a child born in their respective territories.[34] As in Australia and the United Kingdom before them, this change of law and policy obviously added a layer of administrative inconvenience. Nevertheless, the change was considered to be a worthwhile investment to ensure that "citizenship and its benefits are limited to people who have a genuine and ongoing link" to the polity, as a spokesperson for the New Zealand Department of Internal Affairs (the relevant government agency to bear the additional administrative costs) explicitly stated.[35]

Even in the United States, which maintains a pure *jus soli* regime, the logic of administrative convenience is breached when the stakes are presented as "guarding the integrity" of the polity's membership boundaries. Such tensions come to the fore in a variety of situations, many of which are connected to the fact that the natural-born child's citizenship status does not necessarily guard against the deportation of a noncitizen parent.[36] The story of Martha Andazolo-Rivas is representative. As an unmarried mother of two U.S.-born citizen children (one aged six and the other eleven), Martha sought relief from a deportation order issued against her based on the hardship that such removal would cause the citizen children. The immigration judge concluded, after a lengthy discussion, that "the United States citizen children, particularly Tanya [the eleven-year-old], would suffer hardship on an emotional, academic and financial nature." If the children were uprooted from their current nurturing environment and cut from their support system, assessed the judge, the hardship "would be of a daunting level"; the children "face complete upheaval in their lives and hardship that could conceivably ruin their lives." The judge therefore granted the mother a right to lawfully stay in the country with her children based on a cancellation of removal procedure.[37] If the logic of administrative convenience were to rule, the judge's decision should have ended this story on a happy note. Unfortunately, it did not. The mother's case was reopened by government authorities, who appealed against the immigration judge's decision, arguing that the interpretation granted in the original decision to the "exceptional and extremely unusual" hardship standard was too lenient, because after the judge's ruling was rendered, a new (and stricter) interpretation of the hardship standard was adopted.

Instead of rationing the agency's limited administrative and personnel resources by allowing the immigration judge's ruling in favor of the mother to stand—allowing her and her U.S. citizen children the safety and security of remaining in the country of residence to which the children legally and socially belong—the case was argued in a comprehensive oral hearing, which eventually led to the overturn of the original decision in favor of the mother. Martha Andazola-Rivas was instead ordered to leave the country. In effect not only she but her children, too, were deported given her primary care-giving obligations to them as a single mother.[38]

In the cold language of the Immigration and Nationality Act, an adjustment of status for the noncitizen parent based on his or her relationship to a U.S. child can occur only in rare circumstances, after establishing that removal would result in an "exceptional and extremely unusual hardship to the alien's . . . child, who is a citizen of the United States."[39] This "hardship standard" has increasingly been interpreted in a strict way, making it very difficult to establish before an administrative agency or a court of law.[40] As the legislative history predating this provision reveals, this is not an inadvertent result. The intent of this provision is to stringently limit the derivative membership benefits that can be gained from the automatic inclusion of offspring in the American polity. As the Congressional record attests: "a showing that an alien's United States citizen child would be less well-off in the alien's country of nationality than in the United States does not establish 'exceptional' or 'extremely unusual' hardship and thus would not grant [the parent of a U.S. citizen] a relief under this provision. Our immigration law and policy clearly provide that an alien parent may not derive immigration benefits through his or her child who is a United States citizen."[41] In contrast to its public image of inclusiveness, the United States has set up vast regulatory and administrative machinery that guard against expanding the scope of family-based access to membership that might otherwise have grown out of the country's generous *jus soli* membership regime.

Another illustration of the zeal with which governmental agencies are willing to breach the logic of administrative convenience in policing the borders of membership is found in *Karassev* v *Finland,* which was decided by the European Court of Human Rights. In that case, a family entered Finland from the Soviet Union; they held valid short-term tourist visas that were about to expire. Very soon after their arrival, the Karassev family members requested asylum in Finland, a request that was later denied. In the interval, a child was born, named Andrei. He was not conferred Finnish citizenship at birth because Finland follows the parental *(jus sanguinis)* membership-allocation rule and his parents were neither Finnish citizens nor were they granted a residence permit to stay in the country.[42] In the normal course of events, it would have been undisputed that Andrei had not acquired membership status. However, the parents claimed that theirs was an extraordinary situation. By the time that Andrei was born, the former Soviet Union (their country of citizenship) no longer existed as a political entity; it had dissolved into a number of independent states.

Finland's citizenship law, like that of many other countries, includes a provision that is designed to prevent statelessness: a child born in Finland will receive Finnish citizenship at birth (irrespective of the parents' immigration status) if that child "does not receive the citizenship of any foreign [s]tate *at that time,* and does not even have a secondary right to acquire the citizenship of any other foreign [s]tate."[43] Andrei's parents argued that upon birth, their child was stateless: he did not receive Russian citizenship, they claimed, because the family did not return to the former Soviet Union after its collapse and therefore could not have benefited from the provisions of the new Act of Citizenship of the Russian Federation, which recognized persons who were temporarily outside of the country at the time of this political upheaval as citizens if they held full membership status in the former Soviet Union. The Finnish authorities rejected the Karassevs' interpretation of the new Russian citizenship law, holding that Andrei was never stateless at birth and thus could not benefit from the Finnish provision granting citizenship entitlement to children in this vulnerable situation. After exhausting all domestic remedies, the debate surrounding Andrei's birthright status reached the European Court of Human Rights. The court, after lengthy deliberation, sided with Finland, rejecting the family's claim that the child was entitled to citizenship. The ECtHR held that although there was some degree of ambiguity concerning the child's membership status vis-à-vis the Russian Federation (the relevant successor state) on the date of his birth, the decision made by the Finnish authorities (to deny him birthright citizenship) was not unjustifiable. This was because there was no issue of a denial of family reunification under Article 8 of the European Convention for the Protection of Human Rights and Fundamental Freedoms.[44]

The real puzzle raised by this legal saga—which involved almost every important public agency in Finland (including its Supreme Administrative Court, the country's Social Insurance Institution, the Office of Alien Affairs, the Ministry of the Interior, the Population Registration Authority), and at its peak, the President of the Republic himself—is to explain why so much attention was paid by the authorities to a single child's request for acquisition of membership status in his birth country. From the standpoint of administrative convenience, it would have been far more efficient to simply grant the child citizenship and close the case; the dispute over Andrei's entitlement to birthright membership involved such a rare fact pattern that it would have been unlikely to open the flood gates (the typical fear of governmental agencies whose responsibility is to control access to social services and membership benefits). But this legal case was nevertheless fought out all the way to the ECtHR. Apparently, the instinct to guard against the anchoring of legal status for the parents through the locally-born child outweighed the consideration of administrative convenience, especially when dealing with families from the other side of the border. In this case, a border that literally tracks some of the deepest cleavages in the levels of wealth and stability between two neighboring countries. This is a pretty extreme example, but I recite it here because of the general principle that it reveals about the lengths to which prosperous states are prepared to go in order to restrict uninvited access to their midst.

The conclusion that can be drawn from the preceding discussion on administrative convenience is that, taken alone, bureaucratic expediency is not enough to explain a polity's decision to enforce, leave untouched, or, conversely, revise its birthright citizenship regime. Although the desire to "see like a state" (as James Scott once put it) by making the event of birth both legible and recorded surely plays a role in explaining the persistence of *jus soli* and *jus sanguinis* regimes, its significance must not be overestimated.[45] In the real world, polities bent on reconstituting their membership boundaries by revising their birth-centered membership allocation schemes have internalized the costs of increased administrative inconvenience whenever the political will was there to reform preexisting citizenship laws.

Finally, it is not clear, even from the administrative convenience point of view, that the reliance on birth in defining membership in fact represents the most efficient filing criterion, precisely because of the problems of over- and underinclusion that I identified in the previous chapter. It is worth asking whether there are other potential systems that could do an equal, or better, job of tracking the ever-dynamic contours of membership in a world of growing mobility across regulated borderlines.[46]

Arbitrariness-as-Fairness

Another strand of defense of birthright citizenship is found in what we might label the "arbitrariness-as-fairness" argument, which moves beyond pure administrative convenience to provide a stronger normative claim in support of ascriptive membership rules. Instead of criticizing birthright entitlements, the arbitrariness-as-fairness argument suggests that we should value the contingency of existing citizenship laws. The thrust of the argument is this: by making the determination of political membership entirely independent of substantive considerations, we avoid the trap of moral judgment about who deserves to be a citizen. According to this view, it is better to exclude persons on the basis of territoriality and parentage than on the basis of criteria such as political opinion, their expression of patriotic loyalty, or, conversely, their suspected subversion of the polity's basic constitutional norms. As part of his illuminating critique of what he calls the "myth of the civic nation," Bernard Yack claims that "birthright citizenship can promote toleration precisely by *removing* the question of communal membership from the realm of choice and contention about political principles."[47]

The idea that birthright blindness is a blessing seems plausible only if we think of the problem in terms of ensuring internal equality among persons already residing within the same territory. In this case, the need to avoid hard decisions about who belongs and why is seen as so important that it justifies any presumably apolitical rule for conferring the valuable status of citizenship. We need not know the gender, race, creed, or need of a child in order to determine eligibility for birthright membership if such membership is granted automatically. The only thing that matters is whether the child was born in the territory (under a *jus soli* rule), or whether one or both of her parents is already a member of the polity (under a *jus sanguinis* rule).

Although this argument may seem compelling at first glance, *jus soli* and *jus sanguinis* can only be conceptualized artificially as a method by which we can remove the question of communal membership from the political realm. It would be more accurate to suggest that they represent a precommitment to following specific rules and criteria for determining who may become a citizen and who may not. This precommitment is inevitably born out of specific political, contextual, and historical events that have led to the creation of particular membership communities that follow particular membership attribution rules. In a similar way, so are the subsequent revisions or deeper transformations in the self-conception of who may partake in constituting part of the collective "we." Once these inevitably charged aspects of drawing the boundaries of inclusion/exclusion are brought into view, we can no longer pretend that the decision to follow a birthright allocation of citizenship is somehow apolitical.

Even if we lived in a less stratified world, where access to citizenship did not translate into dramatically differentiated life prospects for the individuals involved, the principled point would still hold: citizenship is not a natural ordering, it is (to borrow from Blackstone's discussion of property and inheritance) "a creature of the civil or municipal laws, and accordingly, in all respects regulated by them."[48] Citizenship comes into life with the creation of a political community—it has never been a creature of the state of nature. As such, it is the product of human imagination, coordination, and agency. The transfer of citizenship by birth, just like any other mechanism for distributing scarce resources, is thus anything but free from complex decisions about where to draw the line, whom to benefit, and what allocation matrix to use.

In a world of severe inequality like our own, these determinations become especially vital because of what is at stake. Not only are we dealing with core components that help shape our identity, belonging, and security, we are also inevitably engaging in a process of distributing membership titles or "shares" in a given political community—with all the associated rights, benefits, and opportunities that attach to such membership entitlement. Once we take this broader perspective, the defense of the arbitrariness-as-fairness vision of birthright (as a means to avoid substantive decisions about where to draw the membership line) loses much of its force. Any distribution matrix for citizenship affects not only those it includes but also those it excludes. Thus, even if we suppose for the sake of argument, that birthright citizenship is less offensive than other methods of defining the criteria for membership, we must still face its complementary effect on deciding who not-to-include. The latter aspect has traditionally received far less attention from proponents of arbitrariness-as-fairness than the former, possibly because it leads to a less neat set of conclusions for dealing with problems of boundary-drawing. In the real world, polities routinely use citizenship-attribution principles not only to provide entitlement internally but also to restrict access externally, often drawing a strict line between member and nonmember based on the letter of the law and its vigorous enforcement, in the process potentially shattering established social ties and tearing families apart, as we just saw in the *Andazola-Rivas* case. This citizenship regime is ultimately backed up, as observed by Debra Satz, by "border patrols with guns whose task is to keep out those whose only crime is that they were born outside" the membership community.[49] Consequently, unless we presuppose that people should enjoy entitlement to membership in the community of their parents (or in the territorial community into which they happened to be born), we have only pushed back the question of political membership.[50]

For the argument of arbitrariness-as-fairness to be persuasive, then, it must assume that we know where the boundaries of membership are (or ought to be) drawn; it is within this framework that birthright can indeed appear neutral or apolitical precisely because of its blind application. Yet once we look at these boundaries from the external perspective, of those born on the "wrong side of the tracks" of prosperity and security (just like the five stowaways whose fatal journey to America I recounted in the Introduction), it is impossible to assert that the arbitrariness argument establishes the justness of such inherited artifacts or the fairness of perpetuating them through birthright entitlements.[51] Instead, this becomes the ethical concern that is at issue, which must be confronted rather than taken for granted.

Respect for Distinct Cultural and National Identities

Perhaps the most familiar argument in favor of preserving bounded membership—as an expression of a community's deliberate choice to preserve in this way its distinct cultural identity—is found in the plentiful writings of communitarians and liberal nationalists.[52] Roughly speaking, this rich set of claims can be summarized as follows: members of a political community have the right to both construct and reflect a shared culture, language, history, or collective identity in their joint ethical enterprise as members of a particular state. Decisions about admission and exclusion are here viewed as powerful expressions of a community's identity and autonomy, as well as a means of preserving those particular characteristics. As Michael Walzer, a key representative of this line of argument, has famously put it, without control over such decisions, "there could not be *communities of character,* historically stable, ongoing associations of men and women with some special commitment to one another and some special sense of their commune life."[53] On this account, respecting cultural, social, communal, and historical ties by attributing membership at birth plays a significant role in preserving such communities of character. Such control over definition of collective membership is treated almost as a precondition for "lead[ing] a satisfying life and attain[ing] the respect of others."[54]

Although this clearly is a potent point, highlighting the importance of membership in particular human communities for our self-understanding and sense of place in the world, it still does not explain why we must rely on some form of birthright; it may well be plausible to argue that such attachments can be cultivated by the experience of partaking in the life of a community and effectively joining in its ranks. Unless we assume that people are "hard wired" into a particular culture or language, the determination of how to define admission to the citizenry body must be seen as politically constituted, and thus contested, especially where the results of drawing such lines of inclusion/exclusion may bear dramatic consequences for the individual involved. These almost trivial insights tend to get lost, however, when so much emphasis is placed on identity and national bonds as generators of mutual duties of care and responsibility. To put the point differently, the "communities of character" can become an all-encompassing explanation covering the spectrum of value and meaning of political membership, with the unfortunate result of largely overlooking the wealth-preserving aspects of inherited membership and their substantial distributional effects upon those remaining outside the designated circle of members. Unless one assumes that we should not care about the external implications of our borders, so long as each individual falls inside the scope of some membership community, the cultural-distinctiveness argument may come to serve as a blanket excuse for overlooking the actual disparities of basic protections and services that attach to holding membership in different political communities. Even if we assume that each political community may provide equally gratifying "identity goods," the reality is that they endow their members with dramatically unequal life prospects in terms of provision of basic subsistence requirements. Arguably, both the latter and the former must be considered part of what makes human flourishing possible, let alone meaningful.[55]

In short, the focus and priority given in the literature to the identity-and-belonging dimension of the edifice of citizenship run the risk of making invisible those additional aspects of political membership that are arguably no less significant in enabling human flourishing and well-being. The danger here is that the preoccupation with culture and identity permits this analysis of citizenship to remain largely blind to the manifold wealth and opportunity implications that membership status bears in practice. This problem becomes even more pressing in our world where existing borders divide "not simply one jurisdiction from another but the rich from the poor as well."[56] In this context, birthright principles inevitably become entangled in more than just nation-building or identity-constituting projects.

A slightly different argument in favor of preserving bounded membership communities refers to the concepts of trust and solidarity among co-members to whom we owe special obligations by virtue of our shared existence as a political collective.[57] David Miller is perhaps best associated with this claim. He argues that citizenship is an important source of common identity and trust and further believes that "without a common national identity, there is nothing to hold citizens together."[58] For Miller, cultivating trust is crucial if we are to preserve a robust commitment to social justice among those who belong to the polity and as a means to conjure up voluntary cooperation and the requisite enthusiasm for meaningful democratic participation among fellow citizens.[59]

A significant weakness of this analysis is, however, that it reifies the status quo where the nation-state currently serves as an important source of solidarity, taking it as a given rather than a product of specific political institutions and particular historical trajectories.[60] Yet, if we reverse the order of things, it might well be possible to generate compatriot feelings at other levels of identification as well (for example, the local, regional, or transnational levels), especially if permitted to incubate for a long enough period of time. Leaving aside for a moment this chicken-and-egg problem, it is important to note that even if we were to accept the view that "the duties we owe to our compatriots may be more extensive than the duties we owe to strangers," we still have not yet established that nothing is owed to those outside our guarded communities. Nor have we addressed the core question of how to define who is a member and who is a stranger—other than by relying on preexisting (here, birth-based) citizenship identifications.[61] Instead of squarely confronting this question, including the need to provide some coherent explanation to the puzzle of the persistence of birthright-membership attribution (despite its tension with core tenets of liberal and democratic theory), we find attempts in the literature to replicate a comforting myth: *our* conception of bounded membership is civic and enlightened (in contrast with the presumed *eros* and irrationality of ethnic identification).[62] We have already encountered this civic-ethnic divide in the previous chapter. Here it plays out slightly differently, namely, as proof that collective identification at the national level can be based on allegiance to common values (freedom, toleration, equality, and so on). This represents an important improvement, according to the proponents of liberal and cultural nationalists, on the traditional ethnic model as it downplays the ascriptive element of political membership and belonging.

This is a powerful narrative. Unfortunately, it suffers from an acute legitimacy problem: it shares little with the reality we find in practice. Birth-based mechanisms remain the core legal means engaged to ensure that civic polities (just like ethnic ones) survive beyond the inevitably limited life-expectancy of each generation of members. As we have already seen in previous chapters, inherited citizenship entitlements serve as the primary method for sorting members from nonmembers even in the most self-proclaimed civic and open nations: consider Canada, the United Kingdom, France, and the United States.

Emphasizing the priority of obligations toward those who are already within our community—regardless of how precisely they become included in it—may appear to be the saving grace in overcoming the gap between theory and practice. However, such a strategy does not finish the job, either. Instead, it implicitly relies on a tautological move: a common identity (for instance, distinct "communities of character" or "special relations") is presumed to generate similar feelings that then become the social glue that binds together those citizens who fit within the common identity's definitional perimeters. In other words, this argument runs the risk of becoming hopelessly circular. A person is deemed not to possess the special character that makes one a citizen because she does not belong to the state; then again, she cannot belong to the state precisely because she lacks the special characteristic needed for membership.

Another set of concerns, which go beyond these theoretical debates, is that as a matter of political reality, the appeal to a common cultural or a shared distinguishing characteristic may implicitly validate practices within a diverse or multiethnic political community that privilege those citizens who "truly" belong (linguistically, religiously, racially, ethnically, and so forth), while disadvantaging those who do not because they do not share in that distinctive identity. Such affiliation-based preferences undermine the shared (legal) status of full membership, making some citizens less equal than others.[63]

Taken to its ultimate conclusion, the special relations or "communities of character" approach appears to suggest that the power of a polity to define its own human boundaries should trump other values and considerations.[64] This is a claim that Walzer famously makes in *Spheres of Justice,* arguing that "the distribution of membership is *not* pervasively subject to the constraints of justice . . . [because] the shape of the community that acts in the world, exercises sovereignty, and so on," is at stake.[65]

Yet even for Walzer, this is not a claim that is used to necessarily justify birthright citizenship; rather, it speaks about the permission to sustain a distinct cultural or national composition of a given polity. Indeed, Walzer himself significantly qualifies the reach of his argument about the semisacred shape of the community by asserting unambiguously that once nonmembers are granted first admission they must be granted an opportunity to embark on a path to full inclusion as citizens of that polity.[66] Otherwise, argues Walzer, we risk becoming "tyrants in our political home," turning long-term permanent residents into the equivalent of "live-in servants" excluded from the company of citizens.[67]

Recognition of Constitutive Ties

Another defense of birthright is found in the constitutive-ties approach to citizenship, which emphasizes the particular relationships that shape our human communities.[68] Specially, "[c]hildren are not born into the world as isolated individuals, but as members of established social networks."[69] These social networks serve as the bedrock for establishing moral claims concerning political membership. Instead of focusing primarily on the *vertical* relationships between the individual and the state, this approach looks at the *horizontal* networks and webs of relationships that are created between persons in various public and private settings, including families.[70] Accordingly, it is argued that citizenship laws ought to reflect the central place of families and societal networks in constituting citizens and, in the process, reforming existing membership-attribution rules by infusing them with the values of gender equality and respect for the labor of caregiving.[71] Here, the emphasis is not necessarily on a shared history or distinct culture on the national level. Rather, attention is given to specific relationships with particular others, such as parents, spouses, lovers, or extended families, who mediate one's inclusion in a larger political community. Citizenship laws, in this account, must protect and foster the important contribution of such intimate and family-based relationships and recognize primary caregivers' immense (private) investment in the (public) "reproduction" of the nation. A *jus soli* membership rule reflects these contributions indirectly (for instance, by granting the future generation a chance to establish itself in the parents' new country of residence), but a *jus sanguinis* membership rule does so explicitly. An affiliation-oriented relational approach that takes family ties and intergenerational continuity seriously therefore provides strong support for inherited citizenship entitlements.[72]

This approach is significant in that it provides a powerful rationale for taking constitutive relations seriously in the context of citizenship. It also serves as a fresh reminder of the fact that someone has to do the crucial reproductive labor for the collective to survive—adding a gendered dimension that often gets lost in these debates. Placing relationships first also translates into advocacy in favor of granting unconditional protections to members of families whose very composition reflects transnational affiliations. For instance, if a child is born in a marriage between spouses from different countries, where each parent holds a different nationality, then the feminist-relational approach instructs that the child belongs to both membership communities on the grounds of safeguarding family relationships as well as respecting the principle of gender equality—thus removing the patriarchal streak that has traditionally been part of classic citizenship law.[73] The notion that fathers and mothers should be equally able to transmit membership entitlement to their offspring may seem self-evident today. But the troubling record of gender-based discrimination in citizenship laws worldwide should teach us differently.

Historically, under Roman law, a child acquired citizenship on the basis of his father's status, or according to family links transmitted exclusively through the *pater familias*. In keeping with this tradition, a mother had no right or legal power to pass her citizenship on to her children. Similarly, with the development of the English common-law doctrine of coverture, the father alone could bequeath citizenship to his children born of a valid marriage.[74] A married mother had no similar authority or standing. In fact, she risked losing her own birthright citizenship upon marriage to a noncitizen husband.[75] Tellingly, as Karen Knop importantly observes, discrimination against women in citizenship-attribution rules was first targeted by international law in the early half of the twentieth century not so much out of concern for gender equality, but for fear that such rules might result in statelessness for a child born out of wedlock or to an unknown father.[76]

Today, the majority of the world's countries have repealed the gender-discriminatory provisions of their citizenship laws, though it is disturbing that even civic nations that see themselves as exemplars of the commitment to sex equality still occasionally distinguish today between the capacity of male and female parents to transmit citizenship status to their offspring born abroad.[77] An illustration of just how deeply the legacy of differentiated citizenship-transferring roles for men and women has permeated into modern citizenship laws is found in surprisingly recent constitutional battles fought over these issues in Canada and the United States, with very different results. I briefly discuss each in turn.

In the 1997 *Benner* case, the Canadian Supreme Court was asked to determine whether Section 5 of the Canadian Citizenship Act, which restricted access to Canadian citizenship based on the gender of the parent, violated the equality principle enshrined in the Canadian Charter of Rights and Freedoms.[78] According to the Act, a child born abroad to a Canadian father was automatically entitled to Canadian citizenship upon registration of his or her birth. However, a child born under similar circumstances to a Canadian mother was denied similar entitlement to membership. Instead, that child's eligibility depended on the absence of a criminal record and his or her willingness to swear an oath of allegiance—demands that resemble the realm of immigration but here applied to the citizenship domain and were constitutionally challenged on the grounds of gender equality. Neither of these requirements were imposed on a child born abroad to a Canadian father.[79] The Canadian Supreme Court ruled that this statutory provision violated the equality principle because it restricted access to citizenship "on the basis of something so intimately connected to and so completely beyond the control of the [child] as the gender of his or her Canadian parent."[80] This legislation, in the words of the court, "continues to suggest that, at least in some cases, men and women are not equally capable of passing on whatever it takes to be a good Canadian citizen."[81] Such gender discrimination was ruled unjustifiable in a free and democratic society, and the relevant provision of the Citizenship Act was struck down.

By way of contrast, the United States Supreme Court was asked to review the constitutionality of Section 309 of the Immigration and Nationality Act (INA), which created a two-tiered system distinguishing between American men and women in their ability to transmit U.S. citizenship to their offspring born abroad.[82] Unlike the Canadian Act, the American Act imposed strict requirements for conferring citizenship upon a child born abroad to an unmarried American father, while attributing automatic birthright membership to a child born abroad to an unmarried American mother.

According to the INA, the citizenship of a child born to an American father could not be established unless and until either the father or the child had taken affirmative steps to confirm their relationship. Unlike the immediate recognition of the connection between a mother and her child at birth, which, in turn, established the child's connection to the political community, the Act held that the relationship between father and child must be legally established (for example, through a court order declaring paternity), if the status-entitlement of citizenship was to be conferred upon the child.[83] The Supreme Court affirmed this provision in 1998 in the controversial *Miller* decision, leaving unchanged the Act's gender discriminatory two-tiered citizenship-attribution system.[84] Just three years later, in 2001, the United States Supreme Court was again asked to review this section of the INA in the *Nguyen* case.[85]

Nguyen was born out of wedlock in Vietnam to a Vietnamese mother and an American father. He had been in the care of his American father ever since the relationship between the parents had ended. At the age of six, when his father returned to the United States, Nguyen became a lawful permanent resident of the United States (green card holder) and was raised in Texas by his father. For all practical purposes, he was a full member of the United States. However, at the age of 22, Nguyen pleaded guilty to criminal offenses committed in the United States and, as a noncitizen, was ordered to be deported. Nguyen's father challenged the order, claiming that his son's blood relationship to him and lifelong association with the American polity should render Nguyen eligible for full membership and thus protect him from deportation.[86] The United States Supreme Court rejected the father's plea, however. It ruled that in spite of the fact that a meaningful and lasting parent-child relationship had been established between the American father and his foreign-born son, the failure to follow one of the three affirmative legal steps defined by law for the transmission of citizenship (legitimization, declaration of paternity under oath, or court order of paternity), meant that Nguyen had no entitlement to full membership status in the American polity. In other words, the state was permitted to deny him the property-like protections of citizenship.[87]

The court also held in *Nguyen* that the decision to impose different requirements on unmarried fathers and unmarried mothers was justified by two governmental interests: first, ensuring that a biological parent-child relationship existed; and second, ensuring that the child and the parent had demonstrated a relationship consisting of "real, everyday ties" that provided a meaningful connection between child and citizen parent and, in turn, the state. Ignoring the fact that precisely such a connection had been established between the child, parent, and state in this particular case, the court preferred to twist the language of relationship by collapsing it into biological essentialism. According to the court, the opportunity to develop a meaningful parent-child relationship inheres in the event of birth of a child to a citizen mother, but does not result "as a matter of biological inevitability, in the case of an unwed father."[88] The court further declared that in the context of citizenship-attribution rules, American men are legally relieved of personal responsibility for the results of their sexual actions. As the court put it, "one concern in this context has always been with young people, men for the most part, who are on duty with the Armed Forces in foreign countries."[89] When turning to current conditions, the court continued, it found "even more substantial grounds to justify the statutory distinction [between men and women]. The ease of travel and the willingness of Americans to visit foreign countries have resulted in numbers of trips abroad that must be a real concern when contemplating the prospect [of mandating] . . . citizenship by male parentage."[90]

Thus, the court concluded, the legislature was well within its authority to refuse to embrace a child conceived abroad to an American father and a noncitizen mother as a U.S. citizen.[91] A child born abroad to an unwed American mother, on the other hand, automatically acquires such membership (without any requirement of proof of the establishment of a parent-child relationship) because, again to cite the court's own words, "there is nothing irrational or improper in recognizing that at *the moment of birth* (a critical event in the statutory scheme and tradition of citizenship law) the mother's knowledge of the child and the fact of parenthood have been established."[92] Instead of looking at the establishment of a viable relationship between Nguyen and his father, the court preferred to stick to a gender-based stereotype of female caregiving and bonding as the paradigmatic case of "real, everyday ties" between a parent and a child that merits recognition by the state. The court in *Nguyen* upheld, as the minority put it, "a historic regime that left women with responsibility, and freed men from responsibility, for nonmarital children . . . Rather than confronting the stereotypical notion that mothers must care for these children and fathers may ignore them, [the majority] quietly condones the very stereotype the law condemns."[93] Nguyen and his father lost their case, and we received a fresh reminder of the dangers and biases that may be inherent in a family-relational-based theory of membership attribution.

Although it is theoretically possible to develop a care-based conception of citizenship that truly respects the crucially important role that mothers, fathers, families, and other social networks play in children's lives without repeating the mistakes of the past, the risks are nonetheless daunting. For one, treating family relations as the constitutive basis for our legal ties with the rest of the political community is likely to lead to a situation in which state officials regularly scrutinize intimate relationships. Such concerns are not hypothetical, as the *Benner* and *Nguyen* cases demonstrate.[94] Moreover, related concerns are regularly encountered in immigration law practice, where some of the most sensitive and topical legal cases revolve around the definitions of "marriage," "child," "immediate relative," or "family" for the purposes of acquiring permanent residency and full membership status.[95]

Even if a generous definition of "spouse," "child," or "family member" is adopted, this still fails to resolve the basic difficulty: the determination of which human relationships deserve to be recognized as the basis for citizenship, the most foundational attachment to the state. This complexity arises because any definition of political membership that depends on such relations must inevitably contain a normative judgment about what counts as "family." The risk here is that unmarried cohabitants, gay and lesbian couples, and members of families that do not comply with a standard household stereotype might not only become vulnerable to societal pressure (as they often are today), but also face the detrimental possibility of formal noninclusion in the polity.

This is by no means a hypothetical or unfounded concern. The mediation of political membership through marriage and family relations provides us with all too many alarming illustrations, beyond the ones already described above.[96] Consider, for example, the infamous 1915 *MacKenzie* v. *Hare* decision, in which the U.S. Supreme Court held that in consenting to marry a non-American husband, a U.S. born and bred citizen lost her American citizenship, receiving instead her husband's nationality (under the doctrine of coverture).[97] Or take the saga of *Abdulaziz, Cabales, and Balkandali* v. *the United Kingdom,* decided in 1985 by the European Court of Human Rights, in which the United Kingdom's immigration rules that permitted husbands settled in the country to be joined there by their foreign wives, without allowing settled wives a similarly favorable route to bring in their husbands, were struck down as discriminatory.[98] Following this ruling, the British government decided to stiffen its family reunification rules so that they affected men and women with permanent residence permits in an equally unfavorably way, making it harder for anyone seeking to facilitate admission into the country of their loved ones through marriage.

A final example that is worth noting here refers not to gender, but to sexual orientation. For many years, the United States specified homosexual conduct as a ground for inadmissibility of entry to the country. This legal provision was only officially removed from the law books as recently as 1990. Today, America still refuses to grant same-sex couples and their families the basic immigration protections that are given as a matter of course to members of opposite-sex families, exposing same-sex partners to the punishing dilemma of either keeping their relationship intact (by staying in the country without permission) or following the letter of the law and giving up their ability to share a life together in that country.[99]

These dilemmas have not escaped advocates of the constitutive-ties approach. On the contrary: their strategy has generally been to try to expand the definition of the family and to fight vigorously against the gender-based or sexual-orientation exclusionary constructions of political membership. This commitment to pushing the boundaries of equality of treatment is particularly apt when removing the residual inequalities that still persist in membership-attribution rules, as we have seen in the legal examples just mentioned. It is also gaining traction through regional and international human rights instruments that explicitly protect the right to family unity, for instance, as a limit on state power to deport noncitizens. However, it still remains difficult to conceptualize what a general schema of citizenship that relies primarily on constitutive ties would require in practice, especially given that we live in diverse societies in which not everyone is, or wishes to be, a family member. For example, if citizenship is to be defined based on a web of attachments to meaningful others, should one be deprived of citizenship because of the lack (or breakdown) of relationships? Would residency be required or would it be sufficient to have family members in the host country? Should all persons belonging to an extended transnational family carry multiple affiliations? If so, for how long? A couple of generations, or in perpetuity? Unlike birthright membership, which at least rests on a factual and usually clearly recorded event (birth), reliance on relations for granting access to the good of citizenship almost inevitably invites political, cultural, and legal debate about the values on which acceptable forms of marriage and family are based. A family-based relational approach to citizenship may inadvertently exacerbate these problems, especially if one's definition of a "spouse" or "child" becomes the prime sorting mechanism, for including individuals in the political community. According to the latter scenario, all citizens would have to establish their status in the political community based on their effective ties to the state or its citizens.

This exclusive focus on intimate relations thus proves unnecessarily limiting. It fails to account for constitutive ties that go beyond family life, such as length of residence, intent to stay, participation in a given society and its polity, and so on. Neglecting to account for these additional factors may unintendedly place children and spouses in a dependency trap because their status as members of the polity will rest solely on their ongoing connection to another individual who happens to be a citizen. As such, they lack the security and autonomy that is gained when a person establishes an unmediated relationship with the rest of the political community. In the history of citizenship, the struggle (ongoing in many parts of the globe) to ensure that all adult women and men, rich and poor, literate and illiterate, majorities and minorities, gain equal membership in the state and an equal standing before the law has been no small feat. This achievement was seen as a great victory over the previously mediated relationships in which entities such as the guild, the family, the tribe, or the church defined the set of rights and duties that attached to an individual. It would be unwise to turn back the clock and risk the independence of women (and other historically vulnerable groups) by reintroducing interdependency—here, through family and marriage, instead of church and guild—as a condition for entitlement to equal political standing in the polity.[100]

Intergenerational Bargains

A more calculated defense of the birthright transmission of membership relies on the following logic: it is nearly impossible for people to fulfill their potential and pursue a good life without resource transfers at crucial stages in their life cycle.[101] To address this serious concern, societies rely on the contributions of different generations at different stages in their life cycles. For instance, the working cohort supports the younger generation and, increasingly, the older as well, but it has also benefited from investments by the prior generation (human capital, caregiving, fiscal transfers, to name but a few examples).[102] Such behavior may rely on various motives: self-interest, altruism, a sense of affection, or an expectation of reciprocity. Whatever the reason, economists and demographers have suggested that it relies on an implicit notion of a bargain or contract across generations: a bargain that involves complex investments and transfers from one generation to another at different points in time.[103] This inevitably requires us to take the long view—developments occur on a rolling basis, but this equally makes these bargains prone to problems of reneging, bad behavior, conflicts among different cohorts, or related cleavages.[104] A stable political community that relies on birthright principles in attributing citizenship appears to provide an ideal opportunity to reduce these risks and instead permit predictable and reliable intergenerational transfers to take place.

Although compelling, this argument assumes much of what needs, in fact, to be proven. For example, it is not clear why we need to calculate the bargain at the national level (rather than the familial, local, regional, or international level) or why we should take for granted the high degree of stability in the state that is required for such bargains to remain viable. Related questions emerge: what would happen if particular generations were to renege on these transfers or if a significant number of individuals prefer to leave the community altogether? Can a person simply opt out of one intergenerational contract by moving to another political community?[105] If so, isn't there an obligation by the recipient nation to compensate the source-country for their public investment in the human-capital accretion of its citizens now turned emigrants? This problem becomes more acute if wealthier polities systemically "cream off" the better-educated segments of poorer countries' populations, thus depleting their main source for sustainable intergenerational transfers through the so-called brain drain.[106]

Another weakness of the intergenerational model is that it relies on certain social conventions that are then transformed into actual expectations, many of them reifying traditional family structures with their implicit gendered assumptions about uncompensated domestic labor. To quote a recent study: "free adults are free from debt only because those who have paid for their upbringing do not demand any payment in return, or because they have renounced the claims others have on them."[107] As many feminist scholars have noted, this expected waiver makes the costliness of human reproduction less visible, often to the detriment of mothers who not only give birth but may also provide the bulk of family caregiving work, yet are "naturally" expected to waive any compensation claim that may arise out of this crucial contribution to reproducing the political community.[108] Although very few would support a bluntly calculative approach to caregiving, for any intergenerational contract to be fair, it must take account of these differentiated gender roles and norms.[109] For instance, it may provide delayed transfers to those who provided uncompensated work, such that those involved in human-reproduction labor would not lose out on this particular social contract. Alternatively, the relevant agents may renegotiate their obligations under the contract once they have a viable opportunity to do so. The dramatically declining fertility levels in most advanced industrial societies—with the United States as an exception—has, by and large, coincided with women's entry *en masse* into the workforce and the development of reliable birth control measures, is clear proof of this. The upshot of this population leveling is that societies cannot forever naturally rely on birth (and women's willingness to bear the bulk of the responsibilities associated with human reproduction) as an unwavering source of the nation's stock.

Still, one might argue that considerations of demographic stability and predictability can legitimately serve as another possible defense of birthright. This is certainly sensible in the actuarial sense: any functioning governance unit must have a degree of demographic stability and predictability in place in order for it to plan any social spending that has a long-term trajectory. Reliance on the reproduction capacity of present members thus makes perfect sense as a tool to guarantee that the polity has a stable population base for the future. (Given the changing age and gender structures of many societies, these basic assumptions may require some adjustments, especially in reference to the role of immigrants, as I explain below.) These "taking stock" calculations are particularly important for planning various public policies, ranging from social security to old age pension to investment in early childhood education. The notion of predictability is also important for each member. It provides an individual with the security that her investment in the collective is not just for her generation but also for the next. This can generate an incentive to produce more and improve the cooperative effort that is encapsulated in membership in a given polity.

These ideas resemble familiar lines of arguments from economic debates about the value of inheritance in the realm of property and wealth transfers, some of which we explored in Chapter 1. In that context, the assumption is that if people do not have assurances that they can bequest to their children and grandchildren, they will be less inclined to accumulate wealth, save, conduct themselves responsibly, and so on.[110] In practice, these predictions are awfully difficult to verify or refute. Also, under the current *jus soli* and *jus sanguinis* regimes of birthright, your child will receive an automatic entitlement to membership whether or not you have invested in the polity or contributed to its public good. As such, this system of allocation does not guard against collective action problems of bad behavior or free riding.

To complicate matters even further, these calculations treat the unit of intergenerational bargains as a constant. Yet this is an unstable assumption. It does not accurately reflect the reality of either sending or receiving polities; in most OECD countries, for example, immigrants have become the only real source of growth in the labor market.[111] Under these conditions, the admission of newcomers becomes a crucial avenue for ensuring a society's ability to fulfill its intergenerational commitments (especially from the working-age generation to the elderly). For example, they help pay for social security, old-age pension, and related pay-as-you-go government benefits that are part of the citizenship package in most advanced industrial countries. And yet, these newcomers do not necessarily receive in return a path to citizenship, if they wish to pursue it. Another set of concerns refer to human-capital accretions from the home country; do emigrants owe anything to the community they leave behind? For instance, should a portion of their contribution be directed to compensating the home country for its past investment in these individuals (through public schooling or subsidized college education, where relevant). This may take many forms, including the creation of social security accounts to which emigrants can contribute a portion of the total amount drawn from their income by the country of immigration, to be directed into accounts that become available upon return, or to be directed back to their countries of origin to pay off the investment that society has made in them before they left, providing in turn an additional source of support that may make staying a worthwhile option for those hanging in the balance. If emigration had not taken place, the source country would have recouped taxation, innovation, leadership, or other in-kind returns from these recipients as a result of the public investment the collective has devoted to them in order to better fulfill their potential.

Add to this already complex narrative the fact that it is usually emigrants from poorer countries who now shoulder a substantial share of the paid day-to-day caregiving responsibilities of the old and fragile in well-off polities (through homecare assistance programs, for example). Similarly, certain aspects of care for younger children (the newest members of these political communities) have been contracted out from the family to the paid labor market (through individualized caregiving arrangements, established day-care centers, and so on). The market for caregiving services, at least in the domain of the home, relies in no small part on the contribution of foreign workers, many of them women migrants. This yet again raises a set of sensitive issues: how should we conceptualize the place of these caregivers, who in many cases are not even on the road to membership, in the context of the intergenerational matrix? Specifically, if nonmembers who regularly contribute to the system are not themselves recipients of its significant benefits, we face difficult questions of justice in the allocation of these resources: is it enough to merely pay a fair wage and provide a secure working environment (assuming that the receiving country's labor laws are properly observed)? Or, is there a further reciprocal duty to provide those whose job it is to assist in the continuation of a country's intergenerational bargain (and who directly contribute to its taxation system) access to the social services and political rights of the residence state, even before they reach the point when they become eligible for membership? If so, how quickly do these entitlements establish themselves? The justification for accessing a community's support networks and institutions does not seem to grow out of a collective risk-reduction social-insurance-like scheme (à la Ronald Dworkin's argument), since these nonmembers are not yet part of the decision-making community. A more solid basis for inclusion is that of an earned, Lockean-style entitlement for those who, through their hard work and societal contribution, have made themselves actual members in the chain of intergenerational exchanges.[112]

A final observation on the place of immigrants in the intergenerational matrix is warranted: whereas the bargain among citizens of a shared polity is typically perceived as a voluntary exchange, we increasingly find in immigration law, as Motomura observes, a contract logic which requires that a contribution be made before anyone can claim access to a nation's collective investments or established safety nets. Consider the post-1996 U.S. policy of banning lawful immigrants (namely, green-card holders) from access to any federal social welfare programs in the first five years of their residence in the country.[113] This controversial rule does not grow organically out of a vision of the political community as the generator and keeper of relations of trust and mutual responsibility. It seems instead to rest on a more calculative rationale: since their forefathers did not partake in the intergenerational investment, these newcomers are asked to effectively bail themselves out by first paying into the system before they can claim its benefits. The problem with this vision is that it demands that up-front payments occur precisely during those difficult years when immigrants are establishing themselves in a new environment.[114] The austere undercurrent of this rule comes fully into view when we consider the unforgiving sanction for violating the five-year rule: a lawful permanent resident may not qualify for naturalization if he or she received support during this prohibition period.[115] This contractualist view treats the lawful admission of permanent residents to the country as "just a *temporary* grant of permission that the government can revoke at any time."[116] This conceptual framework in turn highlights the contrast between noncitizens (and recall that we are in this respect talking about the most protected category of immigrants, namely, those who have lawful residence status) and the beneficiaries of automatic membership by inheritance. In this mirror of contrasting images, reliance on birthright in "re-producing" citizens is yet again reconstituted as the norm—only it grants a secure set of expectations and entitlements to those who naturally belong in the pool of members, while offering a harsh take-it-or-leave-it deal to everyone else.[117]

THE DIFFERENT ARGUMENTS in favor of birthright citizenship that I have outlined in this chapter provide a rich panoply of normative and prudential reasons for preserving the idea of bounded membership when it creates a special bond among those sharing a stake in the political unit. Where they all fall short, however, is (1) in explaining where to draw these boundaries in the first place and (2) in justifying a disregard for the profound distributional effects of the citizenship transmission scheme on those left outside their bounty with very limited recourse to overcome the initial lottery of birthright. The latter problem can be addressed, at least in part, by the adoption of the global privilege levy (discussed in Chapter 3). The former, the "demarcation dilemma," requires the introduction of a new principle of membership allocation: *jus nexi.* Articulating the contours of this genuine-connection citizenship principle is the task to which the next chapter is devoted.

CHAPTER SIX

Curtailing Inheritance: Toward a *Jus Nexi* Membership Allocation Principle

Put together by circumstance
he window, she aisle
not a word exchanged
carefully avoiding each other's eyes
he studies her profile
the shape of her fingernails
her thrice-pierced ears
the curve of her breast

The plane jostles—her arm touches his for an instant
a moment of connection—he exists!

He picks up his bag from the carousel
turns sees her looking at him smiling
she reaches for hers
he gently takes it from her hand
they walk together like lovers
absorbed into the crowd . . .

HILDA K. BRITT, *Plane Love* (1993)

THE PREVIOUS CHAPTER critically assessed the explanations currently on offer for upholding birthright-transmission laws in the most profoundly political and public of realms: defining who belongs in the *demos,* or the collective body of the citizenry. Although they fail to articulate a plausible defense for this ascriptive transfer mechanism, they are successful in offering principled arguments in favor of provisionally preserving some degree of bounded membership as a source of security, continuity, and identity—so long as citizenship's enabling and gate-keeping functions are tamed by a mandatory global redistributive scheme along the lines of the birthright privilege levy which I developed earlier in the book.

It is against this background that I will recommend the reform of current citizenship laws in order to encourage a shift toward a *jus nexi,* or genuine-connection principle of membership acquisition, establishing that citizenship must account for more than the mere automatic transmission of entitlement. Instead, some proximity must be established between full membership status in the polity and an actual share in its rights and obligations, responding to the democratic legitimacy concerns raised by both under- and overinclusion.

We saw earlier that even avid defenders of property rights resist endorsing automatic transmission of entitlement from one generation to another in perpetuity: such inheritance regimes are treated as morally weak and objectionable. A similar intuition should gain sway in the realm of citizenship entitlement as well. There is ever-increasing influence in the argument that something more than the mere accident of birth is required in order to determine who is entitled to the good of membership itself. That something else is defined here as a "real and effective link," or the *jus nexi* principle of membership assignment. In its fullest application, *jus nexi* requires a shift away from present ascriptive principles of birthright membership to a genuine-connection principle of citizenship acquisition. In its softer variants, this principle is seen as supplementary to them. I call this genuine connection *jus nexi* because, like *jus soli* and *jus sanguinis,* it conveys the core meaning of the method through which political membership is conveyed: by connection, union, or linkage.

Unlike the often unjust effects that follow from reliance on the legally prescribed territorial or lineage rules, a genuine-connection principle establishes a tie between citizenship and the *social fact of membership* rather than blind reliance upon the accident of birth. Building further on the analogy to property, I consider the relevance of the generational timeline, as well as the nexus of right and duty, in sketching the main implications of the *jus nexi* membership criterion for the most significant test-case categories of potential recipients. These include the *nominal heir:* the child born abroad to parents and families that have long lost their ties with the country of birthright membership. This case represents the problem of overinclusion. At the other extreme, we find the *resident stakeholder:* the person who participates in the life of the polity but lacks citizenship due to the weight presently given to ascriptive factors in defining the *demos.* This category illustrates the underinclusion problem.

In outlining the *jus nexi* membership criterion, I draw upon the growing acceptance of the genuine-connection criterion in court decisions, regulatory regimes, and academic commentaries on the place of residence and the relevance of factual membership and actual ties to the polity. I also explore the idea of a "declining generational entitlement" in property and inheritance theory, as developed by Eugino Rignano, and develop a complementary concept of "ascending membership entitlement." I point to what amounts to a genuine-connection test in some countries with respect to their citizens abroad to lend support to the proposed principle. Where relevant, I also articulate the presence of the genuine-connection idea in the jurisprudence. It is here that the ground is shifting: no longer is birthright the near exclusive and automatic measure for defining entitlement.

Finally, I explore the relevance of the concept of "adverse possession" in thinking through one of the most difficult dilemmas for liberal democracies: how to deal with noncitizen residents whose initial entry breached the law of the admitting states. I argue that here, too, reliance on a property-generated doctrine establishes surprisingly fresh results for citizenship law. Counterintuitively, it offers a powerful precedent for legalizing the status of those who initially entered without permission (unauthorized migrants), countering the claim of "absolute dominion" often raised by those who oppose such legalization.

Taken together, *jus nexi,* declining or ascending membership entitlement, and adverse possession offer important contributions to resolving some of the most pressing local problems in today's citizenship law and practice: overcoming the archaic principles of birthright, which, beyond their severe global distributive consequences (the topic of discussion in previous chapters), are also proving to be poor predictors for defining who will actually belong in the circle of members based on their real and substantive ties rather than any formal, status-based ascriptive factors.

Jus Nexi: A Functional Basis for Gaining Membership Entitlement

The idea of adopting a functional, genuine-connection criterion for defining citizenship finds support from an unexpected source: the jurisprudence of international law. In the landmark 1955 *Nottebohm* decision, the International Court of Justice held that citizenship is not merely an empty "title." It must reflect instead: "a legal bond having as its basis the *social fact of attachment,* a genuine connection of existence, interests and sentiments, together with the existence of reciprocal rights and duties. It may be said to constitute the juridical expression of the fact that the individual upon whom it is conferred . . . is in fact more closely connected with the population of the [s]tate conferring [citizenship] than with any other [s]tate."[1]

In this particular case, the ICJ had to determine whether a citizen of Germany who had resided in Guatemala for most of his adult life and made that country the headquarters of his business activities before acquiring a Lichtensteinian passport was entitled to enjoy protection by one of these countries (Liechtenstein) as against another (Guatemala). This was not an easy case. It required the international court to "pierce the veil" of membership title in the search for that something else that makes citizenship effective at the international law level vis-à-vis another polity. To address this challenge, the ICJ crystallized the principle of *real and effective citizenship:* instead of just looking at the formal status of membership, the court explored and then gave preference to the actual connection "which accorded with the facts." In the *Nottebohm* case, the real and effective ties pointed to Germany (and possibly the place of fixed abode, Guatemala), but certainly not to Liechtenstein, in which Nottebohm had a tenuous connection at best. The more general lesson to be drawn from *Nottebohm* for our discussion is that instead of relying on mere formal status of affiliation, the more important criterion is to examine the social fact of attachment, the genuine connection of the person to the polity as a valid and relevant basis for membership allocation.

Similar developments are occurring on the ground at the local and municipal levels; here we find the rise of city-citizenship definitions, which do not rely on ascription. Instead, cities like Amsterdam grant the local franchise to noncitizens who reside in the metropolis for at least five years, asserting, through their employment, residence, and social attachment to the local community, their genuine connection to it. These city-citizens are then entitled to have their interests and voices represented in city-wide elections and to form political parties.[2] It is through a grounded notion of participation (inhabiting a place, sharing in its risks and promises, and interacting with others, or "rubbing elbows at corner stores" in the colorful language of one court decision) that noncitizens gain political standing and the protection of the enabling locality without reference to their place of birth or bloodline.[3]

In this respect, the *jus nexi* reform I propose is informed by reinvigorated definitions of membership at the international and local levels, as well as a critical reconception of property and related fields of law.[4] These reconceptions have flatly rejected the traditional emphasis on static, blanket formalism, highlighting instead the value of an actual, real, everyday, and meaningful web of relations and human interaction.[5] In carrying out this exercise, we are able to situate the legal analysis of particular disputes or policy questions within a broader social context in which power, social transactions, and enduring relations of interdependence are taken into account.[6] Instead of focusing on the legalese (of contract, marriage, and so on), this type of analysis looks to acts and conduct in light of the surrounding circumstances in which the parties operate in order to determine whether or not an implicit promise, property transfer, or permanent relationship has been established by deed.[7] This approach is widely employed these days in a host of legal arenas, spanning property and contract to family law and resolution of conflicts of law.[8] Consider, for example, the status given to nonmarital cohabitation relationships. Instead of a formalist legal interpretation under which such relationships were categorically unrecognized and unprotected, they are treated today in many jurisdictions as generating a range of actual rights and obligations between partners as well as toward third parties, even without the couple entering into a formal agreement or undertaking registration. In this reading, factors such as the pooling of resources or sharing a household for an extended period of time become evidence of the seriousness of the relationship, and in turn, its legal validity. Another example is found in determinations concerning the best-interest of the child for custody or visitation purposes, which is governed by factual, attentive case-by-case decision making, rather than reliance on fixed and gendered presumptions (as was the case in the past). The growing use of the constructive trust to achieve equitable distribution of shared property among partners based on imputed duties of good faith and fair dealing in the absence of a formal agreement offers yet another illustration of this larger trend.[9] Consider also the relevance of one's place of abode for determining tax liability for foreign residents or in defining eligibility for local voting rights, admission to public schools, access to municipal services, and so on.

Returning to the *Nottebohm* case, which deals directly with our subject of inquiry, namely, illuminating the meaning to be given to the genuine-connection conception of membership, the ICJ articulates several different factors that need to be taken into consideration in identifying whether a real and effective link has been established, granting that the importance (or weight) of these factors might vary from one case to the next. This list of factors (which is illustrative rather than conclusive), includes, in the court's words, "the habitual residence of the individual concerned but also the centre of his [or her] interests, his [or her] family ties, his [or her] participation in public life, attachment shown by him [or her] for a given country and inculcated in his [or her] children, etc." This "center of interests" test is pragmatic and functional; it requires evidence of the establishment of a genuine connection between the individual and the political community. Such a connection need not rely on birthright; instead, it traces the attachment between the individual and the political community on the basis of factual membership and affected interests.[10]

In the same vein, we find a string of influential U.S. court decisions emphasizing the significance of developing ties and identification with the country over time as a basis for bestowing citizenship and its benefits upon long-term residents. This idea we can refer to as the "ascending citizenship model": the longer the person resides in the polity, the deeper his or her ties to its society, the stronger the claim for inclusion in the membership.[11] As one commentator observes, "no matter how strongly our formal laws deny it, our *conduct* [of having persons live, work, and participate in a community over many years] creates the obligation."[12] The idea of making citizenship depend on functional and pragmatic rather than formal criteria finds comprehensive support in the writing of leading scholars of immigration law and theory, including Alexander Aleinikoff, Joseph Carens, Ruth Rubio-Marin, Rainer Bauböck, Seyla Benhabib, and Linda Bosniak, to name but a few in a flourishing academic field. These authors share a commitment to the idea that a generous and ascending scale of rights should be accorded to nonmembers as they extend and deepen their actual participation in a polity over time. This incremental process, in which one's center of life gravity shifts, is central to the *jus nexi* principle. It also finds expression in the jurisprudence: "as the alien's tie grows stronger, so does the strength of his claim to an equal share in that munificence [the bounty that a conscientious sovereign makes available to its citizens]."[13]

By focusing on the "genuine connection of existence, interests and sentiments," as the ICJ puts it, rather than merely looking to formal titles acquired at birth, *jus nexi* provides substance to the idea that real and genuine ties fostered on the ground deserve some form of legal recognition: here, by granting secure membership status based on the social connectedness that has already been established. Such an approach enables us to welcome into the *political* community those who have already become *social* members based on their actual participation in the everyday life and economy of the jurisdiction, and through their interdependence with its legal and governance structures. As Hiroshi Motomura eloquently observes, this emphasis on the ties that bind allows law to "take time into account by acknowledging and giving legal meaning to what has *already* occurred."[14] Instead of asking whether a person happened to have been born in a given country (the focal point of ascriptive citizenship laws), the more significant set of questions under the *jus nexi* framework becomes where he or she actually lives, where his or her center of interests lie, and where, as a result, to place "the legal bond [of citizenship] having as its basis the social fact of attachment."[15]

Political philosophers and democratic theorists have also come to recognize the importance of real, genuine links as a basis for membership entitlement and political participation. As Tomas Hammar observes, "in affluent societies being a member of this population [the country's citizenry] is in itself a valuable social asset which is, however, taken for granted by those who already possess it."[16] This invaluable property of citizenship, as I have called it, "is distributed by them [those already counting as citizens] to others, who have not got membership but who would like to get it."[17] The main bone of contention, of course, is to determine the "correct regulative principle" for such distribution, which, as John Rawls once put it, "depends on the nature of that thing [distributed.]"[18] In the context of our discussion, any new principle for bestowing citizenship needs to correspond better with the actual content associated with this legal status, rather than merely reemphasizing predetermined circumstances of territoriality or descent as the core determinants of membership. For Rainer Bauböck, this implies that, as a result of their involvement and stake in the life of the polity, noncitizen residents become members not by formal designation, but as a matter of fact. A more equitable criterion for allocating citizenship must therefore acknowledge this real and genuine component in defining access to the collective good of citizenship and its accompanying benefits for the individuals involved. We can no longer rely merely on transmission by birthright; any new and more equitable principle of citizenship allotment, here interpreted from the in-state perspective, must take into account the actual interdependence of one's lived experience with the particular political community in which he or she seeks inclusion as a permanent member.[19] This requires us to ask, as Bauböck nicely puts it, "whether an individual's long-term circumstances of life link her own well-being to a particular polity." If the answer is affirmative, serious consideration must be given to granting her the security and dignity that comes with sharing in the collective good of citizenship.

Resolving the Mismatches of Status for the Resident Stakeholder and Nominal Heir through Ascending and Descending Membership Entitlements

For the vast majority of the population, those who carry on the bulk of their lives in the country of birthplace *(jus soli)* or parentage *(jus sanguinis)*, the shift toward *jus nexi* will not make a significant difference: they shall acquire full membership regardless. However, this change could make a significant difference for those who relocate across borders. In particular, it can make a difference for two important constituents: the *nominal heirs* of birthright title (the children or grandchildren of emigrants who have left the country of inherited citizenship) and long-term *resident stakeholders* who are not citizens (those who have settled in a new homeland yet have not received membership in it). As processes of globalization deepen, we will likely see more individuals and families falling into these categories, which highlight, from different angles, the growing inappropriateness of relying on ascriptive definitions of membership in allocating citizenship's legal protections and its accompanying security, voice, and opportunity.

As Christian Joppke pointedly observes, "pure *jus sanguinis* and *jus soli* citizenship rules are equally ill-adjusted to a world of global migration. While pure *jus sanguinis* keeps immigrants forever out of the country, pure *jus soli* has the reverse defect of bestowing the precious good of life-long citizenship on mere transients and passers-by."[20] This is a variant on the familiar problem of over- and underinclusion that we encountered in Chapter 4. Can the proposed *jus nexi* approach overcome these perennial mismatches? I will argue that it can and suggest that by adopting the genuine-connection principle of membership allocation, we can resolve (or at least mitigate) the overinclusion of birthright citizenship by adopting a "declining membership entitlement" scale, while at the same time insisting on an "ascending citizenship matrix" to address the problem of underinclusion for those who are de facto members but lack access to citizenship.

The declining membership entitlement takes into account the generational-timeline factor; it is designed to respond to the challenge posed by those who can be categorized as the *nominal heirs:* the windfall recipients who have never lived in their emigrant parents' or grandparents' country of origin but nonetheless gain full membership standing in it because of the operation of present birthright citizenship regimes. In these circumstances, a graduated set of limits could be introduced to restrict the automatic transfer of citizenship as the number of generations since the time the original member left the polity increases. This proposal would offer a welcome development in curbing the rising trend toward "re-ethnicization" of membership, a term coined by Joppke to refer to distant-in-time emigrants who are seen as part of the nation's stock and thus retain citizenship irrespective of actual ties to the polity.[21]

For *resident stakeholders,* the settled immigrants and their children who have already become intertwined with the polity as a matter of actual attachment, link, identification, center of life, or sheer interdependence an "ascending citizenship matrix" is put into place: the longer the stay, the deeper the social connectedness, the stronger the claim for inclusion in the polity, overcoming the absence of the "correct" bloodline or station of birth. Those who are already members as a matter of social fact thus gain a pathway to citizenship, correcting the problem of underinclusiveness. This type of legal reform is ever-more-urgently needed in light of the mounting anti-immigrant sentiment sweeping many parts of Europe and North America.

Together, these descending and ascending scales reflect concrete and illustrative manifestations of the genuine-connection criterion. Although they apply to different situations, both share a mutual distrust of mere reliance on circumstances of birth as the primary connecting factors that, at present, bestow upon some (and deny to others) the precious title of citizenship without a trace of any actual nexus between right and duty, membership and participation, exercising voice and bearing the consequences of collective decision making, social connectedness and legal entitlement.

The Rignano Principle: Membership Entitlement and the Generational Timeline

The idea of a "declining intergenerational entitlement" structure (as we might call it) resembles an innovative proposal developed by Eugenio Rignano and discussed in Chapter 3.[22] To recap, Rignano was searching for a way to restrict inheritance without destroying the incentives that motivate individuals to work and save. His proposed solution to this dilemma was "to differentiate the right of bequest according to the 'origin' or 'age' of the property to be bequeathed."[23] This required a distinction to be made between the property that a person created or saved during his or her lifetime ("0 transfers"), the property which that person inherited from a prior generation and which came out of the prior generation's own hard work and savings ("1 transfer"), and property that was inherited from persons who themselves inherited it from others ("2 transfers"). The Rignano principle, as it came to be known, stipulates that the higher the number of transfers, the weaker the entitlement of the heir; this in turn permits a steeper rate of taxation on the intergenerational transfer.

The brilliance of Rignano's principle lies in his simple yet elegant idea that inheritance taxation can be progressive in time, reflecting the generational distance from the original acquisition, with a declining moral and legal impetus to continue the chain of transfer as that distance grows. This proposal prefers property and wealth acquired through individuals' own efforts and contributions to that which is attained by transmission from generation to generation.[24]

A Rignano-style scheme of declining entitlement transported into the realm of citizenship entitlement thus calls for a reconstruction of the birthright privilege. It permits a degree of continuity that is important for political communities to fulfill their enabling provisions, without sanctioning the perpetuation of entail-like transmission of merely inherited property, or membership entitlement. Following this idea, it may be argued that entitlement to birthright citizenship is similarly weakened as we get further away from the original point of acquisition; on this declining entitlement account, the attribution of political membership to the 2nd, 3rd, or Nth generation of heirs must be accompanied by genuine links to the relevant political community in order to survive the intergenerational distance.

According to this vision, birthright inheritance does not by itself establish a full right to citizenship; it merely provides a provisional or partial title to the distant-in-time heir. This must be complemented by the recipient's own actual behavior, such as establishing residency in the relevant political community, sending remittances, maintaining links with the country or its diaspora by partaking in intercultural or political exchanges, learning the language of the birthright polity or related activities that indicate the person's connectedness and willingness to share both the risks and benefits of membership in a society in which he or she never lived. If these factors are nonexistent, then the passage of title down the cascading generational line no longer serves as a strong enough basis to automatically extend citizenship and its accompanying goods.

Whereas emigrants who themselves left the home country ("o transfer" in Rignano's terminology) can legitimately claim a continued stake simply by virtue of having the experience of growing up in the country they left and perhaps the expectation of returning there at an older age, as the "distance" from the original acquisition increases, their progeny, namely, the first and second generation (and more so, the third, fourth, fifth, or Nth generation) born abroad have a correspondingly weaker claim to the host of benefits that attach to citizenship. This includes the sticky question of whether voting rights should be granted to those who inherited membership but never lived in the country, which has generated lively debate in both academic and policy-making circles in recent years.[25] Although this is primarily a matter for each political community to determine according to its democratic decision-making processes, the logic of *jus nexi* strongly weighs in favor of the opinion that "democratic participation presupposes a stronger ongoing involvement in the polity than can be transmitted by mere descent."[26]

Put more schematically, the main insight drawn from the world of property and inheritance that is important for the purposes of our discussion of birthright citizenship is this: the greater the generational distance from the original titleholder to the heir, the weaker the recipient's claim for unlimited and uninterrupted transfer of the bequest. Although each generation's claim for the "fruits" of its own initiative is strong, its claim for the inherited "capital" appears to weaken as we get farther away from the original point of acquisition. Instead of the current reality in which hereditary citizenship is still often passed down the generations automatically and perpetually, the declining-membership-entitlement logic requires that as the generational distance from the actual point of last residence in the country increases, some form of substantive connection to, or membership in, the polity may be required before the right to citizenship—and its benefits—are bestowed.[27]

Jus Nexi and Citizens Residing Abroad

A kind of *jus nexi* test has already appeared in relation to citizens residing abroad who have established their lives in an adopted home country, leaving behind the country of origin of their ancestors. For example, the United States has adopted what could be referred to as a "declining intergenerational entitlement" (without giving it this name) with respect to its citizens who live overseas. An example of this is the child born to American parents living outside of the United States who acquires citizenship at birth only if one of its parents resided in the United States at some time prior to the birth. In other words, the parent must have fulfilled the genuine-connection requirement before he or she can transfer title to the next generation.[28] If one of the parents is a noncitizen, then U.S. law further specifies that the citizen parent must have been physically present in the United States for at least five years preceding the birth of the child, two of which must have been after the age of fourteen.[29] In effect, this formalizes into law the requirement that a person through whom the precious entitlement to American citizenship is transmitted must have experienced the lived reality of "*being* an American." (The emphasis on the *experience* of actual membership enables us to avoid charged "identity" and "belonging" questions about what content is or ought to be given to the designation of being an American.) This legal requirement is typically fulfilled by making the country the actual place of residence for a specified number of years. This type of *jus nexi* requirement reflects, as the authors of a leading textbook on citizenship and immigration note, an attempt by the American legislature to "avoid the creation of a class of expatriates who may transmit U.S. citizenship to their children indefinitely, even though the family has had no close contact with actual life in the United States for generations."[30]

This emphasis of real and effective citizenship is by no means unique to the United States. According to the British Nationality Act, a child born abroad can acquire British nationality only when at least one of the parents derived her citizenship not by inheritance-transmission alone.[31] In Canada, too, transmission is not automatic for the beneficiaries of "transfer 2" (in Rignano's typology), that is, children born to parents who *themselves* were born outside Canada. Section 8 of the Citizenship Act proclaims that in order to retain their birthright entitlement to membership, such nominal heirs must (re)activate their connection to the country, for instance, by "[registering] as a citizen and either [residing] in Canada for a period of at least one year immediately preceding the date of his [or her] application or [establishing] a substantial connection with Canada."[32] This connection-establishing or "reactivation" requirement can be met in a number of ways: for example, by residing in the country for more than one year after the age of fourteen; attending a recognized Canadian secondary or postsecondary educational institution; demonstrating adequate knowledge of one of the country's official languages; or being employed in the public service of the collective, whether in Canada or abroad.[33] These various membership-retention strategies are designed to ensure that a real and genuine connection is established between the citizen and the granting polity, over and above the ascription of membership by inherited title. Other countries, impose even stricter terms for preservation of membership, providing in their citizenship laws that children born abroad to parents who themselves have received their entitlement merely by blood must establish residence in the parent's country of origin for a certain period of time before they gain a full and irrevocable membership status.[34] Even Germany, which until recently endorsed an unlimited intergenerational transmission of membership, changed its birthright citizenship law in 2000, putting "a stopping point for extra-territorial citizenship transmission in terms of the second ('grandchild') generation born abroad."[35] For these children, German citizenship is no longer automatic—it is conditional upon their parents' declaration and registration of the child's birth at a German embassy or consulate, within a tight time framework.[36] This resembles, in the analogy to property, an imposition of a "rule against perpetuities" on the previously perpetual and cascading transmission of the inherited entitlement.

Although there is significant diversity in terms of the specific legal requirements for establishing citizenship for children or grandchildren who have received provisional title by perpetual entail, the logic that unites them is that of a declining membership entitlement. Inheritance of membership title—especially as we get further away in time from the last title holder who had a real and effective link to the polity—can no longer serve as the sole criterion for gaining citizenship; something else is required. That something else I label the *genuine-connection principle* of membership acquisition, which holds that citizenship must account for more than mere automatic transmission of entitlement in perpetuity.

Jus Nexi in the Jurisprudence: "The Ties that Bind"

The acknowledgement of the importance of an actual center-of-life connection is most vividly apparent in the jurisprudence of the European Court of Justice, which over the last decades has given greater weight to the genuine-link criterion for defining access to certain benefits of membership in lieu of simply relying on birthright and inheritance as the basis for automatic entitlement.[37] To explain this last point, consider the recent case of *Collins,* decided by the European Court of Justice in 2004.

In this case, the ECJ had to determine whether Brian Francis Collins, a dual citizen of the United States and Ireland, was entitled to claim a jobseeker's allowance in Great Britain—a country where he was not a habitual resident. The facts were as follows: Collins was a well-traveled man. He was born in the United States, and acquired membership there by virtue of the *jus soli* (territoriality) principle. Collins also possessed Irish citizenship based on the *jus sanguinis* (parentage) principle. In 1978, as part of his college education, Collins spent one semester in the United Kingdom. He then worked at part-time jobs in the United Kingdom in 1980 and 1981, before returning to the United States. Almost two decades later (in 1998), Collins returned to the United Kingdom, where he sought employment. It was undisputed that he had a right to seek a job in the United Kingdom, given his European citizenship status (which he had acquired by virtue of his birthright entitlement to an Irish passport). However, less than a month after his arrival in the United Kingdom in 1998, Collins claimed a jobseeker's allowance. His claim was refused because he was not a habitual resident in the United Kingdom; that is, although he clearly inherited a valid membership status (as a birthright citizen of a Member State of the Union), he was lacking, in the court's words, "the real link [to] . . . the geographic employment market" in question. The court, in other words, was not willing to accept Collins' claim that his *inherited* membership status alone made him eligible to immediately enjoy whatever goods and services attached to *actual membership* in the state. Instead, the court ruled that such benefits must be reserved for those who have established, through their actual behavior, a genuine link to the relevant jurisdiction, a link of involvement and interdependency that is distinct from mere ascriptive entitlement to citizenship.

Importantly, the United Kingdom (like most other OECD countries) provides access to basic services (such as emergency medical care) to anyone in its territory on the basis of immediate need; this is the case, regardless of the recipient's membership status or length of stay.[38] But this was not the issue here. Collins was seeking a means-tested social-assistance benefit, which, at least according to the court's ruling, was legitimately understood as a safety net created primarily *by* and *for* those who regularly live in the country, experiencing both the opportunities and risks of its economic and societal infrastructure.

Beyond the specific details of this case, what is most important for the purposes of our discussion is that the court treats birthright membership as a valid source of title but as an insufficient criterion for enjoying, without any additional connection to the polity, the "whole estate." As a recipient of a title that itself was inherited, Collins's "declining entitlement" was not as strong as the entitlement of someone who participated in the collective enterprise; effectively, this meant that he could not automatically draw on the benefits of the inherited entitlement without at least demonstrating his provisional willingness to wed his own fate to that of the political community in question.[39]

The flip-side of the *Collins* case is found in an earlier decision of the ECJ, in *Martinez-Sala.* In that case, the court ruled that a nonworker migrant who has established extended residency and deep social ties to the relevant jurisdiction (Germany, in that particular decision), acquires by virtue of these ties, an entitlement to access the public goods provided by that political community to its population.[40] The rationale for the *Martinez-Sala* decision was the converse of the "declining entitlement" logic: it relied on the *ascending* citizenship matrix, though the legal claim in this case was narrowly defined as applying to social benefits that attach to permanent residence.[41] The court reasoned that the stronger the social ties, the stronger the claim of the person seeking to partake in the full social and economic life of that political community.[42]

This emphasis on providing a growing catalogue of rights and protections for the resident stakeholder through the genuine connection established between that individual and the relevant political community has strong juridical foundations.[43] We have already seen it at work in the *Nottebohm* case in the international context. It further finds expression in positive law in the domestic arena as well. For example, the American jurisprudence dealing with the situation of long-term noncitizen residents emphasizes the idea of earning membership through building actual, genuine ties to the political community and its society. To provide a concrete illustration we should look at section 240A of the Immigration and Nationality Act which provides that even persons subject to a formal removal order in the United States are permitted to ask the government for a waiver that would permit them to stay.[44] In assessing such requests, immigration judges are instructed to consider factors such as the length of residence in the country, family ties, evidence of value and service to the community, employment history, and the extreme hardship that might be incurred by the respondent and her family if deportation were to take place.[45] Related factors to be considered include the person's age, health, ability to travel, lack of criminal record, and other "equities" that can weigh in favor of allowing long-term residents or close family members to remain in the country and adjust their status—overcoming the specific grounds for their removal, which in certain cases may include unlawful presence in the country.[46] In situations where removal amounts to extreme hardship, the various "facts and circumstances of each case," as a leading opinion instructs, must be taken into account.[47] The ties that bind, which can receive retrospective legal recognition, may further include being an active parent in a child's school, volunteering in community service, or caring for a needy relative.[48]

This determination requires probing beyond the formal status of a person's admission into the country, looking to the actual conduct of the person in the context of her social attachments and community ties. As Alexander Aleinikoff lucidly articulated many years ago, this shifts the focus to the "*actual* relationships the individual has developed with a society: a family, friends, a job, association membership, professional acquaintances, opportunities."[49] It is possible to further extend and update this illustrative list to include factors such as caregiving at home and volunteering in civil society or religious organizations in order to ensure a diverse pool of potential recipients; for if only paid participation in the labor force, business ownership, or military service (to pick a few familiar examples) are counted toward proof of establishing the social fact of membership, then we will end up with an impoverished and notoriously distorted vision of the lived world, as well as run the risk of disadvantaging women, linguistic minorities, and others whose life circumstances may prevent them from fully participating in the formal, paid marketplace. With this expansive definition of actual familial and communal ties, even the severity of an initial unlawful entry may be partly diminished over time if one's status is later adjusted; as I mentioned earlier, the longer the time that elapses, the stronger the claim for gaining equal membership entitlement.

Developing the Implications for *Jus Nexi*

Although prolonged residence plays a crucial role in defining the genuine connection to the polity, the legal validation of this connection may take many different forms, reflecting the multidimensional interests and expectations that people bear in relation to this core entitlement. As Bauböck eloquently observes, "a more extensive claim to full membership arises when the social conditions and circumstances an individual finds herself in, or has chosen to live in, link her individual interests to the common good of a particular political community."[50] These connections need not grow out of blood or territory; they may well develop out of experiences of social interaction that takes place under the normative umbrella of a given political community and within a particular geographical location. In this way, *jus nexi* reflects the idea of democratic inclusion, according to which those who are habitually subject to the coercive powers of the state must gain a hand in shaping its laws, if they so choose.

In this respect, *jus nexi* differs from a pure domicile-based principle of membership that would provide automatic naturalization *(ex lege)* for anyone residing in the polity after their presence is deemed permanent, as advanced, for example, by Ruth Rubio-Marin in *Immigration as a Democratic Challenge*. Like the *ex lege* idea, the *jus nexi* principle is normatively designed to shrink the gap between partaking in actual membership and gaining political voice; it views every long-term resident as a citizen-in-the-making. Unlike it, however, *jus nexi* does not force membership upon them. Instead, it creates an eligibility or presumption of inclusion on behalf of those whose life center has already shifted. What is required here is not mere physical presence in the territory but also the passage of time and social connectedness, the latter referring to the requisite "center of life" criteria, which itself can be interpreted in more generous or more stringent ways. The crucial point is, however, that *jus nexi* differs from a conception of membership that makes territorial presence the all-or-nothing criterion.[51] It thus escapes the autonomy-diminishing aspect of an automatic, *ex lege* (and potentially forced) incorporation of individuals into the polity.[52] Another concern is that automatic formal imposition of citizenship title by the country of residence may potentially harm the status of the emigrant in the country of origin if the latter objects to dual nationality.

In contrast, precisely because of its anchoring in social fact, *jus nexi* permits *multiple* citizenship affiliations to remain and flourish; at the same time, it gives priority to the political relationships toward which the real and genuine ties are manifested. Here, the logic of *Nottebohm* can be read (beyond its original articulation) as providing a method for sorting between multiple membership affiliations held by the same person. Instead of asking her to sever such attachments (as does current U.S. naturalization requirements), *jus nexi* honors one's "center of life" and actual (or "active") membership location, while acknowledging that this *locus* itself may change over the course of one's lifetime.

I have already mentioned that *jus nexi* can be viewed either as a complete alternative to *jus soli* and *jus sanguinis* or as a supplementary principle for citizenship acquisition. As a complete alternative, *jus nexi* would treat birthright as a mere component in a larger schema of defining membership boundaries according to social fact and actual manifestation of participation, for instance, through residence or other connection-establishing acts. Any fair and persistent application of the *jus nexi* principle must, however, take account of the relevant distance in time; otherwise it risks breaching any stable notion of intergenerational bargain (discussed in Chapter 5) and depriving members of the political community of any sense of mutual trust or continuity between past and future. This still reserves ample room for change and transformation in the composition of the citizenry body; in this respect, *jus nexi* (especially if combined with more open borders) provides an excellent response to a future with greater cross-border mobility which is not devoid of bounded membership. In the latter scenario, those with no prior ties can become members through deed; they will gain access to a post-natal citizenship title assigned *jure nexi*. Those whose expectations arise out of inherited title, namely individuals who are closer in generational distance, must also be offered ample venues to (re)connect with the bounded community. We have seen this idea in action in the context of Canada's second-generation born abroad retention requirement, which in addition to a registration requirement also clarifies that a substantive connection can be established by way of a one-year residence period, public service abroad on behalf of the nation, or merely demonstration of knowledge of the country's basic constitutional principles, and adequate proficiency in one of its official languages.[53] Under the proposed scheme, a presumption of inclusion initially applies; those who will want to sever ties with the polity will have to opt out of the default rules, thus securing a relatively strong membership claim for up to two descending generations. The entitlement to citizenship does, however, weaken with each successive generation (given the greater distance in time) in the absence of any real connection to the polity. Again, the rationale for this is that in order to fully enjoy the "right-not-to-be-excluded"—that is, to share the privileges and obligations of citizenship—something more than repeated transfers of hereditary bequests is required. We risk otherwise the perpetuation of entail-like inequalities that unfairly exclude nonmembers while enriching those with no connection to the polity aside from a distant bloodline or an accident of birthplace.

The other side of abolishing the privileges of hereditary entitlement is that *jus nexi* offers resident stakeholders a predictable and secure route to becoming full members, irrespective of their lack of birth-based connection to the polity.[54] In this respect, *jus nexi* allows both greater democratic accountability and political equality for those who are most directly affected by the legal authority of the state—namely, those who are regularly subject to the full extent of its coercive powers and governance institutions and whose fundamental rights have come to depend on protections provided by that particular polity (whether or not they were born into its *demos*).

Related processes of gradual incorporation through participation in the life of the polity should be familiar to us from the naturalization procedure, which typically requires a newcomer to fulfill a mandatory residence requirement before he or she can apply for citizenship. The focus here is on the experience of membership for which, in the words of one official report on citizenship, "there can be no substitute."[55] In the same vein, a nominal heir may be asked to reside in the country for a specified period of time before (re)gaining her full membership status.[56] Again, drawing upon existing practices, it is important to note that in certain categories of admission, such as a fiancé or fiancée entering the polity to marry a citizen, the individual is usually able to acquire full membership far more quickly than those in other categories. Similarly, we can imagine a *jus nexi* regime that permits nominal heirs born outside the polity to (re)establish their membership affiliation in the polity under an expedited procedure of, say, one year of residence in the country. What matters is not the concrete threshold defined (for instance, six or twelve or twenty-four months), but rather the acknowledgment that hereditary title alone is no longer a sufficient basis for membership if the person has not physically set foot in her home community or otherwise maintained any meaningful ties with it.

What *jus nexi* demands, then, is a closer correlation between democratic voice, factual membership, and citizenship entitlement. It offers a path for stakeholder residents whose lives have already become deeply intertwined with the bounded community in which they have settled to enjoy legal rights and protections as permanent residents and a predictable path to becoming full members.[57] It also requires the nominal heir whose entitlement diminishes as the age or distance of the inheritance increases to establish some meaningful connection with the polity before claiming the manifold benefits that attach to citizenship's property.

As I alluded to earlier, the reliance on factual, genuine links to the polity in lieu of the traditional insistence on birthright membership could make a substantial difference for two main groups. The first includes long-term resident stakeholders who, after lawfully entering the country, have become a part of the polity's social fabric, sharing the risks and benefits of its economic and political structures. Subject to the polity's sovereign power and legal authority, they have become stakeholders in it despite lacking an ascriptive claim to membership.[58] The second group is composed of those who have acquired membership at birth, but have never made the granting state a part of their lived experience or a centre of their interests. This is the situation of the nominal heir, the windfall beneficiary born abroad to parents who merely inherited the title of citizenship by virtue of entail-like birthright, never themselves establishing a genuine connection to the home community the grandparents left behind. Such perpetual-transmission privileges are curtailed under this proposal, just as the bequests received by repeated transfers of inheritance are gradually eroded under the declining entitlement principle.

On this account, a law-abiding, not-yet-naturalized permanent resident of a given polity may, under certain circumstances, be more entitled to full membership in the polity than a nominal heir birthright titleholder. This might, for example, be the case where the hereditary titleholder received citizenship *jure sanguinis* or *jure soli* but has never lived in the polity or developed any effective and genuine ties to it. Still, under an un-curtailed citizenship-transfer regime that privileges birthright, such an individual is entitled to automatic, unconditional, and irrevocable membership in the polity, while the long-term habitual resident lacks any guaranteed membership stake in it.[59]

In principle, nothing in the rationale of connectedness and democratic inclusion, which is at the heart of the *jus nexi* principle, limits its application strictly within the realm of the bounded community. For at least some collective decisions which clearly have cross-border implications (for example, environmental pollution or its reduction), the genuine-connection principle, here referring to political participation rather than membership, could also be extended beyond borders. Such a transnational variant of *jus nexi* could apply to certain nonmembers outside the territory, at least by granting them democratic voice where crucial decision-making processes that have a significant extraterritorial effect on their lives are at stake. This idea represents a modified and narrow version of the affected interests principle which, in this context, complies perfectly with the logic of *jus nexi:* the stronger the connection to the polity (where an individual adversely affected by a given decision would be considered connected in this way), the stronger the claim for participation.[60]

Addressing the Dual Problem of Under- and Overinclusion

Having explained how *jus nexi* operates in theory, I will now provide two concrete examples of the principle at work. The first example shows how *jus nexi* can rectify the problem of underinclusion in the ascription of citizenship, while the second example addresses overinclusion. That is, *jus nexi* reduces the reliance on chance factors in a way that appears just, whereas *jus soli* and *jus sanguinis* exclude some who feel they should rightly be included while including others who should not.

In Chapter 5, I discussed the sad story of Nguyen, the natural-born son of an American father and a Vietnamese mother, who was born outside the

United States. Nguyen was brought back to the United States with his father. He lawfully received a green card at the tender age of five and lived with his American father in the United States without realizing that he had to go through a registration process before a specific cut-off date in order to acquire full membership. If a *jus nexi* principle were in operation, this child (and any similarly situated person) would not face the threat of deportation as a result of the failure of the child or parent to fulfill the technical requirement of affirming paternity and membership through the formal channels enumerated in the law books. Under a *jus nexi* regime, Nguyen would be able to claim entitlement to American citizenship based on his *actual, real, and genuine connection* to that polity—the country in which he was bred and educated, where his American father lived and raised him, the only place that he knew as his home. Put differently, Nguyen would have benefited from the introduction of the remedial principle of genuine connection. The presumption of inclusion would have been easily validated by his actual membership in the American polity as reflected in the context and reality of his life situation. In the absence of *jus nexi,* Nguyen's case was lost, the nexus denied. Instead, what prevailed were formalistic and birth-centered assumptions about what creates the ties that bind us to a particular political community.

The emphasis on the social fact of membership would have helped resolve not only the problem of legal exclusion by birth affecting children born abroad to an unwed parent (like *Nguyen*), but also those who enter the country at a very young age with their immigrant parents (like *Ortiz-Martinez*), gaining lawful residence but not citizenship. As a particularly vulnerable group, *jus nexi* would grant these children semiautomatic access to citizenship (in both *jus soli* and *jus sanguinis* countries) after they had resided in the admitting polity for a specified number of years or had acquired their formative schooling through its educational system.[61] The Comparative Citizenship Project, conducted by an international group of researchers, has reached a similar conclusion. The group argues that foreign-born children who have entered the United States at an early stage and have at least six years of schooling or ten years of residence are, for all practical purposes, "Americans." Their legal status should therefore reflect this social reality.[62] In other words, these children should receive citizenship by way of *jus nexi;* that is, their membership entitlement should be engendered by their actual, real, and effective links to the only polity that they know as home.[63]

By the same token, the *jus nexi* principle would have barred Sheinbein (whose case is discussed in Chapter 4) from escaping to his father's home country of Israel. The adolescent American murderer, after committing his crime in the United States, fled to Israel. As a nominal heir to Israeli citizenship, he was protected against extradition back to the United States, which was, undisputedly, his active country of citizenship. Sheinbein had never set foot in his father's country of origin, nor did he make any other effort to establish a genuine connection to that polity.[64] According to the *jus nexi* principle, this represents a case where inheritance alone ought not to serve as a sufficient basis for the nominal heir to claim membership-based immunity against facing trial in the home country to which he held real and genuine ties. (A different result may occur if the person seeking to invoke his birthright community's protection is discriminated against by the community of residence because of his legal affiliation with the hereditary-membership state. This was, however, never an issue in this particular case.)

The above examples illustrate the *jus nexi* principle at work and highlight the value inherent in an ascription of citizenship that is based on something substantial rather than accidental. The application of the *jus nexi* principle appears to result in a more balanced outcome, in part because there is an implied notion of reciprocity and joint responsibility that informs the reliance on a genuine-link test for distributing membership and political voice. The substantial-connection test links up access to the rights and benefits of citizenship with the sharing in its obligations.

Adverse Possession and Enforceable Rights for the Noncitizen

Lawful admission to a polity is generally viewed as a necessary step toward the acquisition of citizenship by those without hereditary entitlement. But what happens if this initial condition of authorized admission is violated; for example, in circumstances where the noncitizen entered the country in a clandestine fashion or has overstayed a temporary visa in violation of the admitting state's provisions?[65] Advocates of the resurrect-the-border position (identified in Chapter 2) have adopted an absolutist stance in response to this question. They firmly hold that unauthorized migrants should be barred from admission to the rights and privileges of membership as a result of their "original sin": they broke the law by entering without permission and must therefore be barred from any path that could enable them to regularize their status. Some even go a step further and argue that unauthorized migrants should be deported back to their countries of origin, irrespective of any hardships that such removal may cause or the web of relationships that they have established in the new polity. By contrast, proponents of a vision of global citizenship tend to quibble with the categorization of unauthorized entrants as illegal immigrants, arguing that, on moral grounds, human beings cannot be defined as "illegal." This sentiment is well-captured in slogans such as "no one is illegal," or advocacy calls for granting "status for all." In a rebuttal, however, a sophisticated resurrect-the-border advocate might point out that it is not the *person* who is deemed "illegal," but rather the *procedure* for entering the country; a point which, at least technically, is valid in a world of regulated migration like our own. In today's political climate, however, this answer does not stand up to scrutiny. Consider the fact that lawmakers in the United States introduced a draft immigration bill in 2006 (which eventually did not pass) that defined illegal presence in the country as a felony, blurring the line between action and status and making unauthorized migration a category of criminal culpability.[66]

The debate between these two competing camps is not easily resolved. Each side comes to it with very different presuppositions about the legitimacy of bounded membership and regulated admission (as we saw in Chapter 2). Instead of reentering the fray of that debate, I again draw upon the analogy of property to develop an alternative response to the problem of initial entry without permission. The results are surprising. Consider the property doctrine of "adverse possession," which, just like the institution of fee tail (discussed in Chapter 1), dates back to the early years of the English common law. Both these legal institutions were placed on a statutory footing by Westminster in the late thirteenth century. Yet, unlike the fate of entailed property, now both banned and discredited, the doctrine of adverse possession is still alive and practiced today. This long-standing rule of law holds that "one who . . . possesses property belonging to another for a sufficient period of time *without* the owner's permission acquires title to the property."[67]

Adverse possession thus offers a "startling means of acquiring property."[68] "Startling" because it holds that a *trespasser*—that is, a person who entered without permission—may obtain full title to the property into which he or she initially entered unlawfully, if the occupancy (or in our case, residency) is peaceful, continuous, and visible "for all the world to see if the owner cared to look."[69] To acquire title in this way, however, certain conditions must apply. The most significant of them is that the entrant must have resided in the territory in actual possession for an extended period of time. The precise period of continued occupancy in actual possession differs from one jurisdiction to another even within the United States. For instance, it is currently set at ten years or less in most western states, while most eastern states require a longer period of continued residency.[70] In the United Kingdom, the jurisdiction from which the adverse possession doctrine originated, the time limit typically ranges from ten to twelve years.[71]

Regardless of the specific period, the principle of adverse possession remains the same: it dramatically limits the owners' "right to exclude," if they sleep on their rights and take no action after actual or constructive notice that an uninvited occupant has visibly resided in their territory for an extended period of time. Under such circumstances, the law of property recognizes that relationships and expectations may change over time. As Oliver Wendell Holmes famously put it: "a thing which you have enjoyed and used as your own for a long time, whether property or opinion, takes root in your being [. . .], however you came by it."[72] As with *jus nexi,* the law recognizes that the adverse possessor, or in our case, the unauthorized entrant (again to rely on Holmes' resounding words), "shape[s] his roots to his surroundings, and when the roots have grown to a certain size, cannot be displaced without cutting at his life."

Another illuminating angle on adverse possession is provided by Joseph Singer, who argues that once "*both* parties have acted in ways inconsistent with the formal property rights," it is unfair to turn against the adverse possessor armed with the formalities of title.[73] Instead, we can understand the parties' acquiescence in their informal arrangements as effectively creating an "informal transfer" of entitlement.[74] The right of the entrant to acquire title through adverse possession is not automatic; it is treated as a remedy that becomes operable only after the statute of limitations for recovery has expired. This legal protection guards the interests of the true owner as against the uninvited occupant, manifesting the "right to exclude." This by itself is not unexpected. What is surprising, and radically so, is that once that period of time has passed (that is, once the statute of limitations for recovery has expired), the original owner is *barred* from removing the adverse possessor from the property, despite the fact that the owner never granted permission for such admission in the first place.

If this is true in the context of real property, where we are dealing with private owners who typically have a strong claim to their rights *in rem* (as against the world), then it must apply at least with equal force when dealing with an entitlement such as the property of citizenship. Recall that citizenship is distributed by an act of government, thus bearing more stringent requirements of public accountability and responsibility. If the authorities have chosen to turn a blind eye to the "adverse possession" by *millions* of unauthorized migrants who settled within their territory (after crossing the border without permission or overstaying their visas), then there must be a point in time when they are estopped by their own inaction; in other words, the unauthorized entrants ought to gain immunity from deportation and removal, in addition to being offered an eventual route for legalizing their status.

Part of the explanation for upholding this unusual method of acquiring property is, as we have already seen in Holmes's remarks, that legal formalities in defining title matter greatly, but so does the actual experience of connectedness to a place. This fits nicely with the *jus nexi* rationale, though I should emphasize that adverse possession takes matters a step farther, by providing a route for legalizing the status of those who have entered in breach of the admitting country's initial entry requirements.

Various other justifications have been offered for the doctrine of adverse possession, precisely because it disrupts the conception of absolute dominion of property (as understood by the narrow conception). What makes it particularly interesting for our discussion is the fact that adverse possession cannot be easily dismissed as an insignificant or implausible remedy: it has been part of property law and theory for centuries, dating back to the earliest days of the common law. Utilitarian arguments would be in favor of rewarding those who make productive use of the land at the expense of formal titleholders who sleep on their rights. Efficiency claims would encourage signaling ownership by public occupancy or use of the land, thus minimizing errors by eliminating old claims for ownership (for which evidence may have faded), as well as protecting the interests of *bona fide* third parties who may have relied on the public use of the land by the adverse possessor as evidence of good title. Other theories along the lines of Holmes' argument would emphasize what Margaret Radin calls "protected personhood" interests, arguing that a possessor's interests change over time. Although they were "initially fungible," the claims "become more and more personal;" that is, the longer the passage of time, the stronger the claim for recognition of the special ties that have been established in relation to a particular land/community.[75]

This focus on taking root echoes the emphasis on connectedness as the basis for membership title, as captured by the proposed *jus nexi* principle. If the "original sin" of unlawful admission can be forgiven in the context of property, where the titleholder is presumed to have "sole and despotic dominion . . . in total exclusion of the right of any other individual in the universe" (to evoke Blackstone's magisterial words) then surely a similar logic can apply with equal force to the relations between democratic governments and those entering their prosperous territories.

As with the argument for participation in democratic self-governance, what makes a difference is not the physical act of crossing the border into the territory of a given polity. What counts are "the ties that non-citizens develop over time."[76] This fits flawlessly with the logic of *jus nexi* and the doctrine of adverse possession, and in a similar fashion, provides a remedy only *after* expectations to stay have been established, a process that in most jurisdictions requires the passage of a significant amount of time. Under the immigration laws of most states, a minimum residence period is often required for a waiver to become a relevant option. The time period is typically referred to as no less than five years, though it may range from seven to ten years.[77] The entitlement to remain in a polity through the adverse possession doctrine, if adapted to the realm of political membership, will likely prove most useful for habitual residents who have, in effect, "taken root" in the community and whose presence in the country was, as the case law has it, "generally known and talked of by the public."[78]

The recent debate in the United States over the status of undocumented migrants has produced a number of approaches, including a route for legalization that emphasizes the linkage of the passage of time with the subsequent ties to the country that grow and deepen, much like the path of adverse possession. Under this model, unauthorized entrants who have been in the country for five years (or more) and can provide evidence of their actual membership and community ties would be allowed to remain and eventually acquire secure legal status in the polity that permits them to embark on the road to citizenship. On the other hand, those who have been in the country for shorter periods of time could be asked to leave, unless there are special circumstances (or "equities") that compel their stay.[79] While not fully satisfying the demands of proponents of open-admission borders, who hold that *any* entrant who wishes to remain should acquire a right to do so (irrespective of length of stay or the establishment of "real and effective links"), this legalization route recognizes that social and personal relations are built over time and in the context of certain places and experiences. It further provides a powerful answer to the formalistic argument that is so dear to the resurrect-the-border crowd, which repeatedly emphasizes that unauthorized migrants violated the law upon entry, as if similar breaches are never forgiven in other contexts, including the semisacred realm of private property.

In this chapter I have recommended the adoption of a *jus nexi,* or genuine-connection principle, as either a supplementary or full-fledged alternative to the existing reliance on *jus soli* and *jus sanguinis*. The proposed principle offers a more nuanced way in which to address the question of boundary making, based as it is on actual membership and social attachment rather than mere birthright entitlement. I have supported this proposal by looking to rationales previously used to limit the transmission of property through inheritance and by building on the Rignano principle of declining entitlement. I have also shown that the *jus nexi* criterion provides a path that may help to bypass various problems associated with over- or underinclusion. In developing these ascending and descending routes for inclusion, I have emphasized that, unlike the blind reliance on birthplace or bloodline, these responses recognize the web of relations and expectations informing the social fact of membership. This in turn permits greater democratic accountability, given that all those who reside in the jurisdiction and are regularly affected by the state's authority and coercive legal powers gain the right not to be excluded, and with it, gain a hand in shaping and deploying its self-governance.

In creating a closer tie between actual membership and access to citizenship, the rather rudimentary state of the debate over birthright citizenship is brought into full light: we have not yet developed even the basic vocabulary and analytical categories that would permit the deployment of contextual and fact-rich definitions of "status;" nor have we witnessed the introduction of certain restrictions and limitations on the holding of mere formal or entailed title, restrictions that are routinely employed in other fields of law. In stark contrast, the literature on property and inheritance abounds with such references, as we have seen over the course of this book. Where citizenship is concerned, what is rightly owed to future generations and what should legitimately be devoted to public uses? What portion of the collective inheritance bestowed upon children of well-off polities ought to be reserved to them by the enabling political community as a "social entitlement" in order to fulfill their legitimate expectations? What remainders of the "whole estate" (or part thereof) can justifiably be redirected so as to better the life prospects of those whom chance, not choice, placed outside the membership boundaries? Once we begin to ask these questions, the idea that birthright privilege might be taxed alongside intergenerational wealth and property presents itself as a very real possibility. In the same vein, the property/inheritance analogy permits us to draw upon concepts of declining and ascending scales of title acquisition; the analogy also sheds light upon the possibility of regularizing the status of unauthorized migrants based on an unexpected and surprising source such as the doctrine of adverse possession. These insights, along with changing definitions of membership at both the local and international levels, have informed my development of the *jus nexi* principle.

As I have shown throughout this book, treating birthright citizenship as a special kind of inherited property allows us to import core restrictions and qualifications from the realm of property into the arena of birthright membership. In addition, this provides a rich new resource for generating fresh answers to the old questions of how best to mediate the demands of security and mobility, justice and citizenship, and especially those dealing with ownership, selection, and allocation.

The proposed remedies of *jus nexi*—and the *birthright privilege levy* discussed in the book's first part—share an uncompromising emphasis on the political and social relations of membership and their far-reaching consequences, which may (and often do) bleed across existing legal, territorial, and conceptual borderlines. This book rejects the unwieldy vision of a "castle" of absolute dominion over territory and membership that is asserted (typically with great piety) by those upholding the narrow, and increasingly commodified, conception of property and citizenship. Instead, I have developed a broad, social-relations-centered, inclusive interpretation of what is owed to those locked outside the enclosed circle of members by those who enjoy access to the scarce property of citizenship in a stable and affluent community as a result of inherited entitlement. I have also considered the responsibilities that this endowment should entail, both in terms of enhancing citizenship's enabling dimension domestically and extending its redistributive obligations globally.

I BEGAN THIS JOURNEY as I was about to experience the unmatched miracle of bringing a new life to the world. I end it with a plea for creating a basic infrastructure of opportunity for every child everywhere on the face of the earth by overcoming our rigid structures of automatic transfer of citizenship via birthright; anything else would make a travesty of our membership obligations and the justifications we assert for upholding this invaluable public inheritance. Instead of merely appealing to abstract principles of justice and equality, I have argued here that we can find concrete and tangible bases for redistribution and redefinition of citizenship by drawing on already-tested and existing venues of legal practice in the related realms of property and inheritance. This counterintuitive appeal is a result of real-life experience, not just philosophical musing. I have shown that the existing system of membership allocation did not fall from the sky. It is the result of human agency. We can change it, just as we can preserve it. The latter route simply asks us to continue our complicity in preserving an unfair situation. The former clearly requires hard work: breaking old habits of thought and adopting creative reformulations instead. This is not an easy process. But the stakes are high. We now live in world torn between those who are doomed to an "endless night" and those promised a "sweet delight" due to arbitrary circumstances of station of birth. This is morally wrong, politically unstable, and institutionally unsound: the fossil of a bygone era. Ensuring greater opportunity globally, revamping the enabling dimension of citizenship locally, and matching membership with actual participation—these all offer a more promising path than the one we are on now. As Robert Frost reminds us, the road not taken can make all the difference. Today we stand a real chance of breaking the chain of perpetual entail of membership titles. The time to end the blind reliance on birthright citizenship has arrived.

Notes

References

Index

Notes

Introduction

1. These facts are recounted in *Olga de Leon* v. *Shih Wei Navigation* (2007).
2. *Olga de Leon* v. *Shih Wei Navigation* (2007), 23.
3. International Organization for Migration 2005.
4. See Cholewinski, Perruchoud, and MacDonald 2007; Dauvergne 2007, 489–507.
5. The list of works identifying these changes is too vast to cite. Among its major authors are Saskia Sassen, Yasemin Soysal, David Held, Rainer Bauböck, Linda Bosniak, Iris Young, Seyla Benhabib, Peter Spiro, and Will Kymlicka. I myself have contributed to these discussions about multilevel citizenship in the context of the relationships among the individual, the group, and the state (Shachar 2001).
6. Ford 2001, 210.
7. The analogy here is to property regimes that date back to medieval England; there, we find the (now discredited) institution of the *fee tail* or *entail*. In the language of the early common law, fee tail allowed a landed estate to automatically descend from person A to person B "and the heirs of his body" and to continue on, thus passing through the generational line. I discuss this property regime in detail in Chapter 1. On the origins and technicalities of fee tail, see Simpson 1986.
8. For a concise overview of the statistics concerning the global fragmentation of opportunity with reference to democracy and participation, economic justice, health and education, as well as peace and security, see e.g., UNDP, *Human Development Report 2002;* UNICEF, *The State of the World's Children* 2005.
9. UNDP, *Human Development Report 2005*, World Bank, *World Development Report 2006*.

10. This is the main argument advanced by Schuck and Smith (1985). On this basis, they develop a consent-based model that they view as more consistent with liberal theory. They then controversially apply this theoretical framework to recommend the domestic *restriction* of membership by birth to children of citizens and permanent residents. For a penetrating critique of this constitutional interpretation, see Neuman (1987). My critique of birthright, on the other hand, points instead to the global *expansion* of the distribution of the social benefits of citizenship. I promote a greater access to membership according to one's actual interdependence and genuine connection with the polity, rather than mere reliance on bloodline or territoriality.
11. These are the official international figures. See GCIM 2005, *Migration in an Interconnected World: New Directions for Action,* Annex II; United Nations 2004, *World Economic and Social Survey 2004: International Migration,* 25; UNPFA 2006, *State of World Population 2006,* 6.
12. An exception to this blindness is found in the formative writings of scholars such as Joseph Carens, and more recently, Peter Spiro. See e.g., Carens 1987a, 251–273. My analysis focuses on the value of citizenship but criticizes its *transmission* routes, whereas Carens is consumed by the question of immigration and the right of states to limit mobility across national borderlines. This also leads to different policy conclusions, as elaborated in detail in Chapters 3 and 6. See also Spiro 2008. Feminist and critical scholars have further attempted to demystify the presumed naturalness of various social institutions, such as contract, property, marriage, and sovereignty itself. My work here fits within this tradition. See, for example, Pateman 1988; McClintock 1995; Stevens 1999; Cott 2002.
13. I am here rephrasing the title of an influential book edited by Archibugi, Held, and Köhler in 1998.
14. Concerns about birthright access to membership become aggravated by the fact that international cross-border mobility is not equally open to all. As Paul Hirst and Grahame Thompson bluntly observe, "apart from a 'club class' of internationally mobile, highly skilled professionals . . . the bulk of the world's populations now cannot easily move." Increasingly, they suggest, those "the poor [from developing countries] are unwelcome in advanced countries." See Hirst and Thompson 1999, 267.

    In this respect, the hyperbolic rhetoric of globalization and demise of borders, according to which the allocated good of citizenship has become so "diluted" as to make a very limited difference in one's life, remains a world apart from the reality experienced by the bulk of the global population. I am here drawing on the terminology that appears in Peter J. Spiro's relentlessly upbeat book (Spiro 2008).
15. See, for example, Joppke 2007, 37–48; Bosniak 2000, 447–509.
16. Technically speaking, citizenship regimes preserve stricter and more rigid intergenerational transfer mechanisms than those permitted today in relation to inherited property. The latter have been relaxed to allow expression of individual will whereas the former operate as a nonrevocable and nonamendable set

of default rules, which are regulated and enforced by the state on behalf of the collective of members.

17. The major exceptions here are found in the formative writings of Peter Schuck and Rogers Smith (Schuck and Smith 1985) and Joseph Carens. See Carens 1987a. My analysis focuses on the value of citizenship but criticizes its *transmission* routes, whereas Carens is consumed by the question of immigration and the right of states to limit mobility across national borderlines. This also leads to different policy conclusions, as elaborated in detail in Chapters 3 and 6.
18. For excellent treatment of these questions in recent works, see e.g., Benhabib 2004b; Bosniak 2006; Motomura 2006a; Cole 2000; Gibney 2004.
19. See Shachar 2007.
20. Eisgruber 1997, 59.
21. For further elaboration on the distinction between the "demarcation" and "distributive" functions of membership rules, see Shachar 2001, 49–55.
22. Waldron 1985, 318.
23. Blackstone [1766] 1979, 2.
24. Blackstone [1766] 1979. For critical discussion, see Heller 1999.
25. For a concise overview, see Munzer 2001. This emphasis on "property as relations" is also consistent with various strands of feminist theory, which frequently foregrounds relationships and relatedness. For an illuminating discussion, see Dickenson 2007. For the development of the concept of stewardship in relation to indigenous cultural property, see Carpenter, Katyal, and Riley 2009.
26. For a detailed exploration of this theme, see Kingsbury 1998.
27. Benhabib 2004b, 141.
28. A vintage of recent books aim to break away from this single-country study framework, offering instead a comparative analysis. See, for example, Hansen and Weil 2001.
29. On the tremendous risk and vulnerability of the bare existence associated with statelessness, see Arendt 1968; Agamben 1998.
30. See Bauböck 1997, 1. As Bauböck points out, this Westphalian image of the world cannot account for the political significance of transnational connections and affiliations that many individuals now bear toward their (old and new) home countries, nor can it satisfactorily address the reality of dual nationality.
31. Brubaker 1992, 31.
32. It is well known that some have suggested we are currently in the midst of another transformation, whereby the concept of political membership may become attached to the international, supranational, transnational, postnational, denational, or subnational levels of affiliations—in addition to, or in lieu of, the state. Of this rich literature, see Sassen 2006; Bosniak 2000.
33. On the historical construction of the distinction between legal and illegal migrants, see Ngai 2004. See also Torpey 2000; Zolberg 2006.
34. In other words, birthright citizenship is neither a natural right nor a genetic attribute (like being born short or tall, beautiful or ugly, and so on), but rather a paradigmatic example of a government-created entitlement. This fits in line

with Blackstone's influential view of the right of inheritance not as a "*natural*, but merely a *civil* right." See Blackstone [1766] 1979, 11 [emphasis in original].

35. In the realm of property theory, this point is powerfully made by J. Singer 2000.
36. My analysis here proceeds from the contention that law not only reflects social realities and power relations but partakes in constituting them as well. For related explorations in the context of citizenship regimes, see Lopez 1996; Ngai 2004.
37. See GCIM 2005, Annex II.
38. Joshua Cohen's recent work on global justice inspired the reliance here on Blake (J. Cohen 2007).
39. See UNDP *Human Development Report 2004*, 129.
40. J. Cohen 2007, ix.
41. See World Bank, *Global Millennium Development Goals*, Goal 4, "More than 10 million children die each year in the developing world, the vast majority from causes preventable through a combination of good care, nutrition, and medical treatment. Mortality rates for children under five dropped by 15 percent since 1990, but the rates remain high in developing countries. In developing countries, one child in 10 dies before its fifth birthday, compared with 1 in 143 in high-income countries."
42. Otherwise, the stowaways would have never had to contemplate the possibility of boarding the ship in order to make their unlawful, and ultimately, fatal trip. They could have simply passed, like so many before them, under the deshackled feet of the Statute of Liberty on Ellis Island, the gateway to the golden door, where Emma Lazarus' legendary poem is inscribed in stone. On unauthorized transnational mobility, see Jordan and Düvell 2002.
43. See World Bank, 2006b, *World Development Indicators 2006*.
44. See Schuck and Smith 1985.
45. See Weis 1979, 30.
46. See Locke 1988; Maine [1861] 1986.
47. See Dobrowsky 2007, 630. See also Bosniak 2006.
48. The evidence is prevalent, ranging from tougher immigration laws to more restrictive naturalization procedures in regard to those who-do-not-yet (or may never) belong. See e.g., Shachar 2007; Andreas and Snyder 2000; Joppke 2005.
49. In *The Law of Peoples*, John Rawls expresses an objection to principles of global distributive justice, because, as he put it, they lack a "target and cut-off point," (Rawls 1999a, 115–119). This concern can be addressed here by distinguishing between a minimalist and expansive interpretation of the birthright levy obligation. The former may treat the levy as a transitional remedy that will expire if (and when) the draconian differential in life prospects according to national or regional distribution will flatten, whereas the latter is less consequentialist and emphasizes the moral basis for restricting entailed-like transfers as a way to curtail inherited entitlement. I return to these questions in Chapter 3.
50. Nagel 2005.

51. Here I am in agreement with authors such as Martha Nussbaum, Amartya Sen, Brian Barry, Bhikhu Parekh, Kok-Chor Tan, Andrea Sangiovanni, and others who have affirmed "modest" cosmopolitan principles of distributive justice, while at the same time accepting that special duties, or heightened obligations, apply to co-citizens and co-residents in a shared political unit. For a lucid exposition of this position, which I accept rather than defend in this project, see Caney 2005, 102–147.
52. The standard account suggests that globalization stimulates growth and development worldwide, but the links between economic globalization, economic growth, inequality and poverty are disputed, even among experts in the field. Some suggest that economic globalization itself exacerbates (rather than mitigates) inequality, by making the poor worse off in many parts of the world. For a concise overview, see Held and Koenig-Archibugi 2003. There are also vibrant debates on whether institutional or cultural factors matter most in explaining economic growth. On these competing explanations, see Rodrick 2003; Landes 1999.

1. Reconceptualizing Membership

1. Global Commission on International Migration 2005.
2. The complete list is too long to cite. Some of the most influential contributors to this body of literature include: Alexander Aleinikoff, Brian Barry, Rainer Bauböck, Seyla Benhabib, Rogers Brubaker, Allen Buchanan, Joseph Carens, David Held, Will Kymlicka, David Miller, Margaret Moore, Bhikhu Parekh, Peter Schuck and Rogers Smith, among others.
3. On the idea of democratic reiterations, see Benhabib 2004b.
4. The minimal threshold is just that; it might well be supplemented by more expansive global redistributive efforts. This construction relies on a nonideal anticipatory theory, which, as Gopal Sreenivasan eloquently explains, "makes assumptions about the minimum requirements that any plausible and complete ideal theory of [global] justice will include." See Sreenivasan 2007, 221.
5. See Hacker-Cordon regarding the term "malfare" (Hacker-Cordon 2002).
6. This "ecumenical" strategy (as Debra Satz nicely puts it) can also assist in establishing a broader base of support for the proposed remedy. See Satz 2005, 53; See Pogge 2002. See also B. Barry 1989.
7. The data in this section is compiled from the *World Development Report 2006* (World Bank 2005) and *Human Development Report 2005* (UNDP 2005).
8. For a detailed analysis, see Pogge 2002.
9. Sachs 2005, 20–31.
10. World Bank, *World Development Report 2000/2001*, 2001.
11. This argument is powerfully advanced by Haslett in his classic essay (Haslett 1986). See also Beckert 2008, 13–14.
12. See Dwyer and Menell 1998, 1.
13. For a classic exposition of this legal-realist insight, see Hohfeld 1913. A detailed analysis of the legal-realist account of property is offered by Joseph W. Singer (2000).

14. See e.g., Macpherson 1978.
15. In theory, other levels of governance (those "above" or "below" the state level) can fulfill this enforcement function. In addition, property scholars have traced how people concoct various common property regimes, even without a formal regulatory system. See, for example, Ellickson 1993; However, in a world where states still enjoy a "monopoly of the legitimate use of physical force within a given territory" to use Max Weber's famous words, they offer a reliable system of law and governance for enforcing property rights. See Weber 1964, 48. See also North 1990.
16. Gray 1980, 79.
17. See Hohfeld 1917. For a more elaborate exploration of what's included in the "bundle," see Honoré 1961.
18. For concise discussion on the form and substance of property, see Dagan 2003. For a comprehensive analysis, see Waldron 1988.
19. Calabresi and Melamed distinguish between property, liability, and inalienability rules as offering different degrees of alienability and transfer of such entitlements. See Calabresi and Melamed 1972.
20. For instance, scientific research on the use of stem cells has precipitated a new debate about what constitutes property. See Dickenson 2007.
21. On property's connection to freedom and autonomy, see the classic elaborations by Kant [1797] 1996 and Hegel [1821] 1996; for contemporary accounts, see Reich 1964; Radin 1982; Baker 1986; Waldron 1993; Domenech and Raventos 2007; E. Weinrib 2003.
22. See Waldron 1996, 5.
23. Waldron 1985, 318.
24. See Brubaker 1992, 21.
25. Orlenticher 1998.
26. For an optimistic vision of this transformation of citizenship, see Benhabib 2004b, Mostov 2008.
27. See Falk 2002, 21.
28. Falk 2002, 21.
29. On the scholarly debate over whether the state has lost or retained control over its borders in the age of globalization, see, for example, David Held; Yasemin Soysal; Randall Hansen; Virginie Guiraudon and Galia Lahav; Christian Joppke; Seyla Benhabib.
30. The citizenship clause reads as follows: "Every national of a Member State shall be a citizen of the Union. Citizenship of the Union shall be additional to national citizenship; it shall not replace it."
31. See Reich 1964. Reich referred to governmental largesse, such as welfare entitlements, jobs, and subsidies. He also used the example of occupational licenses as a form of new property, which creates enhanced earning potential for its holder.
32. Membership in a state persists as a meaningful entitlement only so long as the political community to which the individual belongs retains its identity and "incorporation" as a recognized sovereign entity. If the political community ceases to exist, there is little value—other, perhaps, than that of memory—to be attached to holding its citizenship.

33. I thank Barbara Fried for this formulation.
34. See *Schneiderman* v. *United States* (1943).
35. On the distinction between "private" and "common" property regimes (the latter is often referred to by different names, with somewhat different interpretations, such as "group," "collective," "communal," "mixed property," or "limited-access"), see, for example, Bromley 1991; Ciriacy-Wantrup and Bishop 1975; Harris 1995; Heller 1999.
36. See Harris 1995.
37. The distinction between the narrow and broad conceptions draws upon C. B. Macpherson's extensive writings on property, in particular, his essay on "Human Rights as Property Rights" (Macpherson 1977). The analysis is also influenced by the magisterial works of authors such as Gregory Alexander (1997) and Joseph Singer (2000).
38. For a familiar exposition of the narrow view, see Posner 2007. For a sharp critique of this "commodified" understanding of property, see Radin 1996.
39. See Blackstone [1766] 1979.
40. For a critical assessment of this vision of social life, see Radin 1987; Michelman 1981.
41. The term *possessive individualism* was coined by Macpherson (Macpherson 1962). The same behavior is often described by modern neoclassic economists (as well as law-and-economics scholars) as a vehicle for preference satisfaction, based on the assumption that there exists a "human propensity to be a self-interested, rational utility maximizer." See Rose 1990, 41–42.
42. A detailed discussion of this last point is offered by Merrill and Smith (Merrill and Smith 2000). The rights of property owners here can also be limited by the lawful entitlements held by other title holders.
43. See Alexander 1997, 2.
44. Whereas the narrow conception emphasizes individual preferences and market relations, the broad conception reflects an ideal of a society where "property as propriety" is intended to benefit not only the owner, but also the public good. See Rose 1994b. This tradition can also be interpreted as creating an obligation (familiar under the common law) not to do harm to the corpus, and if possible improve the public inheritance that we are bestowed. This is often referred to as the duty to prevent waste; for an illuminating discussion, see McCaffery 2001.
45. This conception is famously traced back to Blackstone's *Commentaries*. See Blackstone [1766] 1979, 2.
46. Dagan and Heller 2005, 38.
47. A classic articulation of this view is offered by Friedman 1962, 7–21.
48. Nedelsky 1990, 207.
49. For a comprehensive discussion of these themes, see Rose 1994a.
50. See Dagan and Heller 2001. There is a rich literature on the commons, and the relationship between property and governance in these communities. For a now-classic discussion, see Ostrom 1990.
51. See Dwyer and Menell 1998, 807–809.
52. See Macpherson 1977, 73.
53. The use of "property" until roughly the seventeenth century correlated with the broad conception, as explained by Macpherson.

54. See *Klapprott* v. *United States* (1949), 616–617.
55. *Schneiderman* v. *United States* (1943).
56. See Alexander 1997; Pocock 1995; Biener 2003.
57. See Macpherson 1977, 73.
58. Hirschman 1970.
59. For an illuminating discussion, see Avi-Yonah 2006. See also Murphy and Nagel 2002.
60. This conception of property as trusteeship or stewardship is expressed, for example, in the civic-republican tradition and has recently been revived by the environmentalist movement. See Sunstein 1988. See also Karp 1993.
61. Interestingly, treating citizenship as a "precious good" is central to Michael Walzer's analysis of membership (Walzer 1983).
62. I make this statement as a descriptive observation of the reality found in practice, not as a normative judgment about whether or not it represents a desirable state of affairs.
63. Brubaker 1992.
64. Interestingly, we find that in medieval England, hereditaments and uses of landed property were firmly protected with one dramatic exception: that of forfeiture for treason. It is hard not to notice that in today's citizenship laws, too, political membership is firmly protected against any form of alienation by fellow members or the government itself, with one dramatic exception: that of treason.
65. These differentiated levels of restriction imposed by immigrant-receiving states are described in Neumayer 2006. Certain barriers to international mobility are also imposed by emigrant-sending states themselves. See McKenzie 2005. In North America, we have seen a similar refortification of the border between the United States and Mexico, as well as the adoption of interdiction policies by Canada to prevent the unwanted or undocumented from even reaching its jurisdictional boundaries. This result is achieved by sending immigration officers abroad in order to regulate access even before a person actually sets foot at the geographical border of the state.
66. See, for example, Volpp 2007 for a fascinating exploration of this point.
67. For further discussion, see Shachar 2007. In the European context, see Vachudova 2000.
68. Held 1991.
69. The security that attaches to full membership is thought to nourish our sense of identity and belonging, with important returns in terms of our ability to fully exercise our autonomy and freedom. Each birthright titleholder is free to enjoy the protections of an inherited membership as a life-estate. Upon the expiration of that life, the membership title reverts back to the state as a trustee.
70. The analogy to property is once again glaring: save for imminent domain, property owners are immune from involuntary deprivation or modification of their ownership rights. See Michelman 1982, 5.
71. Clearly, acquisition of citizenship status per se is no guarantee against the persistence of inequalities between members of the same polity. But it does anchor certain basic interests as nonrevocable once a person is counted in the innermost circle of members.

72. Rose 1994b, "Property as Propriety," 63.
73. A related argument is developed by Christopher L. Eisgruber (Eisgruber 1997).
74. Harris 1995.
75. The idea of fair value of equal liberties is drawn from John Rawls (1999b, 227).
76. The latter interpretation draws on Sen's capabilities approach, see, for example, Sen 1992; Roemer 1998; Nussbaum 2000. Nussbaum makes explicit the claim that these capabilities ought to be fulfilled by governments.
77. For further discussion, see Alstott 2007.
78. Zucker 2001, chaps. 9–11.
79. Murphey and Nagel 2002, 40–75.
80. The right-not-to-be-excluded can therefore serve as a powerful critique of, and grounds for, political action against a state's failure to ensure an adequate level of support and participation for its members. Think of the unacceptable situation of leaving almost 45 million people without medical insurance in a wealthy country like the United States, for example.
81. Importantly, I am not relying here on the historical precedent of treating ownership of property as a precondition for full membership in the polity. As is well recorded, such reliance has worked to drastically restrict access to citizenship, excluding the vast majority of the population from full inclusion as equals. The focus here is different: the aim is to explore the conceptual and functional analogies between the regimes of protected property and bounded citizenship. On the troubling historical record of exclusion, see, for example, R. Smith 1997; Heather 2004; Cott 1998.
82. The foundational historical work here remains Simpson 1986.
83. See Hart 2001, 171–172.
84. See Orth 1992.
85. See Alexander 1997, 38. For further discussion, see Orth 1992.
86. See Orth 1992, 38. The entail was commonly limited to male descendants alone (in the form of primogeniture), as part of the gendered social hierarchy that excluded married women from the possibility of autonomous property ownership. Of the vast body of feminist critique of this hierarchical social order, see Spring 1993; Murray 2004.
87. Y.B. 12, Edw. 4, Mich 25 (1472).
88. For detailed discussion, see Morris 1927.
89. I draw this argument from the elegant analysis offered by Orth 1992.
90. Orth 1992, 40.
91. Hart 2001, 168, citing Jefferson's autobiography.
92. The vast majority of American states quickly followed suit in the post-Revolution era, emulating the example of Virginia in adopting legislation that officially abolished the transfer of entailed estates. See Morris 1927.
93. For an illuminating and meticulous study of Madison's position on entail in the context of a broader historical argument about the inaccuracy of portraying Madison's position on property-rights protection as libertarian rather than republican, see Hart 2001.
94. Alexander 1997, 39.
95. Hart 2001, 168, citing Thomas Jefferson (1892).

96. Hart 2001, 189, citing James Madison (1865, 30).
97. Blackstone [1776] 1979, 116, cited by Orth 1992, 37.
98. On the contrast between virtue and corruption in civic republicanism, see Alexander 1997, 26–88.
99. Preamble, Virginia statute.
100. Act of October 1776, chap. XXVI, reprinted in 9 *Laws of Virginia* 226, ed. William Waller Hening (Richmond: J & G Cochran, 1823).
101. Orth 1992, 42–43.
102. Kettner 1978.
103. The 1790 Naturalization Act prescribed that a free white alien who had resided in the United States for two years might be naturalized, provided the person was of good moral character and took an oath to support the constitution.
104. For a marvelously rich analysis of the history of racial and gendered restrictions that limited access to citizenship, see R. Smith 1997; Lopez 1996, 42–46; Sapiro 1984; Bredbenner 1998.
105. Locke [1689] 1988, 347, §118.
106. Jefferson [1774] 1984, 4.
107. This perpetual structure of hereditary transfer also appears to violate the common-law rule against perpetuities, which has been in effect for centuries, dating back to at least the 1682 decision in the *Duke of Norfolk's Case*.
108. This notion is perhaps best captured in Henry Maine's "from status to contract" typology. See Maine [1861] 1986.

2. Abolishing versus Resurrecting Borders

1. I am borrowing this term from the title of an influential volume on this topic, *Re-imagining Political Community: Studies in Cosmopolitan Democracy* (Archibugi, Held, and Köhler 1998).
2. Claims in favor of cosmopolitan or global citizenship have received much attention in recent years. Among the leading contributions, see Archibugi, Held, and Köhler 1998; Dower and Williams 2002; Vertovec and Cohen 2002; Hutchins and Dannreuther 1999; Gosepath 2001, 145, 162. For an eloquent and comprehensive defense of the idea of denationalizing citizenship, see Bosniak 2000.
3. See Pogge 1992, 49.
4. Bosniak 2006, 24.
5. Held 1995.
6. A strong vision of world citizenship does not stand as a complement to domestic affiliations (or their federated, multilevel interpretations) but rather displaces bounded political membership. Thomas Pogge, for example, "does not presuppose the existence of a community of persons committed first of all to share with one another." (Pogge 1992, 56).
7. Here I combine the core elements of citizenship that can be traced back to the Roman legalistic conception and the Aristotelian tradition of collective self-governance. See Pockock 1995.

8. This view resolves the moral concerns of inequality attaching to bounded membership by diluting (if not altogether erasing) the distinction between the citizen and the noncitizen, highlighting instead the premise of free movement across borders and the universalism of our moral status as people in general rather than as people belonging to some particular political community. See, for example, Goodin 1992, 7. See also Carens 1987a; Nett 1971.
9. My criticism of the world citizenship position is not based on a rejection of the idea that it is possible and indeed desirable to cultivate multilevel governance regimes, networks, and institutions, particularly if they establish cooperative and competitive jurisdictional relations along the lines of joint governance. In *Multicultural Jurisdictions,* I focus on envisioning multilevel governance regimes within the state in order to resolve, or at least ameliorate, the tension between respecting cultural differences and protecting women's rights in the event of a clash. In principle, nothing prohibits the application of joint governance (or what others described as "compounded federalism") at the supra- or subnational level, though attention must be paid to defining which challenges are to be met by such joint governance regimes, who will be involved in their establishment and enforcement, which voices and interests will be represented and protected through joint governance, and how well such a proposal fares in comparison to other alternative remedies. See Shachar 2001.
10. The correlation between a country's wealth and its citizens' well-being can be translated into a host of concrete indicators, among them, the polity's ability to provide conditions that support higher life expectancies. A recent study by the OECD provides comprehensive statistical evidence showing that among its member countries, "higher national income is generally associated with higher life expectancy." See OECD 2005b, Executive Summary, 11.
11. Carens 1992, 27.
12. Van den Anker 2002, 158–168.
13. Weinstock 1999; D. Miller 1995a.
14. I thank Veit Bader for highlighting this point in a private conversation; a similar view is shared by Seyla Benhabib (Benhabib 2004b).
15. Ultimately, these are empirical claims that must be substantiated. I am here referring to the theoretical concerns regarding the democratic and welfare-state arguments, as raised by authors such as Kymlicka 1999; D. Miller 2000; Tamir 1995; and Moore 2001.
16. These political economy arguments, however, do not preclude a move toward greater sharing of responsibility among overlapping membership communities (as is the case, in effect, in existing federal systems). Nor do they suggest that *jus soli* and *jus sanguinis* currently establish the optimal composition for existing polities in terms of size or population. Rather, they serve as a critique of the simplistic assumption that the solution to birthright citizenship lies in abolishing membership boundaries altogether.
17. For a similar theme, see Walzer 2002, which provides a pointed critique of Nussbaum's essay in the same collection.
18. Although we do not yet have any global governance structure, the UN system is the nearest structure in operation; it has witnessed the vagaries and difficulties

of "hearing" the voices of smaller nations. I thank Kate Brookson-Morris for drawing this parallel. An opposite set of concerns, which is familiar from the federal realm, refers to veto power holding by strategic or balance-of-power minorities, which might be replicated at worldwide level, depending on the specific majority rules adopted.

19. The analogue to property is in various semicommons regimes that are relatively egalitarian among members, but rely on a notion of boundary (or other mechanisms of social control) to define access in the first place. See the now-classic work of Olstrom 1990. From a different perspective, see Henry E. Smith on the interchangeability of border and regulation (Smith 2000; Smith 2002).

20. For an influential collection of essays that seeks to identify whether such a loss of control claim is supported by evidence drawn from a comparative study of the efficacy of immigration control measures in leading industrialized countries, see Cornelius, Martin, and Hollifield 1994.

21. J. Singer 2000; Satz 1999; Abizadeh 2008.

22. This places the latter in a position of being owed justification by the former. The demand for justification need not translate into the conclusion that membership boundaries can never be defended as having some legitimate purpose (for many of the reasons I already elaborated in Chapter 1 and those discussed in Chapter 5), but it does place those who seek membership at an equal moral footing, recognizing their capacity to accept (or reject) the justice of the social institutions that restrict their international mobility. This line of argument leads different authors to reach different conclusions about the legitimacy of borders. Of this fast-emerging body of scholarship, see Van Parijs 2007, Benhabib 2004b; Ackerman 1980.

23. Signatories to the Geneva Convention of 1951 on the Status of Refugees (in force since 1954) are bound to provide temporary relief to certain asylum seekers (those that fit the definition of "refugee" as codified in that convention). This obligation is borne by the "first-safe country" entered by the asylum seeker.

24. Although a citizen holds a right to exit her own home country, she holds no corresponding right to enter and remain in another country (with the caveat of seeking asylum). To date, there is no governing international principle that can force a country to adopt one or another method of immigration admission or citizenship transmission. Each political community or country is free to choose its own method of assigning citizenship, manifesting its autonomy and sovereignty. In practice, new democracies face increasing pressures to ensure inclusion in the body politick of long-term permanent residents (even if they do not belong to the ethnocultural nation that that state is said to represent), especially in cases of secession or new state creation; see Orlenticher 1998.

25. See United Nations 2000. This Declaration has been endorsed by 189 countries. For detailed information on the progress made toward achieving the Millennium Development Goals (MDGs), see www.un.org/millenniumgoals and www.mdgmonitor.org.

26. This recognition leads advocates of cosmopolitan citizenship to the opposite conclusion—namely, that we should seek new bonds of transnational solidarity.

27. See UN, *International Migration Report 2002* on the adoption of new measures to restrict immigration by receiving states. The 1996 immigration reform

in the United States represents a specific example of this broader trend. It is also widely recognized that the opening of internal borders in Europe has been consistent with the closing of external borders to non-EU or third-country nationals. The legal changes that followed the events of September 11 in the United States and July 7 in the United Kingdom have only fortified this restrictive trend. For detailed analysis, see Shachar 2007.

28. Ghosh 2000, 10.
29. Koser 2007, 75. Empirical data on current or even past trends is unlikely to lessen the fear of drowning in unwanted migration in the future.
30. Hassner 1998, 278.
31. Shachar 1999.
32. This full list is far too long to cite; among the leading lights are T. H. Marshall; Rogers Smith; Iris Marion Young; Judith Shklar; Kenneth Karst; Linda Bosniak; Leti Volpp; Gershon Shafir; Yoav Peled; Anthony Marx; Ian Haney Lopez; Margaret Somers; and Will Kymlicka.
33. Shafir 2004, 12.
34. Volpp 2007.
35. Roman 2006; Muneer 2007.
36. Flynn 2003, 117.
37. We will encounter similar arguments in Chapter 5 (Respect for Distinct Cultural and National Identities). For further elaboration of the distinction between special and general duties in this context, see Parekh 2003; R. Miller 1998. Others have emphasized that the only reason that justifies restrictions upon free movement is to guard the potential fragility of liberal-democratic institutions, which may be overwhelmed by large numbers of foreigners previously accustomed to authoritarian governance. See, for example, Ackerman 1980, 93–95.
38. For detailed discussion, see Shachar 2006.
39. For a concise human development balance sheet, see UNDP, *Human Development Report 2002,* 10–11. A self-interest rationale also informs Peter Shuck's proposal in favor of proportional burden-sharing. See Shuck 1997.
40. Simon 1986.
41. Radin 1996, 3.
42. Borna and Stearns 2002.
43. Chiswick 1982; Becker 1992.
44. Simon 1986.
45. Trebilcock 2003.
46. Becker 1992.
47. Borna and Stearns 2002, 197.
48. Walzer 1983.
49. See Downes and Janda 1998.
50. This notion is shared by both the common and civil law systems.
51. Radin and Sunder 2005, 10.
52. Weiner 1992.
53. This is a view that is shared by some law-and-economics scholars. See the influential contribution by Calabresi and Melamed (Calabresi and Melamed 1972).
54. Rose-Ackerman 1985. On the inalienability of heritage, see Pretto-Sakmann 2005, 64–165. We can think of the inalienability classification here as removing

the *jus disponendi* (right to dispose or alienate) from the life estate holder, effectively meaning that each member is barred from selling or alienating his or her present and future-oriented stake in the bodypolitick. See McCaffery 2001; Pound 1939. Although each remains free to severe his or her relationship to the political community through formal, public procedure (for instance, by surrendering title to membership through expatriation), he or she is individually and collectively barred from doing so for private material gain. This complex structure, which combines features of individual and shared holdings can be interpreted as averting collective action problems by placing absolutist inalienability restrictions so that they do not encroach on all present and future titleholders. It can also be seen as a by-product of the co-authorship and fiduciary-like relationship to which each is obliged so long as he or she clings to the membership entitlement.

55. Weiner 1992, 6.
56. Radin defines these entitlements as falling into the categories of "status" or "community" inalienability. See Radin 1996, 19. See also Harrison 1999. There is another line of defense for legal rules of inalienability that focuses on efficiency grounds. See Epstein 1985, 972; Rose-Ackerman 1985. Others justify inalienability in cases where permitting trade or transfer would cause subjective harm that is nonquantifiable. See Calabresi and Melamed 1972. For a civil law perspective, see Pretto-Sakmann 2005.
57. Sandel 2005, 122.
58. This is analogous to other common-property regimes that limit the freedom of each individual for the good of the collective. In such collective ownership situations, owners cannot exclude one another but can exclude outsiders from use and decision making. See Bromley 1991, 25–26.
59. See Radin on the distinction between personal and fungible property (Radin 1996, 34–40). Radin here builds on the tradition of Kant and Hegel, both of whom opposed the alienablity of substantive characteristics of personality.
60. See sec. 121(a) of the Immigration Act of 1990, which amended Sec. 203 of INA and provided one million as the minimum investment amount for employment-based immigrants (i.e., EB-5 preference category). In Canada, see sec. 88(1) of the Immigration and Refugee Protection Regulations (IRPR) under Immigration and Refugee Protection Act (IRPA) for the requirement of minimum investment. The U.K. government also issued new guidelines on immigration. See U.K. Border Agency, *Immigration Directorate Instructions,* Chapter 6. For the change in Germany, see sec. 21 of Residence Act of 30 July 2004. It grants a residence permit to a foreigner whose activity brings "positive effects on the economy," meaning at least 500,000 euros invested and 5 jobs created. After three years, the investor and immediate family will receive an unlimited residence permit.
61. Downes and Janda 1998, 55.
62. The notion of treating citizenship as embedded in the language of fiscal federalism and the economic theory of clubs is discussed by Bill Jordan and Frank Düvell (Jordan and Düvell 2003).
63. Spiro 2008, 134. Spiro believes that civil society can step in to remedy these relations, along with other nonterritorial forms of affiliation that operate alongside that of national membership. Spiro 2008, 137–163.

64. In political philosophy, Arendt's writing remains among the most powerful set of reflections of the perils of statelessness. See Arendt 1968. On the bare life of the "homo sacer," see Agamben 1998. In International law, the classic text remains Weis 1979.
65. This is the familiar theme of the Marshalian concept of membership, spanning citizenship rights from civil to political to social, and more recently, cultural rights as well. But this emphasis on citizenship's expansion (both in terms of who is included and what rights are granted to them as members) is a familiar theme raised by many contemporary authors on citizenship (feminists, multiculturalists, even globalists). See, for example, Marshall 1950; Shklar 1991; Kymlicka 1995; Brysk and Shafir 2004.
66. For example, imagine a national heritage treasure displayed at an art museum in Italy; this "property" is legally inalienable; it is banned from market exchange (because of its nonpecuniary value). See Pretto-Sakmann 2005, 164. It may nevertheless have an estimated marketplace dollar value placed on it for insurance purposes.
67. Bauböck 2003b, 701; Mostov 2008.
68. Ruggie 1993; Sassen 2006. See also Held et al. 1999.
69. The full list is too long to cite. Among the most influential interventions in these debates, see Sosyal 1994; Sassen 1996; Bosniak 2000; Jacobson 1996; Spiro 2008.
70. Jacobson 1996, 9.
71. Sassen 2006. See also Held, McGrew, Goldblatt and Perraton 1999; Bosniak 2006, 23–33.
72. Soysal 1994, 3.
73. Soysal 1994, 3.
74. Sassen 2006; Bauböck 2003b; Faist 2000.
75. Ong 1999. See also Mostov 2008.
76. Soysal 1994, 142.
77. Bosniak 2006.
78. Andreas and Snyder 2000.
79. I discuss these recent developments in Shachar 2007.
80. Brouwer and Kumin 2003.
81. Jacobson 1996, 9.
82. For further discussion of these developments, see Shachar 2007.
83. Guiraudon and Lahav 2000.
84. See, for example, Aleinikoff 1994; Chuang 1998; Shachar 2007; Redpath 2007; these examples demonstrate that border controls and membership boundaries continue to play a significant role in an increasingly globalizing world. For a revealing account of the relationship between globalization and the "crackdown" or extralegal migration; see Dauvergne 2008.
85. Another concern here has been the inability of the detainees' countries of citizenship to adequately protect their nationals' rights or secure their return from Guantanamo; even here, the "heft of citizenship" is not equal among different countries. See Macklin 2007.
86. Of course, there are many other dimensions to explore, such as the rise of transnational civil society organizations; the activities of international institu-

tions with a issue-specific mandate (think of the WHO, UNESCO, or the ILO); the grass-roots mobilization as well as mass-media campaigns to end poverty, and so on. All of these tell a far more complex story about the unbundling or perhaps rebundling of different components of voice, agency, and political mobility. This broader canvass permits us to find some important bright lights in the new world order.

87. Peter Spiro's work offers an excellent example of the "one among many" theme. See Spiro 2007. On the local level, see New Havens' identity card for the undocumented (Holtz 2007). For a theoretical defense, see Hefler 1999.
88. Of the growing body of literature on transnational participation and global civil society, see, for example, Archibugi, Held, and Köhler 1998; Connolly 1991; Held 1995; Dryzek 1999; Fraser 2005; Benhabib 2004a; Blank 2007. This vision differs from the world citizenship image, that may require the creation of a superstate or alter demos.
89. This point is elegantly made by Linda Bosniak (Bosniak 2006).
90. A familiar example of this pattern at work is the Bhopal gas disaster victims' transnational litigation.
91. The North American Agreement on Environmental Cooperation (NAAEC), which is supplemental to NAFTA, provides that "any non-governmental organization or person" can submit a complaint directly to the Commission for Environmental Cooperation (CEC) asserting that a party state fails to effectively enforce its environmental laws. The CEC established under NAAEC imposes duties on each party to "address regional environmental concerns, help prevent potential trade and environmental conflicts, and promote the effective enforcement of environmental laws." See CEC website, Part Three, Section B, Article 14 (Submissions of Enforcement Matters). For a comprehensive discussion of NAAEC, see Markell and Knox 2003. Other less formalized methods of participatory opposition in a global civil society include campus students' protests against producing university memorabilia in sweathouses around the world or civil society protests in different cities around the world against poverty, violations of women's human rights, unsustainable development, and so on. For further discussion, see Dower 2000.
92. This transition would imply the internal "commodification" of citizenship; see, for example, Somers 2006.
93. Related concerns about the erosion of citizenship's collective aspects are raised by Fudge 2005; D. Abraham 2007.
94. This conclusion shares much with Saskia Sasssen's observation regarding the interactive processes between the national and global, or what she labels as "de-nationalizing" and "re-nationalizing" dynamics in a global era. See Sassen 2006.

3. A New Basis for Global Redistribution

1. For a comprehensive argument that suggests that the assumed tension between our local (here understood as defined by bounded membership) and global commitments is superficial, see Tan 2004; see also Parekh 2003; Sangiovanni 2007.

2. Note that I distinguish here between the wealth-preserving (or quantifiable) aspects that a legal regime of birthright citizenship preserves, and its non-material aspects, relating, for example, to its identity-bonding function. The strategy of taxation obviously refers to the former and not the latter.
3. In Chapter 5, I discuss in detail the various values (such as democratic self-governance, concern for distinct cultural identities, and constitutive relations, among other justifications) that make bounded membership worth preserving as a provisional matter—at least until we can envisage new transnational or international equivalents.
4. GCIM 2005.
5. The main exception here is that refugee and asylum seekers, as well as those eligible to legalization or amnesty provisions, are exempted from the first "gate" of lawful admission—they must still comply, however, with the second and third gates of permanent residence and naturalization. Hammar 1990, 20–25.
6. Global migration flows are typically defined as falling into three main categories: family reunification (allowing family members of citizens and permanent residents privileged access to the destination country); labor migration (providing admission to the receiving economy according to the immigrant's human capital accretion or specialized labor skills); and humanitarian admission (guaranteeing a safe haven to refugee and asylum seekers who have fled their home country due to well-founded fears of persecution or related infringements of their basic human rights). The only unrestricted migration stream that few countries uphold is reserved for their returning sons and daughters, and even that has been restricted in some cases. See, for example, Germany's change of its citizenship law. Joppke 2005, 204–218.
7. In the United States, for example, a complex preference system is in place for categorizing admissions in the family category. There is also an intricate "ceilings" scheme, defined annually per category and per country. These ceilings have a particularly harsh effect on high-admission countries, such as Mexico or the Phillippines, where those falling into the "close relative" category may wait for more than ten years until a visa becomes available to them. For an overview of the U.S. family-preference categories, see Aleinikoff, Martin, and Motomura 2003, 274–287.
8. Martin 2004, 443.
9. Kymlicka 2001, 250.
10. See, for example, Trebilcock 2003.
11. Martin 2004, 443. The WTO's General Agreement on Trade and Services (GATS) "Mode 4" applies to labor as an internationally tradable service. See Mattoo and Carzaniga 2003.
12. This is evident, for example, in European Union law, where the "four freedoms" refer to the mobility of goods, services, persons, and capital. The free movement of knowledge has recently been added as the "fifth freedom" in the EU context.
13. There is a rich literature here. See, for example, Krugman and Obstfield 1991; Trebilcock and Howse 2005; Chang 1997.
14. For a comprehensive exploration of the arguments for and against open-admission policies, see, for example, Carens 1987a; Nett 1971; Goodin 1992; Moellendorf 2002; Caney 2005; Bader 2005.

15. This distinction is drawn from Veit Bader's insightful analysis (Bader 2000). The freedom and equality arguments are based on a notion of volitional mobility, which tend to underemphasize the growing concern about *forced* migration across borders.
16. Bader 2005, 337–340.
17. Carens 1992, 25.
18. Goodin 1992, 8.
19. Bader 2000, 42.
20. Kymlicka 2001, 250.
21. Moral intuitions may well change with new background conditions or transformed social expectations. A similar point is made by Michael Blake (Blake 2005).
22. I thank Jennie Rubio for *The Canterbury Tales* reference.
23. Joppke 2005.
24. This is an aspirational view, not a representation of the legal reality of international migration. Although people are, at least in principle, free to leave their countries of origin (although they often face too many restrictions in practice), emigrants have *no* guaranteed right of entry into a new political community. In other words, there is little symmetry between the right to exit and the right to enter. The latter is strictly reserved only to citizens. See Zilbershats 2002.
25. In cases of forced migration and human trafficking, the assumption of choice and agency obviously becomes contested. See Chuang 1998.
26. For empirical research on the impact of international migration on poverty reduction in emigration countries, see Adams and Page 2003.
27. See United Nations 2006, 5–6.
28. Martin 2004, 444; United Nations 2006, 4; UNPFA 2006, 7.
29. See World Bank 2006a.
30. Ratha 2007, 2. See also International Organization for Migration 2005.
31. Economists have been critical of the fact that recipients of remittances are using them for consumption rather than investment, but this is a quibble that must be read in the broader context of general appreciation of the significant role of remittances in supporting the economy of certain emigrant-sending countries. Critics of global inequality patterns raise another concern: these transnational income transfers are hardly changing the basic structure of the global accumulation of wealth, which remains drastically stratified and concentrated mostly outside the developing regions of the world.
32. Martin 2004, 442.
33. Hamilton and Whalley 1984, 70. A more conservative (but still substantial) estimate is offered by Winters 2003. See also Chang 1998.
34. Martin 2004, 445–446.
35. In studying these problems, scholars associated with the new economics of labor migration theory emphasize that migration decisions are not made by isolated individuals, but often within larger units of interrelated persons—typically families or households. See, for example, Stark 1991. Others have stressed the importance of migration networks that often provide the necessary links between specific emigration and immigration countries. This leads

to a concentration of migrants in certain destination areas, who, in turn, channel the later cohorts of migrants to take the same cross-border path. See, for example, Massey et al. 1998.

36. The literature on international migration aims to strictly distinguish between voluntary and forced migrants, although in practice the two often bleed into each other's domain. The forced category refers to people who have been forced to leave their own home country, for instance, for reasons of ethnic conflict or persecution, or due to environmental disasters leading to drought and famine. Not all forced migrants are categorized as refugees, however, given that this legal term is granted a specific content according to both domestic and international law. Another major bone of contention is whether to define those who cross borders to escape dire economic conditions as falling into the category of voluntary or forced migration.
37. Note that many "push" countries are simultaneously "pull" countries—Mexico is a classic example of this pattern at work; its southern border is a gateway for migrants arriving from other parts of Latin America, while its northern border offers a passage to the United States to Mexicans and other nationals.
38. Torpey 2001, 163.
39. Canada and the United States have recently moved toward creating a shared infrastructure at certain ports-of-entry, allowing "reverse inspections" of information; this allows the two countries to collect biographical and biometric data on persons entering and exiting their shared border. Add to this the third-country agreement that prohibits refugees who entered one of these countries to seek refuge in the other, again tightening the control over admission to their respective territories and membership regimes.
40. Neumayer 2006, 75. See also Andreas and Snyder 2000.
41. Neumayer 2006, 80.
42. For instance, international air carriers are obliged to transport at their own expense inadmissible passangers back to their countries of departure. With the guidelines established by the 1944 Convention on International Civil Aviation (ICAP), air carriers have increasingly been required to enforce immigration rules by ensuring that passengers have the necessary travel and visa documents. Since the 1990s, airline companies have been subject to hefty fines if they fail to fulfill these regulatory responsibilities at international "zones" (such as international airports). See Guiraudon and Lahav 2000,184–186.
43. Joesph Carens has developed these arguments in a series of seminal articles, including Carens 1987a and Carens 1992.
44. This concise presentation of Carens's argument is offered by P. Cole 2000, 142–148. Others have added to this list the importance of trust in democratic societies (a polity may impose certain restrictions on migration in order to protect conditions of trust and stability to maintain the democratic decision-making process); and the social-welfare argument, according to which some degree of closure is required in order to protect existing labor and welfare standards in advanced industrial countries from a "race to the bottom" in a fully open global market. Bader 2001, 51–53.
45. See Macedo, 1995; Galston 1995.

46. Lahiri's book was later adapted into a movie with the same title, *The Namesake* 2006.
47. UNPFA 2006, 7.
48. See Borjas 1999 on economic impact; on the cultural aspect see Huntington 2004.
49. See Wright 2008.
50. United Nations 2006, 8.
51. United Nations 2006, 8, table 2.
52. There are also growing debates about the effects of international migration on development and developing countries. See, for example, UN 2003.
53. On a more mundane level, this lack of coordination increases the vulnerability of migrants at the destination country, manifested, for example, in the difficulties caused by double taxation or lack of social insurance transfers between these polities.
54. Ghosh 2000, 1.
55. This approach may change in the years to come given growing international recognition of the need to coordinate human mobility across borderlines. See, for example, GCIM 2005.
56. Canada Immigration and Refugee Protection Act, SC 2001, c. 27.
57. Ghosh 2000; GCIM 2005.
58. Chuang 1998; Macklin 2005.
59. Knight 2000.
60. United Nations 2006, 8.
61. A recent OECD study found that the percentage of noncitizens (that is, people who have not naturalized) is lower in each of these countries, estimated at 6.6 percent of the total population in the United States, 5.3 percent in Canada, and 7.4 percent in Australia. See OECD 2005a, 120.
62. United Nations 2006.
63. Aleinikoff, Martin, and Motomura 2003, 283, citing the INS Statistical Yearbook, FY 2003, table 8.
64. For instance, it is estimated that as many as 2.5 to 4 million migrants cross international borders *without* authorization each year. As Khalid Koser observes, this pressure might be building because "more people than ever before want to move, but there are proportionally fewer legal opportunities for them to do so." See Koser 2007, 54.
65. Walzer 1983.
66. Recent research on the causes and patterns of international migration also reveals that migrants are quite shrewd and calculated in setting their goals and in determining where to move.
67. P. Cole 2000, 161.
68. P. Cole 2000, 161.
69. For example, during the period of 1990–2002, "admissions of refugees and humanitarian cases accounted for 11 percent of all immigrants to Australia and to the United States, and 13 percent of those to Canada." See UN 2002c, 14.
70. Ottonelli 2002, 234.
71. Economists differentiate between extreme poverty (or absolute deprivation) and relative poverty/deprivation. Extreme poverty refers to situations in which

people are "chronically hungry, unable to access health care, lack the amenities of safe drinking water and sanitation, cannot afford education for some or all of the children, and perhaps lack rudimentary shelter." Relative poverty as the name indicates is other-referential. It is calculated as a minimal household income level below a given proportion of average national income. Relative poverty generally refers to the situation of the least well-off in high-income countries, where extreme poverty occurs primarily in developing countries. For a concise exposition, see Sachs 2005, 20–24.

72. Clearly, some of the derivative benefits that attach to membership, such as a sense of identity, belonging, and security, fall on the personal side of property definitions, and, as such, are not transferable (nor should they be). But citizenship's more fungible and material dimensions (for instance, the inherited wealth that is passed down to the heirs of title) represents a different kettle of fish: it is possible to distribute them beyond borders without trivializing bounded membership for those who remain inside.
73. Haslett 1986.
74. Henderson 1926, 12–13.
75. Obviously, the topics of property and inheritance have been the subject of fierce ideological controversy in the modern era. To provide just a glimpse into these charged debates, compare William Blackstone's bold claim that "[t]here is nothing that strikes the imagination, and engages the affections of mankind, as the right of property, or that sole and despotic dominion which one man claims and exercises over external things of the world" (Blackstone [1766] 1979, 2) to Karl Marx and Friedrich Engels' contrasting view that property is the fount of inequality and the source of splintering communities into hyperindividualized social environments. Their critique culminates in the famous assertion in the *Communist Manifesto* that "in the most advanced countries, the following [measures] will be pretty generally applicable: 1. Abolition of property in land . . . 2. Absolution of all right of inheritance." See Marx and Engels [1848] 1977, 237. For an illuminating analysis of the ownership-regime implications of these competing views, see Ellickson 1993.
76. Even an ultralibertarian like Robert Nozick accepts this point; see his critical discussion of intergenerational transfers in Nozick 1989, 30–31.
77. Tawney 1964, 120.
78. Kant [1797] 1991, 3.
79. Blackstone [1766] 1979, 10–13.
80. Thomas Jefferson, Letter to James Madison dated Sept. 6, 1789, 7 *Jefferson's Works* 454 (Monticello ed. 1904).
81. Jeremy Bentham, 1882, 122.
82. Bentham 1882, 177.
83. Levi 1983, 552.
84. West 1893, 110.
85. Mill [1848] 1977, vol. 2, 811.
86. Levi 1983, 552.
87. Rose 2004.
88. Mill [1848] 1977, 221.
89. Mill [1848] 1977, 221–222.

90. Rignano 1924 (English translation).
91. Erreygers 1997, 40.
92. Rawls [1970] 1999b, 278.
93. Rawls [1970] 1999b, 277.
94. Dworkin 1981a; Dworkin 1981b.
95. Nozick 1974, 150–153. For Nozick, a just acquisition is restricted by the "Lockean Proviso," a requirement that is regularly breached in the context of citizenship. This may call into question any subsequent transfer of membership title, even according to the narrow conception of property. I thank Daniel Weinstock for this illuminating point.
96. Nozick 1989, 30.
97. Nozick 1989, 31.
98. B. Barry 1989, 452.
99. Within the context of well-off communities, related ideas referring to the child trust fund have recently gained traction. See, for example, Ackerman and Alstott 1999.
100. Pikeety and Saez 2007.
101. On this revenue and expenditure combination, see Alstott 2007.
102. Rose 2004.
103. This signaling effect holds true irrespective of the specific subsequent usages of a given tax revenue.
104. Gingiss 2005, 1.
105. Brittain 1977, 6–7.
106. Alstott 2007; Isbister 2001, 102.
107. Considerations of generational distance may unduly complicate the calculation of the birthright levy obligation; I discuss the possible implications of a Rignano-style "distant in time, weaker in right" logic in developing the *jus nexi* membership principle in Chapter 6.
108. This means that a share of the privilege levy will also fall on long-term residents who, as I explain in Chapter 6, are given a path to citizenship in the country of habitual residence under the proposed *jus nexi* principle. Given that the privilege levy assumes global progressivity as its condition (that is, transfers must flow from richer to poorer countries), it is consistent to demand that the same condition also apply domestically, meaning that a heavier burden falls within each contributing society on those at the top of its distributional matrix. We saw earlier that according to the broad conception of property, "[s]ociety plays a crucial role in every individual's acquisitive activities. [It] determines the rules by which individuals acquire property. Society also educates (to one extent or another) every individual. And society enacts and enforces laws that protect individuals' enjoyment of what they acquire." (Ascher 1991, 86). If a society's wealthiest are those who have benefited most from the cooperative enterprise of citizenship, they can legitimately be asked to bear a more substantial share of their country's obligation towards the rest of the world.
109. Many authors writing on foreign aid and so-called development strategies acknowledge past failures, urging instead a more sustained commitment to investment in infrastructure and human capital, seeing economic development

as a core vehicle for ending the deadly traps of absolute deprivation. See Sachs 2005. Others see the global economic system itself as implicated in the problem of extreme poverty. See Pogge 2002.

110. J. Cohen 2007, xi.

111. These efforts must be coordinated, indeed preferably initiated, by local communities in the recipient countries and implemented with their cooperation and guidance to avoid repeating the past mistakes of paternalistic do-gooders. Working at the grassroots level with community activists assists in overcoming these serious concerns. It also provides a powerful response to the standard critique of international aid programs as going to corrupt and unaccountable leaders instead of the needy.

112. This differs from natural resource global taxation proposals such as Steiner's or Pogge's—which begin from the assumption that the whole world once belonged to all and can therefore be reallocated (Steiner's argument) or apply globally the Rawlsian difference principle (Pogge's argument). The birthright privilege levy, on the other hand, targets the artificiality and inevitability of the legally constructed process of determining who is a citizen by birth and in the process tries to denaturalize this very construction. I discuss these proposals below. On the potential malleability of *jus soli* and *jus sanguinis* rules, see Stevens 1999.

113. One of the most powerful articulations of the claim that rich countries owe a humanitarian obligation to aid poor countries is still found in P. Singer 1972. On the distinction between the duties of humanity and the duties of justice, see Barry 1989. For a critique of the moral imperative line of argument, see Franck 1982. Thomas Pogge has done much in recent years to develop the claim that extreme poverty is a violation of human rights, see, for example, Pogge 2002.

114. This is a crucial basis for David Miller's defense of a noncosmopolitan theory of global justice. See Miller 2007. Similarly, Philippe Van Parijs points out that some transfer of economic resources from one country to another may be supported by those who do not endorse global distributive justice, so long as they fit under the category of compensation for past wrong, fair trade, or cooperative bargains. However, there are serious causal constraints in establishing liability for past wrong the more distant the occasion of the harm. See Van Parijs 2006. On the limits of such compensation, see Kukathas 2003. A different restitution line of argument is represented in Hillel Steiner's work. See, for example, Steiner 2001.

115. Sachs 2005; UNDP 2005, chap. 3.

116. See B. Barry 1989, 454. As a preliminary matter, we should add that extensive consultations will have to be undertaken with representatives of the various countries involved were the birthright levy, in any of its variations, to become operative. Elaborating these various procedures goes beyond the limited space available here. My intention, as just mentioned, is to develop the core idea of taxing birthright privilege, not the various technicalities.

117. Other considerations that might be taken into account in defining these cross-border responsibilities between countries are colonial ties, regional proximity, networking effects of migration, and the like.

118. I thank David Owen and Yoav Peled who offered comments on earlier drafts, highlighting the idea of substitution plans along the lines described above.
119. Building on this infrastructure, we can also imagine that certain countries from different groupings which share tighter historical, economic, linguistic, or geopolitical ties may negotiate extended exchange or tax-substitution programs. Such programs could reflect their interdependence and special relationship once the basic birthright levy scheme of redistribution is operational on a global scale. Many of these types of closer affiliations already exist. Think of the Commonwealth of Nations (a voluntary association of more than 50 sovereign states, which today constitute approximately 30 percent of the world's population, sharing an imperial/colonial past) or La Francophonie (an international organization of French-speaking peoples, that, just like the Commonwealth, brings together more than 50 countries from five different continents).
120. This vision does not require dislocation and resettlement, which is part of what international migration through open admission policies inevitably involves. By improving the life prospects at the home country, it allows individuals and families to stay put.
121. On different ways to materialize this goal, see Sachs 2005. In this context, we can think of the birthright privilege levy as a way to motivate wealthy countries to fulfill their publicly pledged obligations to provide international development assistance at the target rate of 0.7 percent of their gross national product (GNP). This repeated commitment was initially made in a landmark 1970 UN General Assembly Resolution. It was reaffirmed and reiterated in 2002, as part of the Monterrey Consensus as part of the Millennium Development Goals: "we urge developed countries that have not done so to make concrete efforts towards the target of 0.7 percent of gross national product (GNP) as ODA to developing countries and 0.15 to 0.20 percent of GNP of developed countries to least developed countries." See United Nations, *Report of the Conference on Financing for Development* 2002b, para. 42. Despite these declarations, many contributors are still lagging behind: the United States, for instance, provided just 0.22 percent of its GNP to official development assistance in 2006—and this is an improvement in comparison to its prior level of 0.14 percent in 2000.
122. UNICEF 2006.
123. The sad reality is that many of these children are kept out of school not only as a result of mega-structural problems (such as gender inequality or systemic under-investment in rural or minority areas) but also because their families cannot afford school and uniform fees. Providing a reliable source of funding for targeted educational projects in lieu of these user fees is but one tangible illustration of how the funds from the global birthright levy could be used to a make a difference. Similarly, sponsoring free school meals (using locally produced foods) is another way in which the birthright privilege levy can make a tremendous contribution in terms of both improving access to education and ending child hunger. These types of on-the-ground interventions "can be taken immediately within existing capacities to produce dramatic results [. . .], bring[ing] vital gains in well-being to millions of people." (United Nations Millennium Project 2006, 4).

124. P. Andreas 1999.
125. Reisen 2002, 1. Tobin originally contemplated a tax rate of 1 percent, but this was subsequently lowered to anywhere between 0.05 percent and 0.25 percent.

4. Blood and Soil

1. The normative critique of exclusion in the context of immigration, rather than birthright citizenship, is well developed. Of this growing body of literature, see Bauböck 1994; Benhabib 2004b; Bosniak 2006; Carens 2005a; P. Cole 2000; Rubio-Marin 2000.
2. A similar attempt to expand the boundaries of our citizenship imagination is found in the work of scholars writing on local, regional, supranational, and international membership definitions. See Bauböck 2004; Blank 2007; Bosniak 2000.
3. *Calvin's Case* (1608 England), 382. For a concise overview, see Houston 2000, 698–701.
4. Polly J. Price offers a detailed analysis of this case in Price 1997. See also Holdsworth 1982, vol. 9, 75.
5. Salyer 2005, 52.
6. Hansen 2002.
7. *Pochi* v. *Macphee* (1982 Australia).
8. Price 1997, 74.
9. *Calvin's Case* (1608 England), 381.
10. This landmark case is part of a larger narrative about the historical ties between land law in England and the rise of nationality law. As one author notes, "the crucial point came when the alien could no longer hold land in England. Whereas formerly the tenure of land was the sine qua non of allegiance, then the quality of being a subject born became the sine qua non of tenure." See Nygh 1963, 176. A similar theme is discussed by Dummett and Nichol 1990.
11. *Calvin's Case* (1608 England), 407.
12. Weil 2001.
13. Joppke 2006, 75.
14. On this historical irony, see Weil 1996.
15. As we shall later see, this remains an absolute rule in Canada and the United States, but this is no longer the case in other common-law jurisdictions. For instance, the United Kingdom, Australia, Ireland, and New Zealand have in recent years modified their version of *jus soli* to apply automatically only to children of citizens and permanent residents.
16. In the United States, birthright citizenship is entrenched in the Fourteenth Amendment of the Constitution: "All persons born or naturalized in the United States, and subject to the jurisdiction thereof, are citizens of the United States and of the State wherein they reside."
17. See *United States* v. *Wong Kim Ark* (1898), 693 (Justice Gray). This decision has been interpreted to hold that children born to unauthorized migrants in the United States are citizens at birth. Thus, even if the child's parents entered a country unlawfully, thereby spoiling their own chances for acquisition of mem-

bership, the child is not made to pay for her parents' misdeed. For a challenge to the common and inclusive interpretation of *Wong Kim Ark,* see Schuck and Smith 1985. For a defense of the jurisprudential tradition of full inclusion, irrespective of the parent's membership status, see "The Birthright Citizenship Amendment: A Threat to Equality" 1994; Schwartz 1986. This debate is no longer limited to legal academics. The past decades have witnessed a number of legislative proposals aimed at restricting entitlement to birthright citizenship in the United States. Similar debates emerged in Canada, which also subscribes to a pure *jus soli* application. See Buhler 2002.

18. British Nationality Act, 1981, section 1, changed the previous common-law rule (where the place of birth was the sole determination in citizenship) to a birthright principle that now takes into account the parents' status and residence considerations. For further discussion, see Dummett and Nicol 1990.
19. British Nationality Act 1981.
20. Australia restricted its automatic *jus soli* citizenship regime in 1986. See Australian Citizenship Act, 1948, s. 10. For commentary, see Rubenstien 2002. Ireland was a country of automatic *jus soli* up until 2004, when a constitutional referendum and subsequent legislative changes introduced descent- and residence-based components, designed to approximate the idea of a "genuine" connection to the polity. See Irish Nationality and Citizenship Act 1956.
21. Joppke 2008, 4.
22. As Joseph Carens points out, this example is often given by those who wish to restrict the application of the territorial birthright principle in the United States to children of citizens and legal resident aliens (thus excluding children born to undocumented migrants from automatic entitlement to American citizenship). See Carens 1987b, 413.
23. The exception to the rule is the status of children born to foreign diplomats. The present jurisprudential debate refers to the interpretation that ought to be given to the phrase "subject to the jurisdiction thereof" in the 14th Amendment Citizenship Clause.
24. Carens 1987b, 413. Although the NAFTA could have expanded the scope of citizenship rights by providing a common ("North American") citizenship to the residents of Canada, the United States and Mexico, it still remains primarily a trade agreement and not a common citizenship project. See Cassise 1996; Pastor 2001.
25. See INA (especially post 1996 provisions), also some measures of the USA Patriot Act of 2001; the Homeland Security Act of 2002; and the REAL ID Act of 2005. Similar provisions are in effect in Canada. See, for example, The Anti-Terrorism Act 2001; Immigration and Refugee Protection Act 2001; Ahani 1995; Chiarelli 1992.
26. See the jurisprudence of the European Court of Human Rights on this matter, for example, *Beljoudi* v. *France* (1992).
27. *Romans* v. *Canada* (2004). Leave to appeal to the Supreme Court of Canada was not granted. See *Romans* v. *Canada* (2001). Romans also filed a complaint to the UN Human Rights Committee, which proved unsuccessful. See *Romans* v. *Canada* (2004).
28. Motomura 1998.

29. Motomura 2006a, 10.
30. In a comprehensive study of citizenship policies, Alexander Aleinikoff and Douglas Klusmeyer label foreign-born children caught in this predicament the "1.5-generation." They recommend that whenever these children of lawful immigrants spend their formative years in the country of immigration, they should conceptually be treated in the same way as children born in the country: that is, they should receive automatic or near-automatic citizenship. See Aleinikoff and Klusmeyer 2002, 9, 14–15.
31. *Matter of Ortiz-Martinez* (2007). In this case, the BIA overturned a decision by the immigration judge to grant the applicant a cancelation of removal, pursuant to section 240A of the Immigration and Nationality Act. The decision is currently under appeal.
32. U.S. Child Citizenship Act of 2000. Similar legislation passed in Canada in 2007. For a brief introduction to the provisions of this amendment, see Citizenship and Immigration Canada (CIC), 2006.
33. To acquire citizenship under the Act, three cumulative requirements must be fulfilled: at least one parent is a U.S. citizen (permanent residence by lawful immigrants is *not* sufficient here, leaving children of immigrants in a vulnerable, nonmember position); the child is under the age of eighteen; and is residing in the United States in the legal and physical custody of the citizen parent. 8 U.S.C. § 1431 (2005). The court held that the statute does not have retroactive effect. See, for example, *Nehme* v. *INS* (2001), 431–433.
34. The Immigration and Nationality Act (INA) provides a statutory *jus sanguinis* route for attributing birthright citizenship to biological children born abroad to American parents; the Child Citizenship Act supplements these provisions.
35. For a critical account, see Romero 2001. For its effects, for example, *Santos* v. *Gonzales* (2007).
36. Aleinikoff and Klusmeyer 2002, 14.
37. If the parents hold the nationality of different countries, the children will become a dual citizen by birth. For an illuminating discussion, see Knop 2001. See also Waldrauch 2006.
38. Weil 2001, 19.
39. Brubaker 1992, 39.
40. Weil 2001, 21.
41. For illuminating discussion on Japan's birthright citizenship regime, see Kashiwazaki 2000, 437–439.
42. Ohliger 2005.
43. Put differently, the heterogeneity of the communities that *jus soli* and *jus sanguinis* engender depends as much on their immigration and naturalization policies as it does on the chosen birthright principles. A similar observation is made by Brubaker 1989; and Weil 2001.
44. For a critical discussion of such selective admission, see Joppke 2005. See also Shachar 1999.
45. Hailbronner 1989.
46. This convergence trend is highlighted by Hansen and Weil 2001.
47. *Sheinbein* v. *Attorney General* (1999 Israel [Hebrew]); *State of Israel* v. *Sheinbein* (1999 Israel [Hebrew]).

48. In this way, he escaped the threat of a heavier punishment, which would most likely have been imposed upon him in the United States. For example, Israeli law does not permit the death penalty for a convicted criminal offender, whereas various American states both allow and implement such punishment.
49. In all likelihood, Sheinbein would *not* have been entitled to receive Israeli citizenship by virtue of the Law of Return, because section 2(B) of that law was interpreted to bar admissibility on grounds of criminality that might endanger the public welfare. See the Israel Supreme Court decision in H.C. 442/71, *Lansky* v. *Minister of the Interior* (1972 Israel [Hebrew]). For further discussion, see Shachar 1999, 240–241.
50. In accordance with the Israel Supreme Court decision and to the dismay of both the Israeli Ministry of Justice and the U.S. Justice Department, Sheinbein was not extradited to the United States. Instead, his trial for murder took place in Israel. He pleaded guilty and was sentenced to 24 years in jail. He is now serving his term in an Israeli prison.
51. The civic-ethnic dichotomy is commonly used in the literature on nationalism. See, for example, Smith 1991; Greenfeld 1992. For a more journalistic account, see Igantieff 1995.
52. For a detailed discussion, see Schuck and Smith 1985, 9–22.
53. They must also acquire basic protections against abuse of power by the state, including the security that their membership will not be unilaterally revoked by the government, no matter how critical they are of their government's actions.
54. The diachronic dimension of citizenship law is elegantly captured by Donald Galloway (Galloway 1999).
55. For those who think that the answer to birthright arbitration lies simply in adopting more open naturalization policies to reward those who take risks and show initiative by leaving their home countries and emigrating to a new society, it is important to remember that migrant stock in the world's population currently stands at less than 3 per cent. This means that 97 per cent of the world's citizens are still living in their country of birth. Moreover, the number of governments adopting more restrictive immigration measures has risen dramatically over the past decades, from 6 per cent in 1976 to 40 per cent in 2001.
56. See Canada Citizenship Act, R.S.C. 1985. Canada here followed the British tradition of *jus soli,* codifying into legislation (the original 1947 Citizenship Act, and the current 1997 Citizenship Act) the common law principles set out in *Calvin's Case.* For a brief historical overview, see Buhler 2002, 94–97.
57. Most EU countries emphasize the principle of simultaneous acquisition of citizenship by minors and their parents, which means that as soon as the parents naturalize, their children too become full members *ex lege.* For further discussion, see Waldrauch 2006. A powerful normative justification of this relational and gender-neutral family-unity rule is articulated by Karen Knop (Knop 2001).
58. Aleinikoff and Klusmeyer 2002, 14.
59. This is an absolute rule in Canada and the United States. As mentioned above, the United Kingdom, Australia, and mostly recently, Ireland, and New Zealand, have modified their versions of the birthright principle to apply only to children of citizens and permanent residents.

60. Some may object to such expressions of loyalty for reasons of religion or conscience, in which case specific clauses need to be established (as in the case of military exemptions). Any exemptions represent the exception, however, rather than the rule.
61. Isin and Turner 2007, 11.
62. In the rare instances where citizens specifically declare their intent to give up citizenship, such formal renunciation usually requires approval by the political community before it takes effect. The approval process is handled by the relevant government agencies within the country or its representatives abroad.
63. World Bank 2001, 1.
64. The exception is if they are subject to persecution in their home country (or former residence) and thus fit the 1951 Convention definition of refugee status. This demands that a host country provide them with a temporary shelter and provides that they may not be returned home if such a step would place them in real danger—the right of *nonrefoulement.*
65. As mentioned above, *jus soli* and *jus sanguinis* do diverge on at least one critical issue: the status of children born to noncitizens who have made the host country their permanent home (the second generation problem). Traditionally, *jus soli* countries have addressed this problem more adequately. In the United States and Canada, for example, children born to illegal immigrants within the nation's borders are automatically entitled to unconditional membership. In recent years, however, many *jus soli* countries have added a combination of descent and residence components before a child born to noncitizens can gain membership. At the same time, various *jus sanguinis* countries have added a territorial component to their citizenship laws, making it easier for children of noncitizens to gain membership. See Hansen and Weil 2001.
66. This is the case because of choice provisions built into German and other citizenship laws in relation to dual citizens by birth, who after the age of majority must make an actual determination as to which membership affiliation they wish to preserve as their own.
67. *United States* v. *Wong Kim Ark* (1898).
68. A narrow exception is made for those seeking asylum from persecution in their home country; only citizens are entitled to entry. The exception here is the obligation taken upon themselves by those nations that were signatories to the 1951 Refugee Convention to provide a safe haven to persons who qualify as refugees. Even where an individual is granted asylum, the receiving country is only obliged to provide temporary shelter, not necessarily long-term residency. See the 1951 Convention Relating to the Status of Refugees as amended by the Protocol Relation to the Status of Refugees 1967.
69. UN 2006.
70. For comprehensive research examining these trends, see National Intelligence Council, U.S.A. 2001. For a comparative perspective, see Castles and Davidson 2000.
71. This again highlights the value of recognizing special relations among individuals as the basis for gaining admission to membership in the body politic, this time in relation to a chosen partner, rather than a biological (or adopted) child.

72. *Landon* v. *Plasencia* (1982), 32.
73. *Landon* v. *Plasencia* (1982), 33.
74. This legal reality in the United States has been the subject of harsh critique in the rich writings of authors such as Linda Bosniak, Leti Volpo, and David Cole, among others.
75. INA §335(a).
76. For a powerful critique of the contract conception in immigration, see Motomura 2006a.
77. Joppke 2008.
78. T. Miller 2003.
79. The situation here differs from jurisdiction to jurisdiction, and may also depend on the specific grounds for exclusion and other facts of the case. In Australia, see *Al-Kateb* v. *Godwin* 2004. In the United States, see *Shaughnessy* v. *United States ex. rel. Mezei* 1953; *Zadvydas* v. *Davis* 2001. In the United Kingdom, see *A* v. *Secretary of State for the Home Department* 2004 UKHL 56, [2005] A.C. 68 (appeal taken from England). See also Kerber 2006, 150.
80. The symbolic meaning of such acts is discussed by Sanford Levinson (Levinson 1986).
81. See Aleinikoff 1994; Motomura 1998; Bosniak 2007, 391.
82. For a detailed account of this trend, which I elsewhere call the "global race for talent," see Shachar 2006.
83. At the same time, wealthy destination countries are trying to do whatever they can within the bounds of legality to fend off unwanted immigrants that they see as falling into the net-burden category. See Flynn 2005.
84. Shachar 2006.
85. Barry 2006, 36.
86. Bauböck 2003b.
87. Bhabha 2004, 235. See also Benhabib and Resnik 2009. For a feminist critique of the gendered dimensions of Lockean conceptions of property, see, for example, Radin 1993.
88. Broude 2007, 13.
89. UNPFA 1999, chap. 2, fig. 5.

5. Popular Defenses of Birthright Citizenship

1. Walzer 1983, 32 [emphasis added].
2. Dahl 1989. An illuminating account of the importance of the responsiveness principle in justifying the United States *jus soli* rule is found in Eisgruber 1997.
3. This traditional view is best expressed in Oppenheim's *International Law,* which pronounces that "it is not for international law but for the internal law of each State to determine who is, and who is not, to be considered its [citizen]." See Oppenheim 2008, 852. It is reflected in various international instruments. Consider Article 1 of the Convention on Certain Questions Relating to Conflict of Nationality Laws ("1930 Hague Convention"): "it is for each State to determine under its own laws who are its nationals."

4. The younger generation will begin to exercise this right upon reaching the age of majority.
5. An eloquent expression of this set of ideas is found in an influential contribution to the debate over national and global justice by Thomas Nagel. See Nagel 2005.
6. In theory, it is possible to separate the right to membership from the right to vote. However, this may take us down the slippery slope of maintaining a privileged group that is entitled to full citizenship, while everyone else must settle for less. This solution was famously rejected by the German Constitutional Court in the late 1970s and early 1990s. See, for example, BVerfG, 83, II, Nr. 3, 37, 1990. It also does not resolve the problem at issue: how to distinguish what (if any) are good grounds for excluding people from the *demos*.
7. Conversely, natural-born citizens who acquired membership through their parents, regardless of how long ago an ancestor had actually lived in the country of origin and whether the birthright citizen developed any real ties to the nation, are granted an equal right to participate in the polity without necessarily bearing the brunt of their political choices if they permanently reside outside the territorial and jurisdictional reach of the home state. See López-Guerra 2005.
8. Bauböck 2005b.
9. I am not taking a stand on whether deliberative democracy ought to be the standard here; any type of participation in the political process as adopted by a given state in relation to its own citizens would suffice as a standard for inclusion of those who currently do not enjoy access to political voice.
10. See Benhabib's discussion of Germany's debate about democratic voice for nonmembers (Benhabib 2004b). New guest workers programs are also threatening to gain momentum in the United States and other advanced economies. See Ruths 2005. Also see Rodriguez 2007.
11. For a detailed and illuminating exploration of precisely this problem, see Rubio-Marín 2000.
12. Eisgruber 1997, 72 [emphasis added].
13. Dahl 1989, 122.
14. Blake 2001.
15. Blake 2001.
16. Miller 2007, 13–14 [emphasis added].
17. Many of these types of closer affiliations already exist. Think of the Commonwealth of Nations (a voluntary association of more than fifty sovereign states, which today constitute approximately 30 percent of the world's population, sharing an imperial/colonial past) or La Francophonie (an international organization of French-speaking peoples, that, just like the Commonwealth, brings together more than fifty countries from five different continents).
18. Whelan 1983, 13.
19. Steiner 2001, 83, Note that Steiner's account refers to appropriating land whereas my analysis focuses on the acquisition of citizenship title per se.
20. Shapiro and Hacker-Cordon 1999, 1.

21. See, for example, Abizadeh 2008; Goodin 2007.
22. Abizadeh 2008, 38 [emphasis added]; Debra Satz takes a somewhat different route, arguing that "saying that citizens of a state have [special] obligations to one another does not mean that they have the right to determine the conditions of entry and exit from their state." See Satz 1999, 79.
23. Goodin 2007, 68.
24. Brubaker 1989.
25. Even this factual assertion must be qualified: the reliance on birth assumes a state bureaucracy that is capable of accurately and systemically documenting birth as a citizenship-establishing event. This is not necessarily the case in all countries and regions. See UNICEF 2007, 42. A recent study has shown, for example, that large numbers of unauthorized migrants in India have managed to establish themselves as citizens based on false, forged or locally-produced birth documentation. See Sadig 2008.
26. Torpey 2000.
27. For an overview of these legislative provisions, see Waldrauch 2006.
28. Waldrauch 2006; Weil 2001; Aleinikoff and Klusmeyer 2001, 17–35.
29. Sec. 12(1) of Australian Citizenship Act 2007 provides that "(1) A person born in Australia is an Australian citizen if and only if: (b) the person is ordinarily resident in Australia throughout the period of 10 years beginning on the day the person is born."
30. Sec. 1(4) of Part I of BNA 1981 states that, "A person born in the United Kingdom after commencement who is not a British citizen by virtue of subsection (1) or (2) shall be entitled, on an application for his registration as a British citizen made at any time after he has attained the age of ten years, to be registered as such a citizen if, as regards each of the first ten years of that person's life, the number of days on which he was absent from the United Kingdom in that year does not exceed 90."
31. Home Office 1980, 8, para. 43.
32. Home Office 1980, 8, para. 44.
33. Home Office 1980, 8, para. 44.
34. The Twenty-seventh Amendment of the Constitution Act 2004, inserted a new provision into the Irish Constitution at Article 9, which provides as follows: "Notwithstanding any other provision of this Constitution, a person born in the island of Ireland, which includes its islands and seas, who does not have, at the time of his or her birth, at least one parent who is an Irish citizen or entitled to be an Irish citizen is not entitled to Irish citizenship or nationality, unless otherwise provided by law." This constitutional amendment qualified Article 2 of the Constitution. See Irish Nationality and Citizenship Bill 2004, Explanatory Memorandum. This restriction was somewhat softened by the enactment in 2004 of the Irish Nationality and Citizenship Act, which permits a child of nonnational parents to gain citizenship in Ireland if one of her parents resided in that country for a period of three years within the four years preceding the child's birth. See Irish Nationality and Citizenship Act, 1956 [consolidated version, as amended by the Irish Nationality and Citizenship Act 2004, no. 38 of 2004], article 6A.

35. Tony Wallace, Spokesperson for Internal Affairs (New Zealand), January 1, 2006.
36. A child is permitted to legally sponsor the parent after reaching the age of twenty-one; subject to the parent's inadmissability on other grounds (such as unlawful entry or purchase and use of forged identity documents).
37. The relief was in the form of a cancellation of removal under section 204A(b) of the INA. See *Matter of Andazola-Rivas,* 23 Immigration and Nationality Decisions 319 (BIA 2002).
38. For further discussion of the tension of choosing between "home and family," see Bhabha 2004.
39. See Immigration and Nationality Act sec. 240A(b)(1)(D).
40. The burden of establishing the hardship standard as set out in the statutory language lies on the person seeking the remedy of "cancellation of removal" or adjustment of status. See *Matter of Monreal,* 23 I&N Dec. 56 (BIA 2001), 65.
41. H.R. Conf. Rep. 104–828, 104th Congress, 2nd Session 230 (1996).
42. The mother petitioned the state for maternity benefits, but her claim was denied because neither she nor the child had been granted a residence permit to stay in the country. The municipality stepped in to assist them with donations of various supplies for the newborn baby, but this was an act of charity, not a duty of law.
43. See Finland Nationality Act, sec. 9 (1) (3).
44. *Karassev* v. *Finland* (1999 European Court of Human Rights), 16. The relevant provision is Article 8 of the ECHR, which guarantees the right to respect of everyone's private and family life. The Commission and the Court have interpreted this provision as extending to cases where minors were seeking entry into the territory in order to join their parents. See *Gul* v. *Switzerland* (1996 European Court of Human Rights). See also *Nsona* v. *the Netherlands* (1996); *Ahmut* v. *the Netherlands* (1996).
45. J. Scott 1998.
46. To this we must add the disturbing recognition that millions of children born in the world's poorest nations have not had their birth registered with any governmental agency. This leaves them at a particularly precarious situation: unregistered children remain administratively invisible, without the basic identity documents required to claim the services and protections due to them as citizens and as beneficiaries of regional and international human rights and development initiatives.
47. Yack 1996, 208.
48. Blackstone [1776] 1979/2001, 13.
49. Satz 1999, 79. Note that Satz' critique emphasizes the over-significance given to crossing the territorial edges of states, but the same line of argument applies with equal force to membership boundaries more generally.
50. Carens 1987. Even *after* a birthright citizenship law is put into place, it must set out the parameters of eligibility and then apply them in reference to those seeking inclusion, a sorting process that may lead to serious controversies in particular instances, as we have seen in the *Karassev* case (*Karassev* v. *Finland* 1999).

51. In fact, this is the very line of critique that Yack himself raises against defenders of the myth of a civic nation, in particular, Jurgen Habermas. See Yack 1996, 197–200.
52. The full list is too long to cite, and there are numerous variants to this approach. Among the most influential accounts, see Kymlicka 1989; MacIntyre 1984; D. Miller 1995b; Sandel 1982; Tamir 1993; Taylor 1989.
53. Walzer 1983, 62.
54. Tamir 1993, 73.
55. Sen 2000.
56. Blake 2001, 257.
57. On trust in multicultural societies, see the important contribution of Daniel Weinstock (Weinstock 1999).
58. See, for example, D. Miller 1998, 48; D. Miller 1989, 245. For a critical account of these claims, see Abizadeh 2002.
59. For detailed elaboration, see D. Miller 1995b.
60. Miller acknowledges (and dismisses) this line of critique in Miller 2007.
61. See Miller 1988, 647.
62. Weiler 1999.
63. Of this rich body of literature, see, for example, Peled 1992; R. Smith 1997; Volpp 2007. It may also shape a country's immigration regime. As Christian Joppke has recently shown, a surprisingly large number of democratic polities select among potential immigrants on the basis of considerations such as ethnicity and linguistic, cultural, or religious affiliation; these policies serve as concrete manifestations of the community's desire to maintain a distinct cultural heritage or national identity. For a comprehensive analysis, see Joppke 2005. Although there are conceivable circumstances under which this may be a fair argument for a minority community to raise against the dominant majority (for instance, when that minority is struggling to preserve its identity in the face of severe assimilation pressures), it is far harder to justify the right of a party to exclude persons on the same basis. Examining the justifications and limits of cultural nationalism of this sort is at the heart of Chaim Gans's incisive analysis in Gans 2003.
64. In its strongest interpretation, this claim may lead to overt discrimination and permanent exclusion along the lines of the worst interpretations of ethnonationalism. That said, it is possible to defend a weaker vision under which political communities may legitimately wish to preserve their collective special character or the value of special relations, so long as these aspirations are tamed by commitment to other values, such as democratic inclusiveness and the accommodation of cultural identities held by minority group members. Michael Walzer's analysis fits the latter approach.
65. Walzer 1983, 61–62.
66. Walzer 1983, 52: "one might insist, as I shall ultimately do, that the same standards apply to naturalization as to immigration, that every immigrant and every resident is a citizen—or, at least, a potential citizen. That is why territorial admission is so serious a matter. The members must be prepared to accept, as their equals in a world of shared obligations, the men and women they admit."
67. Walzer 1983, 55.

68. For a concise overview, see Nedelsky 2001. The legal implications of this approach are elegantly articulated by Karen Knop (Knop 2001).
69. Carens 1987b, 424.
70. For further elaboration of a feminist theory of relational rights, see, for example, Minow and Shanley 1997. More generally, see Tronto 1993.
71. Nedelsky 2001.
72. Motomura 2006b.
73. See Knop 2001. As Knop explains, this approach has been adopted by the new *European Convention on Nationality,* Nov. 6, 1997, ETS no.166. See also Council of Europe 1998.
74. For a detailed discussion, see Bredbenner 1998.
75. For illuminating critiques of this gender-biased rule, see Sapiro 1984; Cott 1998. Such discrimination continued until late into the twentieth century, when married women in most countries finally acquired the right to transmit their nationality to their children independently. For further discussion, see International Law Association 2000.
76. Knop 2001; see International Law Association 2000.
77. Stratton 1992.
78. *Benner* v. *Canada* (1997).
79. See Canada Citizenship Act, R.S.C., ch. C-29, sec. 5(2)(b) (1985) (Can).
80. *Benner* v. *Canada* (1997), 401.
81. *Benner* v. *Canada* (1997), 403.
82. See Immigration and Nationality Act, sec. 309; sec. 1409.
83. *Miller* v. *Albright* (1998), 434.
84. International law, on the other hand, clearly provides that men and women deserve equal rights to acquire, change, or retain their nationality and to confer citizenship on their children. See, for example, UN, 1979, Article 9.
85. *Nguyen* v. *INS.* (2001).
86. Nguyen's father obtained an order of parentage from a state court, based on DNA testing, proving their blood relationship as father and son. See *Nguyen* v. *INS.* (2001), 2057.
87. *Nguyen* v. *INS.* (2001), 2060.
88. *Nguyen* v. *INS.* (2001), 2061.
89. *Nguyen* v. *INS.* (2001), 2061–2062.
90. *Nguyen* v. *INS.* (2001), 2062.
91. *Nguyen* v. *INS.* (2001), 2062.
92. *Nguyen* v. *INS.* (2001), 2063 [emphasis added].
93. *Nguyen* v. *INS.* (2001), 2066 (O'Connor J., dissenting) (internal quotation marks omitted).
94. Immigration agencies are criticized for their "invasions of privacy [in marriage-based immigration] which even the boldest of government agencies have heretofore been hesitant to enter." See *Chan* v. *Bell* (1978), 130, n.13; *Stokes* v. *INS* (1976) (consent judgment) (ordering particular procedural guidelines for New York INS marital fraud investigation processes); *Doe* v. *Miller* (1983) (granting an injunction against implementation of state policies that forced undocumented alien parents to withdraw food stamp applications or disclose information about their alien status).

95. Unlike the automatic nature of citizenship attribution at birth, a noncitizen seeking admission on the basis of marriage has to prove his or her eligibility for such inclusion. The burden is on the applicant to show that the relationship is genuine, that is, it is not merely a pretext for gaining access to the rights and benefits of full membership.
96. For further discussion, see Abrams 2007.
97. *MacKenzie* v. *Hare* (1915). For a perceptive analysis of the role of marriage in defining the boundaries of the nation, see Cott 2002.
98. *Abdulaziz, Cabales, and Balkandali* v. *the United Kingdom* (1985 European Court of Human Rights).
99. See Francoeur 2007.
100. For the now-established body of feminist literature on this problem, see, for example, Young 1995. For illuminating discussions of the complex intersections between family and immigration law, see Calvo 1991; Abrams 2007.
101. Collard 2001, 54.
102. Most advanced industrial countries are currently ageing, making the structure of the generational pyramid such that it is expected that the current working-age generation will have to rely more heavily on the younger generation when they reach retirement age. See Auerbach, Kotlikoff, and Leibfritz 1999. These patterns of "generational accounting" become more complicated in ageing economies. See World Bank 1994; Wallace 2001; Giannakouris 2008.
103. For a now-classic exposition, see Laslett and Fishkin 1992.
104. See, for example, Kotlikoff and Burns 2004.
105. For a discussion of related concerns, see Goodin 1999.
106. See, for example, Shachar 2006.
107. Lindh, Malmberg, and Palme 2005, 447.
108. Pateman 1988.
109. Radin 1996.
110. Ascher 1990.
111. For example, it is estimated in the GCIM Report 2005 that foreign workers make up more than 5 percent of the labor force in eight European countries and that "in certain countries, whole sectors of the economy and many public services have become highly dependent on migrant labour, and would collapse overnight if those workers were no longer available." (GCIM Report 2005, 6).
112. On this account, participation in the labor market becomes the main criterion for gaining access to full membership title. Yet this seems problematic on several accounts. For one, it seems both too crude (equating citizenship with employment) *and* too specific: what about the situation of the stay-at-home-parent who is engaged in uncompensated yet crucial intergenerational caregiving labor? Or the grandparent who may serve as the core stabilizing force that permits the working generation to pursue their education or establish themselves professionally and financially during the crucial child-bearing and child-rearing years? Another important point refers to unlawful migrants, who in many cases pay taxes and work in the receiving state's market: should they too benefit from earned citizenship? The current proposal to regulate migrants'

unauthorized status through a measure of earned citizenship supports this view, and I concur.

113. For example, the Personal Responsibility and Work Opportunity Reconciliaton Act and the Illegal Immigrant Reform and Immigration Responsibility Act, both passed in 1996, which restricted access to government services of aliens lawfully residing in the United States. See *Abreu* v. *Callahan* (1997).
114. Motomura 2006a.
115. Motomura 2006a.
116. Motomura 2006a, 10. The strict contractualist approach further suffers from the familiar weaknesses of unequal bargaining power, and, in this case, no real negotiation is even possible given that the government's offer is a fixed one, nor is it clear that newcomers are fully aware of the type of possible grounds-for-exclusion which they have implicitly incurred. See Motomura 2006a, 38–62.
117. What is more, the contract vision provides no recognition of anything but the strict legal dimension of the terms and conditions of admission (and possible removal); it grants no recognition of the actual social relations and genuine ties to the polity and its people that might have grown out of continued membership within its society. It thus smacks of an exclusionary undertone, guarding access to the polity's pot of benefits for those who are seen to truly belong: namely, those whose title originates in intergenerational transfer rather than any other route of admission. This also seems to inform the charge of robbing our nation by America's conservative opponents of its automatic *jus soli* principle, which they see as a venue for undeserving foreigners to establish for their children an unfair advantage, no matter how long the parents or the children have actually lived in the country. In contrast, the *jus nexi* principle that I develop in Chapter 6 captures these ongoing ties, making them part of the equation of establishing membership in the state without necessarily relying on birthright.

6. Curtailing Inheritance

1. See *Liechtenstein* v. *Guatemala* (*The Nottebohm* Case, 1955 ICJ), 23.
2. Rath 1990, 139; Benhabib 2004b, 157. The definition of residence here follows the provisions of the Netherlands Aliens Act 2000, Article 8.
3. In the United States, noncitizens are already voting in several local elections, for instance, in certain communities in Maryland. In Chicago, noncitizens can vote in school board elections. Other metropolitan areas, including New York City, are considering the adoption of noncitizen voting rights as well. These current practices revive a forgotten tradition in American history which permitted noncitizens to vote in various local, state, and federal levels. On this fascinating history, see Hayduk 2006. In granting noncitizens voting rights, these cities (and other subnational entities, such as provinces and cantons) are functioning as semiautonomous political communities, nested within larger multilevel governance units. In other contexts, local authorities hold a more limited set of powers, operating primarily as organs of a central authority. On this distinction, see Blank 2007.

4. See Blackman 1998; Bauböck 2003a, 139.
5. For an illuminating discussion, see Munzer 2001.
6. Of this rich literature, see Nedelsky 1989; Nedelsky 2001; Knop 2001; Minow and Shanley 1997; Bowman and Cornish 1992.
7. See Morris and Cheshire 1940; Knop 2001; Munzer 2001.
8. On the functional, "proper" law, or modern approach in conflicts of law resolution, see Collins et al. 2008.
9. L. Weinrib 2002.
10. There is a growing body of literature on the moral and legal foundation of transnational claims, much of which is inspired by Rainer Bauböck's influential writings. See, for example, Bauböck 2003b.
11. This model is referred to as "citizenship as affiliation" by Motomura (Motomura 2006a); see also Carens 2005a.
12. Lopez 1981, 696.
13. *Mathews* v. *Diaz* (1976), 80. See also *Landon* v. *Plasecnia* (1982), 33.
14. Motomura 2006b, 250. See also Bosniak 2007.
15. *Nottebohm* (1995 ICJ), 23.
16. Hammar 1990, 20.
17. Hammar 1990, 20.
18. Rawls [1970] 1999b, 25.
19. Bauböck 2005c, 5.
20. Joppke 2008, 135.
21. Joppke 2005, 241–247. Joppke draws here on the recent citizenship law reforms in France, Italy, Portugal, and Spain.
22. See Rignano 1924.
23. See Erreygers 1997, 40.
24. See Rignano 1924; Kiesling 1992, 157–159. As its critics have shown, the difficulty with this proposal lies in the practical complexity of distinguishing between "earned" and "inherited" wealth, though this is not a problem for our application in the realm of citizenship. See Wedgwood 1929.
25. See Bauböck 2005b; K. Barry 2006; Itzigshon 2000; Lopez-Guerra 2005. On the policy implementation front, see the articles in the special collection on "Diasporas and Transnationalism" (Duncan 2006).
26. Bauböck 2005c, 17.
27. A classic example of a birthright citizenship law that grants automatic and perpetual passage of membership title is found in Article 1 of the Greek Citizenship Act: "The child of a Greek acquires the Greek nationality as from the time of his/her birth." Note the lack of any territoriality requirements or a generational timeline stop-point at which the automatic transmission of title comes to a halt.
28. See INA sec. 301(c); *Weedin* v. *Chin Bow* (1927).
29. Sec. 301(g) of INA provides that "a person born outside the geographical limits of the United States and its outlying possessions of parents one of whom is an alien, and the other a citizen of the United States who, prior to the birth of such person, was physically present in the United States or its outlying possessions for a period or periods totaling not less than five years, at least two of which were after attaining the age of fourteen years."

30. Aleinikoff, Martin, and Motomura 2003, 33. Those serving abroad in the military are treated as if their children were born in the home country; in other words, taking arms up on behalf of the collective establishes the required nexus, or, where relevant, such service counts as serving toward the fulfillment of the physical-presence requirements of sec. 301(g) of the INA.
31. Lagarde 1984, 483.
32. Canada Citizenship Act, sec. 8.
33. Sec. 16(b) (Substantial Connection with Canada Criteria) of Citizenship Regulations 1993 authorized by Citizenship Act (Can.). This provision of Canada's citizenship law is set to change in 2009, adopting a stricter intergenerational transmission scheme.
34. See Bauböck 2005a, 14; Bauböck et al. 2006.
35. Joppke 2006, 76.
36. Joppke 2005, 241.
37. Note that the ECJ has refrained from taking the further step of using residence as a basis for acquisition of citizenship itself. Instead, it restricted the residence criteria to defining who has access to what derivative benefits of membership, which accrue after that person has already established membership in one of the EU member-states, and through so doing, gained EU citizenship.
38. Aleinikoff and Klusmeyer 2002.
39. The court leaves open the question of how precisely to define this genuine link, stating instead that in principle such a link must be established by a "reasonable period" that is proportional to the legitimate aims of the national legislation at issue. In so ruling, the court held that as a corollary to freedom of movement within the union, it is permissible to impose a residence-based genuine connection requirement in governing access to a noncontributory means-tested benefit. As the text of the decision indicates, the court was clearly concerned with the problem of "benefit tourism" (in the court's words), where potential entrants engage in forum-shopping, seeking a jurisdiction that provides the greatest benefits to them without sharing in the risks and responsibilities of membership. This is the concern about opportunism and the devaluation of citizenship. It is quite different, however, from the situation of a person who has already settled in the relevant jurisdiction, meaning that he or she must share the burdens as well as the rights that attach to membership, given that the enabling goods of citizenship are always the result of a collective effort.
40. See *Martinez Sala* v. *Freistaat Bayern* (1998 European Court of Justice). This line of argument is also defended by various political theorists. See, for example, Carens 2008; Rubio-Marin 2000.
41. The conditions for the bestowing of a Member State's citizenship, and derivatively, Union citizenship, remains at the national level.
42. A related ascending-membership rationale is manifested in the European Council's "long-term resident directive," which holds that certain non-European Union citizens who have resided legally and permanently in the territory of one of the Member States for a period of at least five years, gain, after meeting each admitting polity's integration requirements, a level of security and mobility that nearly imitates that enjoyed by citizens. See Council Directive 2003/109/EC, OJ 2004, L16/44. For commentary, see Halleskov 2005.

43. See Garot 1998, 229–248. This insistence on a "real and substantive link" is not unique to the European Union. Even Canada, a country which supports a generous network of social welfare programs, nevertheless imposes minimal residency requirements (typically a three months' period) before citizens and residents can access primary services such as universal health care. Although the specifics of the residence requirement may vary, they generally rely on a two-fold structure in order to gain legitimacy: first, residence is treated as a factual element, thus all that is required is for the clock to tick. In our Canadian example, once a given period of three months has passed, the claimant becomes eligible for the benefit. Importantly, basic rights protections formally apply irrespective of one's legal status or length of stay in the country.
44. This was the legal basis for the children's and mother's claim in the case of *Martha Andazolo-Rivas,* discussed in Chapter 4. See sec. 240A(a) of INA, which provides that "The Attorney General may cancel removal in the case of an alien who is inadmissible or deportable from the United States if the alien (1) has been an alien lawfully admitted for permanent residence for not less than 5 years, (2) has resided in the United States continuously for 7 years after having been admitted in any status, and (3) has not been convicted of any aggravated felony." Those subject to a removal order based on an aggravated felony are not eligible for the waiver. A more lenient standard was in effect until 1996.
45. See *Matter of C-V-T* (1998 Board of Immigration Appeals); *Matter of Martin* (1978 Board of Immigration Appeals).
46. These factors were listed in proposed rules issued in 1979 by the INS that sought to identify the relevant consideration for the discretion in removal matters. See Federal Register, vol. 44, 1979, 36191. These guidelines were later withdrawn, because it "is impossible to list or foresee all of the adverse or favorable factors which may be present in any given set of circumstances." See Federal Register, vol. 46, 1981, 9119. For further discussion, see Roberts 1975. More recently, see Neuman 2006.
47. *Matter of Cervantes-Gonzalez* (1999 Board of Immigration Appeal).
48. See, for example, the case of *Maria Teresa Garcia De Nunez* (2007 Administrative Appeal Office).
49. Aleinikoff 1983, 244.
50. Bauböck 2005c.
51. Bosniak 2007.
52. On this latter point, see Bauböck 2005c.
53. Granted, the situation of a nominal heir (who has ancestral ties to the political community) is not fully analogous to that of the person who has recently emigrated to it, that is, the former appears to have, *prima facie,* a stronger claim to inclusion, both the newcomer and the returning nominal heir can be legitimately asked to establish a real and effective link to the polity before they can enjoy its full range of rights and obligations. The distinction is therefore a matter of degree, rather than that of principle.
54. The most extensive proposal in favor of making social membership a path to inclusion in the bounds of the relevant democratic polity is found in Ruth Rubio-Marin's elegant treatment of the subject in her book, *Immigration as a Democratic Challenge: Citizenship and Inclusion in Germany and the United States*

(Rubio-Marin 2000). Rubio-Marin argues that automatic incorporation into the polity is mandated on democratic grounds after the passage of a fixed number of years of residence on its territory, a conclusion that has been challenged by authors who are otherwise sympathetic to her project. See Bauböck 2005b, 766.

55. See Canada *Report of the Standing Committee on Citizenship and Immigration* 1994, 12.

56. In Canada and the United States, would-be citizens are required to fulfill a mandatory threshold residence period (at least three years in Canada, five in the United States), rubbing elbows with members of those societies before they can lay a claim to citizenship. These immigrants are not required to prove their economic self-sufficiency or involvement in the job market as a precondition for gaining full membership status. See Canada *Pourghasemi* (*Re*)(1993), 260. In most European countries in which naturalization is discretionary (rather than representing an as-of-right system) elements of self-sufficiency are often taken into account. See Brubaker 1989, Hansen and Weil 2001.

57. Note that membership here is not automatically bestowed on the person as in a *jus domicili* regime. Instead, as in naturalization, the stakeholder resident must apply for citizenship and comply with its requirements. In this, it differs from the analysis offered by territorial inclusion scholars in the context of regularizing unauthorized immigrants' status.

58. I here share much of Rainer Bauböck's vision of "stakeholder citizenship." See Bauböck 2005b, 766–767. In this and other works, Bauböck analyzes with great lucidity and persuasion the scope of rights that should be awarded to noncitizen residents (or stakeholders) and to nonresident citizens (sometimes referred to as external citizens). Unlike Bauböck, however, I am focusing on the basis for membership and entitlement, rather than its specific institutional implications, such as whether external citizens ought to maintain (or gain) political rights in the home country they left behind.

59. This raises vital issues of democratic legitimacy; addressed in Chapters 4 and 5.

60. See Shapiro 1999, 1–3; this principle has been criticized as either too strong (Bauböck 2005b) or too weak (Goodin 2007). This vision of increased participation option does not amount, however, to a full-fledged claim for acquisition of membership entitlement. NAFTA's environmental protocol, which allows citizens of Canada, Mexico, and the United States to bring forward environmental violation claims against any one of the participating countries, is a nice example of the participatory-oriented transnational *jus nexi* principle at work.

61. A related emphasis on connectedness informs the proposed Dream Act legislation, which would grant temporary legal status (on the road to full membership) to undocumented children when they graduate from high school or enroll in college, if they were 16 or younger upon entry to the country and have been residing in it for at least five years. As with any other legalization program, the applicant must be of good moral character and meet other admission criteria. In perfect compliance with the *jus nexi* rationale, this graduated membership process culminates by allowing those who have already become members an option to legally ascend to citizenship. For commentary on the proposed Development, Relief, and Education for Alien Minors (Dream) Act (Dream Act 2007), see Gonzales 2007; Sharron 2007.

62. Aleinikoff and Klusmeyer 2002, 15.
63. In 2005, Israel adopted a *jus nexi* policy in regard to children of labor migrants to the country, which granted secure legal status to them and their families. These children must meet a set of criteria, including living in the country for six consecutive years (this requirement was later reduced to four years and nine months). They must speak Hebrew and attend at least one year of elementary school in Israel. In a distinctively republican fashion, the Israeli application of the *jus nexi* principle grants these children permanent residence status with the option of gaining entitlement to citizenship if they are willing to take arms on behalf of the nation by enlisting in the military. For an illuminating analysis of this governmental policy, which applies to undocumented children of labor migrants but not to undocumented Palestinian children, see Kemp 2007.
64. Given the criminal charges against him, Sheinbein would not have been eligible to claim a right to return to Israel under its Law of Return.
65. For different modes of entry of unauthorized migrants living in the United States, see the statistics by Pew Hispanic Center (Pew Hispanic Center 2006).
66. See H.R. 4437 [109th], *The Border Protection, Anti-Terrorism, and Illegal Immigration Control Act of 2005*, approved by the House of Representatives in December 2005. Currently, unauthorized migrants are in violation of immigration law. The proposed Act, on the other hand, would have made unlawful residence in the United States a federal criminal offense. It further defined any relative, lawyer, employer, co-workers, clergyman, or friend who in some way interacted with an undocumented migrant as an alien smuggler—even if they acted innocently and in good faith, assisting the unauthorized migrant—thus detracting attention from the real problem of human smuggling.
67. J. Singer 2000, 45.
68. Dwyer and Menell 1998, 76.
69. Hovenkamp and Kurtz 2001, 55.
70. Dwyer and Menell 1998, 80.
71. With regard to registered land, see Land Regulation Act 2002, secs. 96, 97, 98, and schedule 6.
72. Holmes 1897, 477.
73. Singer 2000, 46 [emphasis added].
74. Singer 2000, 46.
75. Radin 1986, 748–749.
76. Motomura 2006b, 246.
77. See sec. 240A of INA. On the historical background, see Ngai 2004.
78. See U.S. *Adams* v. *Slattery* (1956).
79. This proposal was part of the *Comprehensive Immigration Reform Act of 2006*. Consideration of administrative convenience may eventually lead to a more simplified procedure whereby unlawful residents who have continuously resided and worked in the country or otherwise participated in its society and economy for a statutory predefined period of time (in this example, two or five years) become eligible to apply for a temporary visa, on the road to regularizing their legal status. This simplified procedure was the approach included in the *Comprehensive Immigration Reform Act of 2007*. Neither proposal became binding law.

References

Books and Journals

Abizadeh, Arash. 2002. "Does Liberal Democracy Presuppose a Cultural Nation? Four Arguments." *American Political Science Review* 96: 495–509.

———. 2008. "Democracy and Border Control: No Right to Unilaterally Control Your Own Borders." *Political Theory* 36(1): 37–65.

Abraham, David. 2007. "The Boundaries and Bonds of Citizenship: Recognition and Redistribution in the United States, Germany, and Israel." In *Migration in History: Human Migration in Comparative Perspective,* ed. Marc S. Rodriguez and Anthony Grafton. Rochester, New York: The University of Rochester Press.

Abrams, Kerry. 2007. "Immigration Law and the Regulation of Marriage." *Minnesota Law Review* 91(6): 1625–1709.

Ackerman, Bruce A. 1980. *Social Justice in the Liberal State.* New Haven: Yale University Press.

Ackerman, Bruce A., and Anne Alstott. 1999. *The Stakeholder Society.* New Haven: Yale University Press.

Adams, Richard H., and John Page. 2003. "International Migration, Remittances, and Poverty in Developing Countries." *World Bank Policy Research Working Paper Series,* WPS 3179.

Agamben, Giorgio. 1998. *Homo Sacer: Sovereign Power and Bare Life.* Trans. Daniel Heller-Roazen. Stanford, Calif.: Stanford University Press.

Aleinikoff, Thomas Alexander. 1983. "Aliens, Due Process and 'Community Ties': A Response to Martin." *University of Pittsburgh Law Review* 44(2): 237–260.

———. 1994. "The Tightening Circle of Membership." *Hastings Constitutional Law Quarterly* 22(4): 915–924.

Aleinikoff, Thomas Alexander, and Douglas Klusmeyer, eds. 2000. *From Migrants to Citizens: Membership in a Changing World.* Washington, DC: Brookings Institution Press.

———. 2001. *Citizenship Today: Global Perspectives and Practices.* Washington, D.C.: Carnegie Endowment for International Peace.

———. 2002. *Citizenship Policies for an Age of Migration.* Washington, D.C.: Carnegie Endowment for International Peace.

Aleinikoff, Thomas Alexander, David A. Martin, and Hiroshi Motomura. 2003. *Immigration and Citizenship: Process and Policy.* 5th ed. St. Paul, Minn.: Thomson West.

Alexander, Gregory S. 1997. *Commodity and Propriety: Competing Visions of Property in American Legal Thought, 1776–1970.* Chicago: University of Chicago Press.

Alstott, Anne L. 2007. "Equal Opportunity and Inheritance Taxation." *Harvard Law Review* 121(2): 469–542.

Anderson, Elizabeth S. 1999. "What Is the Point of Equality?" *Ethics* 109(2): 287–337.

Andreas, Peter. 1999. "The Escalation of U.S. Immigration Control in the Post-NAFTA Era." *Political Science Quarterly* 113(4): 591–615.

Andreas, Peter, and Thomas J. Biersteker, eds. 2003. *The Rebordering of North America: Integration and Exclusion in a New Security Context.* New York: Routledge.

Andreas, Peter, and Timothy Snyder, eds. 2000. *The Wall Around the West: State Borders and Immigration Controls in North America and Europe.* Lanham, Md: Rowman and Littlefield.

Archibugi, Daniele, David Held, and Martin Köhler, eds. 1998. *Re-Imagining Political Community: Studies in Cosmopolitan Democracy.* Stanford, Calif.: Stanford University Press.

Arendt, Hannah. 1968. *The Origins of Totalitarianism.* New York: Harvest Books.

Arneson, Richard J. 1989. "Equality and Equality of Opportunity for Welfare." *Philosophical Studies* 56(1): 77–93.

Ascher, Mark L. 1990. "Curtailing Inherited Wealth." *Michigan Law Review* 89 (1): 69–151.

Auerbach, Alan J., Laurence J. Kotlikoff, and Willi Leibfritz, eds. 1999. *Generational Accounting Around the World.* Chicago: University of Chicago Press.

Avi-Yonah, Reuven S. 2006. "The Three Goals of Taxation." *Tax Law Review* 60 (October 2006): 1–28.

Bader, Veit-Michael. 2000. "Practical Philosophy and First Admission." *SAIS Review* 20(1): 39–59.

———. 2005. "The Ethics of Migration." *Constellations* 12(3): 331–361.

Baker, C. Edwin. 1986. "Property and Its Relation to Constitutionally Protected Liberty." *University of Pennsylvania Law Review* 134(4): 741–816.

Barry, Brian. 1989. "Humanity and Justice in Global Perspective." In *Democracy, Power, and Justice: Essays in Political Theory.* Oxford: Clarendon Press.

Barry, Kim. 2006. "Home and Away: The Construction of Citizenship in an Emigration Context." *New York University Law Review* 81(1): 11–59.

Bauböck, Rainer. 1994. *Transnational Citizenship: Membership and Rights in International Migration.* Aldershot, Hants, England: Edward Elgar.

———. 1997. *Citizenship and National Identities in the European Union.* Harvard Jean Monnet working paper series no. 97/4. Cambridge, Mass.: Harvard Law School.

———. 2003a. "Reinventing Urban Citizenship." *Citizenship Studies* 7(2): 139–160.

———. 2003b. "Toward a Political Theory of Migrant Transnationalism." *International Migration Review* 37(3): 700–723.

———. 2004. "The Shape of a New Species: Citizenship and Territorial Borders in the EU Polity." In *The State of Europe: Transformations of Statehood from a European Perspective,* ed. Sonja Puntscher Riekmann, Monika Mokre and Michael Latzer. Frankfurt: Campus Verlag.

———. 2005a. "Citizenship Policies: International, State, Migrant, and Democratic Perspectives." *Global Migration Perspectives Papers* No. 19. Geneva: United Nations/Global Commission on International Immigration.

———. 2005b. "Expansive Citizenship—Voting beyond Territory and Membership." *Political Science and Politics* 38(4): 683–688.

———. 2005c. "Stakeholder Citizenship and Democratic Participation in Migration Contexts." In Conference: The Ties That Bind: Accommodating Complex Diversity in Canada and the European Union. Brussels (November 17–19, 2005).

Bauböck, Rainer, Eva Ersboll, Kees Groenendijk, and Harald Waldrauch, eds. 2006. *Acquisition and Loss of Nationality: Policies and Trends in 15 European States, Vol. 1: Comparative Analyses.* Amsterdam: Amsterdam University Press.

Becker, Gary S. 1992. "An Open Door for Immigration—The Auction." *The Wall Street Journal,* October 14, 1992, A14.

Beckert, Jens. 2007. *Inherited Wealth.* Trans. Thomas Dunlap. Princeton, N.J.: Princeton University Press.

Beiner, Ronald. 1992. *What's the Matter with Liberalism?* Berkeley: University of California Press.

———. 2003. *Liberalism, Nationalism, Citizenship: Essays on the Problem of Political Community.* Vancouver: UBC Press.

Benhabib, Seyla. 2004a. "The Law of Peoples, Distributive Justice and Migrations." *Fordham Law Review* 72(5): 1761–1787.

———. 2004b. *The Rights of Others: Aliens, Residents and Citizens.* Cambridge: Cambridge University Press.

Bentham, Jeremy. 1795. *Supply without Burthen or Escheat vice Taxation.* London: J. Debrett.

———. 1882. "Principles of the Civil Code." In *The Theory of Legislation.* 4th ed. Trans. Richard Hildreth. London: Trübner.

Bhabha, Jacqueline. 2004. "Demography and Rights: Women, Children, and Access to Asylum." *International Journal of Refugee Law* 16(2): 227–243.

"The Birthright Citizenship Amendment: A Threat to Equality." 1994. *Harvard Law Review* 107(5): 1026–1043.

Blackman, Jeffrey L. 1998. "State Succession and Statelessness: The Emerging Right to an Effective Nationality under International Law." *Michigan Journal of International Law* 19(4): 1141–1194.

Blackstone, William. [1766] 1979. *Commentaries on the Laws of England*. Vol. 2. Repr. Chicago: University of Chicago Press.

Blake, Michael. 2001. "Distributive Justice, State Coercion, and Autonomy." *Philosophy & Public Affairs* 30(3): 257–296.

———. 2005. "International Justice." *Stanford Encyclopedia of Philosophy*. www.plato.stanford.edu/entries/international-justice.

Blank, Yishai. 2007. "Spheres of Citizenship." *Theoretical Inquiries in Law* 8(2): 411–452.

Borjas, George J. 1999. *Heaven's Door: Immigration Policy and the American Economy*. Princeton, N.J.: Princeton University Press.

Borna, Shaheen, and James M. Stearns. 2002. "The Ethics and Efficacy of Selling National Citizenship." *Journal of Business Ethics* 37(2): 193–207.

Bosniak, Linda. 2000. "Citizenship Denationalized." *Indiana Journal of Global Legal Studies* 7(2): 447–509.

———. 2006. *The Citizen and the Alien: Dilemmas of Contemporary Membership*. Princeton, N.J.: Princeton University Press.

———. 2007. "Being Here: Ethical Territoriality and the Rights of Immigrants." *Theoretical Inquiries in Law* 8(2): 389–410.

Bowman, Craig A., and Blake M. Cornish. 1992. "A More Perfect Union: A Legal and Social Analysis of Domestic Partnership Ordinances." *Columbia Law Review* 92(6): 1164–1211.

Bredbenner, Candice Lewis. 1998. *A Nationality of Her Own: Women, Marriage and the Law of Citizenship*. Berkeley: University of California Press.

Brittain, John A. 1977. *The Inheritance of Economic Status*. Washington D.C.: Brookings Institution.

Bromley, Daniel W. 1991. *Environment and Economy: Property Rights and Public Policy*. Oxford: Blackwell.

Broude, Tomer. 2007. "The WTO/GATS Mode 4, International Labor Migration Regimes and Global Justice." International Law Forum of the Hebrew University of Jerusalem Law Faculty, Research Paper No. 7–07 (May 2007).

Brouwer, Andrew, and Judith Kumin. 2003. "Interception and Asylum: When Migration Control and Human Rights Collide." *Refuge* 21(4): 6–24.

Brubaker, W. Rogers, ed. 1989. *Immigration and the Politics of Citizenship in Europe and North America*. Lanham, Md.: University Press of America.

———. 1992. *Citizenship and Nationhood in France and Germany*. Cambridge, Mass: Harvard University Press.

———. 2001. "The Return of Assimilation? Changing Perspectives on Immigration and Its Sequels in France, Germany, and the United States." *Ethnic and Racial Studies* 24(4): 531–548.

Brysk, Alison, and Gershon Shafir, eds. 2004. *People Out of Place: Globalization, Human Rights, and the Citizenship Gap*. New York: Routledge.

Buchanan, Allen. 1991. *Secession: The Morality of Political Divorce from Fort Sumter to Lithuania to Quebec*. Boulder, Colo.: Westview.

Buhler, Sarah. 2002. "Babies as Bargaining Chips? In Defense of Birthright Citizenship in Canada." *Journal of Law and Social Policy* 17: 87–114.

Calabresi, Guido, and A. Douglas Melamed. 1972. "Property Rules, Liability Rules, and Inalienability: One View of the Cathedral." *Harvard Law Review* 85(6): 1089–1128.

Calvo, Janet M. 1991. "Spouse-Based Immigration Laws: The Legacies of Coverture." *San Diego Law Review* 28(3): 593–644.

Caney, Simon. 2005. *Justice Beyond Borders: A Global Political Theory.* Oxford: Oxford University Press.

Carens, Joseph H. 1987a. "Aliens and Citizens: The Case for Open Borders." *The Review of Politics* 49(2): 251–273.

———. 1987b. "Who Belongs? Theoretical and Legal Questions about Birthright Citizenship in the United States." *University of Toronto Law Journal* 37(4): 413–444.

———. 1992. "Migration and Morality: A Liberal Egalitarian Perspective." In *Free Movement: Ethical Issues in the Transnational Migration of People and of Money,* ed. Brian Barry and Robert E. Goodin, 25–47. University Park, Pa.: Pennsylvania State University Press.

———. 2005a. "On Belonging: What We Owe People Who Stay." *Boston Review* 30 (Summer 2005).

———. 2008. "Immigration, Democracy, and Citizenship," in *Of States, Rights, and Social Closure: Governing Migration and Citizenship,* ed. Saime Ozcurumez and Oliver Schmidte, 17–36. New York: Palgrave Macmillian.

Carpenter, Kristen A., Sonia Katyal, and Angela Riley. 2009. "In Defense of Property." *Yale Law Journal* 118(7).

Cassise, Christopher J. 1996. "The European Union v. the United States under the NAFTA: A Comparative Analysis of the Free Movement of Persons within the Regions." *Syracuse Law Review* 46(4): 1343–1368.

Castles, Stephen, and Alastair Davidson. 2000. *Citizenship and Migration: Globalization and the Politics of Belonging.* New York: Routledge.

Chang, Howard F. 1997. "Liberalized Immigration as Free Trade: Economic Welfare and the Optimal Immigration Policy." *University of Pennsylvania Law Review* 145(5): 1147–1244.

———. 1998. "Migration as International Trade: The Economic Gains from the Liberalized Movement of Labor." *UCLA Journal of International Law and Foreign Affairs* 3(2): 371–414.

Chester, Ronald. 1982. *Inheritance, Wealth, and Society.* Bloomington: Indiana University Press.

Chiswick, Barry R. 1982. "The Impact of Immigration on the Level and Distribution of Economic Well-Being." In *The Gateway: U.S. Immigration Issues and Policies,* ed. Barry R. Chiswick, 289–313. Washington, D.C.: American Enterprise Institute for Public Policy Research.

Cholewinski, Ryszard, Richard Perruchoud, and Euan MacDonald, eds. 2007. *International Migration Law: Developing Paradigms and Key Challenges.* The Hague: T.M.C. Asser Press.

Chuang, Janie. 1998. "Redefining the Debate over Trafficking in Women: Definitions, Paradigms, and Contexts." *Harvard Human Rights Journal* 11: 65–107.

Ciriacy-Wantrop, S. V. and Richard C. Bishop. 1975. "'Common Property' as a Concept in Natural Resources Policy." *Natural Resources Journal* 15(4): 713–727.

Citizenship and Immigration Canada (CIC). 2006. Amendment to the *Citizenship Act:* Adoption. Backgrounder, 15 May 2006.

Cohen, Jerry. 1989. "On the Currency of Egalitarian Justice." *Ethics* 99(4): 906–944.

Cohen, Joshua. 2007. "Forward." In *Making Aid Work*. Abhijit Vinayak Banerjee. Cambridge, Mass: MIT Press.

Cole, Daniel H. 2002. *Pollution and Property: Comparing Ownership Institutions for Environmental Protection.* Cambridge: Cambridge University Press.

Cole, Phillip. 2000. *Philosophies of Exclusion: Liberal Political Theory and Immigration.* Edinburgh: Edinburgh University Press.

Collard, David. 2001. "The Generational Bargain." *International Journal of Social Welfare* 10(1): 54–65.

Collins et. al. 2008. *Dicey, Morris and Collins on the Conflict of Laws.* 14th ed. London: Sweet and Maxwell.

Commission for Environmental Cooperation (CEC). "Who We Are." www.cec.org/home/index.cfm?varlan=english

Connolly, William E. 1991. "Democracy and Territoriality." *Millennium: Journal of International Studies* 20(3): 463–484.

Cornelius, Wayne A., Philip L. Martin, and James F. Hollifield, eds. 1994. *Controlling Immigration: A Global Perspective.* Stanford, Calif.: Stanford University Press.

Cott, Nancy F. 1998. "Marriage and Women's Citizenship in the United States, 1830–1934." *American Historical Review* 103(5): 1440–1474.

———. 2002. *Public Vows: A History of Marriage and the Nation.* Cambridge, Mass.: Harvard University Press.

Council of Europe. 1998. *European Convention on Nationality and Explanatory Report.* Strasburg: Council of Europe Publishing.

Dagan, Hanoch. 2003. "The Craft of Property." *California Law Review* 91(6): 1517–1571.

Dagan, Hanoch, and Michael Heller. 2001. "The Liberal Commons." *Yale Law Journal* 110(4): 549–624.

———. 2005. "Conflicts in Property." *Theoretical Inquires in Law* 6(1): 37–58.

Dahl, Robert Alan. 1989. *Democracy and Its Critics.* New Haven: Yale University Press.

Dauvergne, Catherine. 2007. "Citizenship with a Vengeance." *Theoretical Inquiries in Law* 8(2): 489–507.

———. 2008. *Making People Illegal: What Globalization Means for Migration and Law.* Cambridge: Cambridge University Press.

De Búrca, Gráinne, and J. H. H. Weiler. 2001. *The European Court of Justice.* Oxford: Oxford University Press.

Demsetz, Harold. 1967. "Toward a Theory of Property Rights." *The American Economic Review* 57(2): 347–359.

Dickenson, Donna. 2007. *Property in the Body: Feminist Perspectives.* Cambridge: Cambridge University Press.

Dobrowsky, Alexandra. 2007. "(In)security and Citizenship: Security, Immigration and Shrinking Citizenship Regimes." *Theoretical Inquires in Law* 8(2): 629–661.

Domenech, Antoni, and Daniel Raventos. 2007. "Property and Republican Freedom: An Institutional Approach to Basic Income." *Basic Income Studies* 2(2).

Dower, Nigel. 2000. "The Idea of Global Citizenship—A Sympathetic Assessment." *Global Society* 14(4): 553–567.

Dower, Nigel, and John Williams, eds. 2002. *Global Citizenship: A Critical Introduction.* New York: Routledge.

Downes, Daniel M., and Richard Janda. 1998. "Virtual Citizenship." *Canadian Journal of Law and Society* 13(2): 27–61.

Dryzek, John S. 1999. "Transnational Democracy." *Journal of Political Philosophy* 7: 30–51.

Duff, David. 1993. "Taxing Inherited Wealth: A Philosophical Account." *Canadian Journal of Law and Jurisprudence* 6(1): 3–64.

Dummett, Ann, and Andrew Nicol. 1990. *Subjects, Citizens, Aliens and Others: Nationality and Immigration Law.* London: Weidenfeld and Nicolson.

Duncan, Howard. 2006. "Diasporas and Transnationalism." *Metropolis World Bulletin* 6 (September 2006). Ottawa: Metropolis Canada.

Dworkin, Ronald, 1981a. "What Is Equality? Part 1: Equality of Welfare." *Philosophy and Public Affairs* 10(3): 185–246.

———. 1981b. "What Is Equality? Part 2: Equality of Resources." *Philosophy and Public Affairs* 10(4): 283–345.

Dwyer, John P., and Peter S. Menell. 1998. *Property Law and Policy: A Comparative Institutional Framework.* Westbury, N.Y.: Foundation Press.

The Earth Institute at Columbia University. 2005. *Facts on International Aid* (part of "facts on poverty" in *The End of Poverty: Economics Possibilities for Our Time,* Jeffrey D. Sachs). New York: Penguin Group. www.earth.columbia.edu/pages/endofpoverty/oda.

The Economist. 2006. "Inequality in America," Special Report. June 17, 2006.

Eisgruber, Christopher L. 1997. "Birthright Citizenship and the Constitution." *New York University Law Review* 72(1): 54–96.

Ellickson, Robert. 1993. "Property in Land." *Yale Law Journal* 102(6): 1315–1400.

Epstein, Richard A. 1985. "Why Restrain Alienation?" *Columbia Law Review* 85 (5): 970–990.

Erreygers, Guido. 1997. "Inheritance in the History of Economic Thought." In *Is Inheritance Legitimate? Ethical and Economic Aspects of Wealth Transfers,* ed. Guido Erreygers and Toon Vandeveldge, 16–53. New York: Springer.

Erreygers, Guido, and Giovanni Di Bartolomeo. 2007. "The Debates on Eugenio Rignano's Inheritance Tax Proposals." *History of Political Economy* 39(4): 605–638.

Faist, Thomas. 2000. *The Volume and Dynamic of International Migration and Transnational Social Spaces.* Oxford: Clarendon Press.

Falk, Richard. 2002. "An Emergent Matrix of Citizenship: Complex, Uneven, and Fluid." In *Global Citizenship: A Critical Introduction,* ed. Nigel Dower and John Williams. 15–29. New York: Routledge.

Flynn, Don. 2005. "New Borders, New Management: The Dilemmas of Modern Immigration Policies." *Ethnic and Racial Studies* 28(3): 463–490.

Flynn, Stephen E. 2003. "The False Conundrum: Continental Integration Versus Homeland Security." In *The Rebordering of North America,* ed. Peter Andreas and Thomas J. Biersteker. 110–127. New York: Routledge.

Ford, Richard T. 2001. "City-States and Citizenship." In *Citizenship Today: Global Perspectives and Practices,* ed. T. Alexander Aleinikoff and Douglas Klusmeyer, 209–233. Washington, D.C.: Carnegie Endowment for International Peace.

Franck, Thomas M. 1982. "Political Functionalism and Philosophical Imperatives in the Fight for a New Economic Order." In *NOMOS: Ethics, Economics, and the Law,* ed. J. Roland Pennock and John W. Chapman, 268–274. New York: New York University Press.

Francoeur, Adam. 2007. "The Enemy Within: Constructions of U.S. Immigration Law and Policy and the Homoterrorist Threat." *Stanford Journal of Civil Rights and Civil Liberties* 3(2): 345–376.

Friedman, Milton. 1962. *Capitalism and Freedom.* Chicago: University of Chicago Press.

Fudge, Judy. 2005. "After Industrial Citizenship: Market Citizenship or Citizenship at Work?" *Relations Industrielles/Industrial Relations* 60(4): 631–656.

Galloway, Donald. 1999. "The Dilemmas of Canadian Citizenship Law." *Georgetown Immigration Law Journal* 13(2): 201–231.

Galston, William A. 1995. "Two Concepts of Liberalism." *Ethics* 105(3): 516–534.

Gans, Chaim. 2003. *The Limits of Nationalism.* Cambridge: Cambridge University Press.

Garot, Marie-José. 1998. "A New Basis for European Citizenship: Residence?" In *European Citizenship: An Institutional Challenge,* ed. Massimo La Torre, 229–248. The Hague: Kluwer Law International.

Ghosh, Bimal. 2000. "Toward a New International Regime for Orderly Movements of People." In *Managing Migration: Time for a New International Regime?* ed. Bimal Ghosh, 6–26. Oxford: Oxford University Press.

Giannakouris, Konstantinos. 2008. "Ageing Characterises the Demographic Perspectives of the European Societies." *Eurostat: Statistics in Focus* 72/2008. Luxembourg: European Communities.

Gibney, Matthew J. 2004. *The Ethics of Politics and Asylum: Liberal Democracy and the Response to Refuges.* Cambridge: Cambridge University Press.

Global Commission on International Migration (GCIM). 2005. *Migration in an Interconnected World: New Directions for Action.* Geneva: United Nations/ GCIM.

Gonzales, Roberto G. 2007. "Wasted Talent and Broken Dreams: The Lost Potential of Undocumented Students." *Immigration Policy in Focus,* 5/13. Washington D.C.: Immigration Policy Center.

Goodin, Robert E. 1992. "If People Were Money . . ." In *Free Movement: Ethical Issues in the Transnational Migration of People and Money,* ed. Brian Barry and Robert E. Goodin, 3–22. University Park, Pa.: Pennsylvania State University Press.

———. 1999. "Treating Likes Alike, Intergenerationally and Internationally." *Policy Sciences* 32(2): 189–206.

———. 2007. "Enfranchising All Affected Interests, and Its Alternatives." *Philosophy and Public Affairs* 35(1): 40–68.

Goodwin-Gill, Guy S., and Jane McAdam. 2007. *The Refugee in International Law.* 3rd ed. Oxford: Oxford University Press.

Gosepath, Stefan. 2001. "The Global Scope of Justice." In *Global Justice,* ed. Thomas W. Pogge, 145–168. Oxford: Blackwell.

Gray, Thomas C. 1980. "The Disintegration of Property." In *Property*, ed. J. Roland Pennock and John W. Chapman, 69–85. New York: New York University Press.

Greenfeld, Liah. 1992. *Nationalism: Five Roads to Modernity.* Cambridge, Mass: Harvard University Press.

Guiraudon, Virginie, and Galia Lahav. 2000. "A Reappraisal of the State Sovereignty Debate: The Case of Migration Control." *Comparative Political Studies* 33 (2): 163–195.

Hacker-Cordon, Casiano A. W. 2002. *Global Injustice and Human Malfare.* Unpublished Ph.D. Dissertation. New Haven: Yale University.

Hailbronner, Kay. 1989. "Citizenship and Nationhood in Germany." In *Immigration and the Politics of Citizenship in Europe and North America*, ed. William Rogers Brubaker, 67–79. Lanham, Md.: University Press of America.

Halleskov, Louise. 2005. "The Long-Term Residents Directive: A Fulfillment of the Tampere Objective of Near-Equality?" *European Journal of Migration and Law* 7(2): 181–202.

Hamilton, Bob, and John Whalley. 1984. "Efficiency and Distributional Implications of Global Restrictions on Labor Mobility." *Journal of Development Economics* 14(1): 61–75.

Hammar, Tomas. 1990. *Democracy and the Nation State: Aliens, Denizens and Citizens in a World of International Migration.* Aldershot, U.K.: Avebury.

Hansen, Randall. 2002. "Globalization, Embedded Realism, and Path Dependence: The Other Immigrants to Europe." *Comparative Political Studies* 35(3): 259–283.

Hansen, Randall, and Patrick Weil, eds. 2001. *Towards a European Nationality: Citizenship, Immigration, and Nationality Law in the EU.* New York: Palgrave.

Harris, J. W. 1995. "Private and Non-Private Property: What Is the Difference?" *The Law Quarterly* 111: 421–444.

———. 1996. *Property and Justice.* Oxford: Clarendon Press.

Harrison, Simon. 1999. "Identity as a Scarce Resource." *Social Anthropology* 7(3): 239–251.

Hart, John F. 2001. "A Less Proportion of Idle Proprietors: Madison, Property Rights, and the Abolition of Fee Tail." *Washington & Lee Law Review* 58(1): 167–194.

Haslett, J. S. 1986. "Is Inheritance Justified?" *Philosophy and Public Affairs* 15(2): 122–155.

Hassner, Pierre. 1998. "Refugees: A Special Case for Cosmopolitan Citizenship." In *Re-imagining Political Community: Studies in Cosmopolitan Democracy*, ed. Daniele Archibugi, David Held and Martin Köhler, 273–286. Stanford, Calif.: Stanford University Press.

Hay, Peter, Russell J. Weintraub, and Patrick J. Borchers. 2004. *Conflict of Laws: Cases and Materials*, 12th ed. New York: Foundation Press.

Hayduk, Ron. 2006. *Democracy for All: Restoring Immigrant Voting Rights in the United States.* New York: Routledge.

Heather, Derek B. 2004. *A Brief History of Citizenship.* New York: New York University Press.

Hegel, Georg Wilhelm Friedrich. [1821] 1991. *Elements of the Philosophy of Right.* Ed. Allen W. Wood. Trans. H. B. Nisbit. Cambridge: Cambridge University Press.

Held, David. 1991. "Between State and Civil Society: Citizenship." In *Citizenship,* ed. Geoff Andrews, 19–25. London: Lawrence & Wishart.

———. 1995. *Democracy and the Global Order: From the Modern State to Cosmopolitan Governance.* Stanford, Calif.: Stanford University Press.

Held, David, and Mathis Koenig-Archibugi, eds. 2003. *Taming Globalization: Frontiers of Governance.* Cambridge: Polity Press.

Held, David, Anthony McGrew, David Goldblatt, and Jonathan Perraton. 1999. *Global Transformations: Politics, Economics and Culture.* Stanford, Calif.: Stanford University Press.

Helfer, Laurence R. 1999. "Forum Shopping for Human Rights." *University of Pennsylvania Law Review* 148(2): 285–400.

Heller, Michael A. 1999. "The Boundaries of Private Property." *Yale Law Journal* 108(6): 1163–1223.

Henderson, Hubert Douglas. 1926. *Inheritance and Inequality: A Practical Proposal.* London: The Daily News.

Hening, William Waller, ed. 1819–1823. The Statutes at Large; Being a Collection of All the Laws of Virginia, from the First Session of the Legislature in the Year 1619. vol. 9. New York: Printed for the editor.

Hirschman, Albert O. 1970. *Exit, Voice, and Loyalty: Responses to Decline in Firms, Organizations, and States.* Cambridge, Mass.: Harvard University Press.

Hirst, Paul, and Grahame Thompson. 1999. *Globalization in Question: The International Economy and the Possibilities of Governance,* 2nd ed. Cambridge: Polity Press.

Hohfeld, Wesley Newcomb. 1913. "Some Fundamental Legal Conceptions as Applied in Judicial Reasoning." *Yale Law Journal* 23(1): 16–59.

———. 1917. "Fundamental Legal Conceptions as Applied in Judicial Reasoning." *Yale Law Journal* 26(8): 710–770.

Holdsworth, William Searle. 1982. *A History of English Law.* vol. 9. London: Sweet and Maxwell.

Holmes, Oliver Wendell, Jr. 1897. "The Path of Law." *Harvard Law Review* 10(8): 457–479.

Holtz, Jeff. 2007. "This Summer's Surprise Hit: An Elm City ID." *The New York Times.* September 16, 2007.

Home Office. 1980; *British Nationality Law: Outline of Proposed Legislation* (White Paper). London: Her Majesty's Stationery Office, Cmnd. 7987.

Honoré, A. M. 1961. "Owenership." In *Oxford Essays in Jurisprudence, A Collaborative Work,* ed. Anthony Gordon Guest, 107–147. Oxford: Oxford University Press.

Houston, Michael Robert W. 2000. "Birthright Citizenship in the United Kingdom and the United States: A Comparative Analysis of the Common Law Basis for Granting Citizenship to Children Born of Illegal Immigrants." *Vanderbilt Journal of Transnational Law* 33(3): 693–738.

Hovenkamp, Herbert, and Sheldon F. Kurtz. 2001. *The Law of Property: An Introductory Survey,* 5th ed. St. Paul, Minn.: West Group.

Huntington, Samuel P. 2004. *Who Are We? The Challenges to America's National Identity.* New York: Simon & Schuster.

Hutchins, Kimberly, and Roland Dannreuther, eds. 1999. *Cosmopolitan Citizenship.* New York: St. Martin's Press.

Igantieff, Michael. 1995. *Blood and Belonging: Journeys into the New Nationalism.* New York: Farrar, Straus and Giroux.

International Law Association/Committee on Feminism and International Law, 2000. *Final Report on Women's Equality and Nationality in International Law.* London: International Law Association.

International Organization for Migration. 2005. *World Migration 2005: Costs and Benefits of International Migration,* World Migration Report Series 3. Geneva: International Organization for Migration.

Isbister, John. 2001. *Capitalism and Justice: Envisioning Social and Economic Fairness.* Bloomfield, Conn.: Kumarian Press.

Isin, Engin F., and Bryan S. Turner. 2007. "Investigating Citizenship: An Agenda for Citizenship Studies." In *Citizenship Between Past and Present,* ed. Engin F. Isin, Peter Nyers, and Bryan S. Turner. New York: Routledge.

Itzigshon, Jose. 2000. "Immigration and the Boundaries of Citizenship: The Institution of Immigrants' Political Transnationalism." *International Migration Review* 34(4): 1126–1154.

Jacobson, David. 1996. *Rights Across Borders: Immigration and the Decline of Citizenship.* Baltimore: John Hopkins University.

Jefferson, Thomas. 1892. "Autobiography 1743–1790." In *The Writings of Thomas Jefferson,* ed. Paul Leicester Ford. New York: G.P. Putnam's Sons.

———. 1984. "Summary View of the Rights of British America." In *Writings/ Thomas Jefferson.* New York: Viking Press.

Joppke, Christian. 2001. "The Legal-Domestic Sources of Immigrant Rights: The United States, Germany and European Union." *Comparative Political Studies* 34(4): 339–366.

———. 2005. *Selecting by Origin: Ethnic Migration in the Liberal State.* Cambridge, Mass.: Harvard University Press.

———. 2006. "Citizenship between De- and Re-Ethnicization." In *Migration, Citizenship, Ethnos,* ed. Y. Michal Bodemann and Gokce Yurdakul, 63–91. New York: Palgrave Macmillan.

———. 2007. "Transformation of Citizenship: Status, Rights, Identity." *Citizenship Studies* 11(1): 37–48.

———. 2008. "Comparative Citizenship: A Restrictive Turn in Europe?" *Journal of Law and Ethics of Human Rights* 2(1): 128–169.

Jordan, Bill, and Frank Düvell. 2002. *Irregular Migration: The Dilemmas of Transnational Mobility.* Cheltenham, U.K.: Edward Elgar.

———. 2003. *Migration: The Boundaries of Equality and Justice.* Cambridge: Polity Press.

Kant, Immanuel. [1797] 1991. *Kant: Political Writings.* Ed. Hans Reiss. Trans. H. B. Nisbet. Cambridge: Cambridge University Press.

———. 1996. *The Metaphysics of Morals.* Trans. and ed. Mary Gregor. Cambridge: Cambridge University Press.

Karp, James P. 1993. "A Private Property Duty to Stewardship: Changing Our Land Ethics." *Environmental Law* 23(3): 735–762.

Karst, Kenneth L. 1989. *Belonging to America: Equal Citizenship and the Constitution*. New Haven: Yale University Press.

Kashiwazaki, Chickako. 2000. "Citizenship in Japan: Legal Practice and Contemporary Development." In *From Migrants to Citizens: Membership in a Changing World,* ed. T. Alexander Aleinikoff and Douglas Klusmeyer, 434–471. Washington, D.C.: Brookings Institution Press.

Kemp, Adriana. 2007. "Managing Migration, Reprioritizing National Citizenship: Undocumented Migrant Workers' Children and Policy Reforms in Israel." *Theoretical Inquiries in Law* 8(2): 663–691.

Kerber, Linda K. 2006. "Toward a History of Statelessness in America." In *Legal Borderlands: Law and the Construction of American Borders,* ed. Mary L. Dudziak and Leti Volpp, 135–157. Baltimore: John Hopkins University Press.

Kettner, James H. 1978. *The Development of American Citizenship, 1608–1870*. Chapel Hill: University of North Carolina Press.

Kiesling, Herbert. 1992. *Taxation and Public Goods: A Welfare-Economic Critique of Tax Policy Analysis*. Ann Arbor: University of Michigan Press.

Kingsbury, Benedict. 1998. "Sovereignty and Inequality." *European Journal of International Law* 9(4): 599–625.

Knight, Stephen M. 2000. "Defining Due Process Down: Expedited Removal in the United States." *Refuge* 19(4): 41–47.

Knop, Karen. 2001. "Relational Nationality: On Gender and Nationality in International Law." In *Citizenship Today: Global Perspectives and Practices,* ed. T. Alexander Aleinikoff and Douglas Klusmeyer, 89–124. Washington D.C.: Brookings Institution Press.

Koser, Khalid. 2007. *International Migration: A Very Short Introduction*. Oxford: Oxford University Press.

Kotlikoff, Laurence J., and Scott Burns. 2004. *The Coming Generational Storm: What You Need to Know about America's Economic Future*. Cambridge, Mass.: MIT Press.

Krugman, Paul, and Maurcie Obstfield. 1991. *International Economics*. New York: Harper and Collins.

Kukathas, Chandran. 2003. "Responsibility for Past Injustice: How to Shift the Burden." *Politics, Philosophy, and Economics* 2(2): 165–190.

Kymlicka, Will. 1989. *Liberalism, Community, and Culture*. Oxford: Clarendon Press.

———. 1995. *Multicultural Citizenship: A Liberal Theory of Minority Rights*. Oxford: Clarendon Press.

———. 1999. "Citizenship in an Era of Globalization: Commentary on Held." In *Democracy's Edges,* ed. Ian Shapiro and Casiano Hacker-Cordón, 112–126. Cambridge: Cambridge University Press.

———. 2001. "Territorial Boundaries: A Liberal Egalitarian Perspective." In *Boundaries and Justice: Diverse Ethical Perspectives,* ed. David Miller and Sohail H. Hashimi, 249–275. Princeton, N.J.: Princeton University Press.

Lahiri, Jhumpa. 2004. *The Namesake*. Boston: Mariner Books.

Landes, David. 1999. *The Wealth and Poverty of Nations: Why Some Are So Rich and Some So Poor.* New York: W. W. Norton.

Laslett, Peter, and James S. Fishkin, eds. 1992. *Justice Between Generations: Philosophy, Politics, and Society.* Oxford: Blackwell.

Levinson, Sanford. 1986. "Constituting Communities through Words that Bind: Reflections on Loyalty Oaths." *Michigan Law Review* 84(7): 1440–1470.

Levy, Michael. 1983. "Liberal Equality and Inherited Wealth." *Political Theory* 11 (4): 545–564.

Lindh, Thomas, Bo Malmberg, and Joakim Palme. 2005. "Generations at War or Sustainable Social Policy in Aging Societies?" *Journal of Political Philosophy* 13(4): 470–489.

Locke, John. [1689] 1988. *Two Treatises of Government,* 3rd ed. Ed. Peter Laslett. Cambridge: Cambridge University Press.

Lopez, Gerald. 1981. "Undocumented Mexican Migration: In Search of a Just Immigration Law and Policy." *UCLA Law Review* 28: 615–714.

Lopez, Ian F. Haney. 1996. *White by Law: The Legal Construction of Race.* New York: New York University Press.

Lopez-Guerra, Claudio. 2005. "Should Expatriates Vote?" *Journal of Political Philosophy* 13(2): 216–334.

Macedo, Stephen. 1995. "Liberal Civic Education and Religious Fundamentalism: The Case of God v. John Rawls?" *Ethics* 105(3): 468–496.

Macklin, Audrey. 2005. "Disappearing Refugees: Reflections on the Canada-U.S. Safe Third Country Agreement." *Columbia Human Rights Law Review* 36 (2): 365–426.

———. 2007. "Who Is the Citizen's Other: Considering the Heft of Citizenship." *Theoretical Inquiries in Law* 8(2): 333–366.

MacIntyre, Alasdair C. 1984. *After Virtue,* 2nd ed. Notre Dame, Ind.: University of Notre Dame Press.

Macpherson, Crawford B. 1962. *The Political Theory of Possessive Individualism: Hobbes to Locke.* Oxford: Clarendon Press.

———. 1977. "Human Rights as Property Rights." *Dissent* 24 (Winter 1977): 72–77.

———. 1978. "The Meaning of Property." In *Property, Mainstream and Critical Positions,* ed. Crawford B. Macpherson. Toronto: University of Toronto Press.

Madison, James. 1865. "Notes on Suffrage." In *Letters and Other Writings of James Madison,* vol. 4. Philadelphia: J. B. Lippincott & Co.

Maine, Henry Summer. [1861] 1986. *Ancient Law: Its Connection with the Early History of Society, and Its Relation to Modern Ideas.* Repr. Tucson: University of Arizona Press.

Markell, David L., and John H. Knox, eds. 2003. *Greening NAFTA: The North American Commission for Environmental Cooperation.* Stanford, Calif.: Stanford Law and Politics.

Marshall, T. H. 1950. *Citizenship and Social Class and Other Essays.* Cambridge: Cambridge University Press.

Martin, Philip. 2004. "Migration." In *Global Crises, Global Solutions,* ed. Bjørn Lomborg, 443–477. Cambridge: Cambridge University Press.

Marx, Anthony W. 2003. *Faith in Nation: Exclusionary Origins of Nationalism.* Oxford: Oxford University Press.

Marx, Karl and Friedrich Engels. [1848] 2000. "The Communist Manifesto." In *Karl Marx, Selected Writings,* 2nd ed. Ed. David McLellan. Oxford: Oxford University Press.

Massey, Douglas S. et al. 2005. *Worlds in Motion: Understanding International Migration at the End of the Millennium.* Oxford: Clarendon Press.

Mattoo, Aaditya, and Antonia Carzaniga, eds. 2003. *Moving People to Deliver Services.* Washington, D.C.: World Bank/Oxford University Press.

Mayhew, Robert. 1993. "Aristotle on Property." *The Review of Metaphysics* 46 803–831.

McCaffery, Edward. 2001. "Must We Have the Right to Waste?" In *New Essays in the Legal and Political Theory of Property,* ed. Steve Munzer, 76–105. Cambridge: Cambridge University Press.

McClintock, Anne. 1995. *Imperial Leather: Race, Gender, and Sexuality in Colonial Contest.* New York: Routledge.

McKenzie, David J. 2005. "Paper Walls Are Easier to Tear Down: Passport Costs and Legal Barriers to Emigration." *World Bank Policy Research Working Paper Series,* WPS 3783.

Merrill, Thomas W., and Henry E. Smith. 2000. "Optimal Standardization in the Law of Property: The *Numerus Clasus* Principle." *Yale Law Journal* 110(1): 1–70.

Michelman, Frank I. 1981. "Property as a Constitutional Right." *Washington & Lee Law Review* 38(4): 1097–1114.

———. 1982. "Ethics, Economics, and the Law of Property." In *NOMOS: Ethics, Economics, and the Law,* ed. J. Roland Pennock and John W. Chapman, 3–40. New York: New York University Press.

Milanovic, Branko. 2007. "Globalization and Inequality." In *Global Inequality: Patterns and Explanations,* ed. David Held and Ayse Kaya, 26–49. Cambridge: Polity Press.

Mill, John Stuart. [1848] 1977. *Principles of Political Economy: with Some of Their Applications to Social Philosophy.* vol. 2. Textual ed. J. M. Robson. Repr. Toronto: University of Toronto Press.

Miller, David. 1988. "The Ethical Significance of Nationality." *Ethics* 98(4): 647–662.

———. 1989. *Market, State, and Community: Theoretical Foundations of Market Socialism.* Oxford: Clarendon Press.

———. 1995a. "Citizenship and Pluralism." *Political Studies* 43: 432–450.

———. 1995b. *On Nationality.* Oxford: Clarendon Press.

———. 1998. "The Left, the Nation-State, and European Citizenship." *Dissent* 45(3): 47–51.

———. 2000. *Citizenship and National Identity.* Cambridge: Polity Press.

———. 2007. *National Responsibility and Global Justice.* Oxford: Oxford University Press.

Miller, Richard. 1998. "Cosmopolitan Respect and Patriotic Concern." *Philosophy & Public Affairs* 27(3): 202–224.

Miller, Teresa A. 2003. "Citizenship and Severity: Recent Immigration Reforms and the New Penology." *Georgetown Immigration Law Journal* 17(4): 611–666.

Minow, Martha, and Mary Lyndon Shanley. 1997. "Revisioning the Family: Relational Rights and Responsibilities." In *Reconstructing Political Theory: Feminist Perspectives,* ed. Mary Lyndon Shanley and Uma Narayan, 84–108. University Park, Penn.: Pennsylvania State University Press.

Moellendorf, Darrel. 2002. *Cosmopolitan Justice.* Boulder, Colo.: Westview Press.

Moore, Margaret. 2001. "Normative Justifications for Liberal Nationalism: Justice, Democracy, and National Identity." *Nations and Nationalism* 7(1): 1–20.

Morris, Richard B. 1927. "Primogeniture and Entailed Estates in America." *Columbia Law Review* 27(1): 24–51.

Mostov, Julie. 2008. *Soft Borders: Rethinking Sovereignty and Democracy.* New York: Palgrave Macmillan.

Motomura, Hiroshi. 1998. "Alienage Classifications in a Nation of Immigrants: Three Models of Permanent Residence." In *Immigration and Citizenship in the Twenty-first Century,* ed. Noah M. J. Pickus, 191–220. Lanham, Md.: Rowman & Littlefield.

———. 2006a. *Americans in Waiting: The Lost Story of Immigration and Citizenship in the United States.* Oxford: Oxford University Press.

———. 2006b. "We Asked for Workers, But Families Came: Time, Law, and the Family in Immigration and Citizenship." *Virginia Journal of Social Policy & the Law* 14(1): 103–118.

Munzer, Stephen R. 2001. "Property as Social Relations." In *New Essays in the Legal and Political Theory of Property,* ed. Stephen R. Munzer, 36–75. Cambridge: Cambridge University Press.

Murphy, Liam, and Thomas Nagel. 2002. *The Myth of Ownership: Taxes and Justice.* Oxford: Oxford University Press.

Murray, Mary. 2004. "Primogeniture, Patrilineage, and the Displacement of Women." In *Women, Property, and the Letters of the Law in Early Modern England,* ed. Nancy E. Wright, Margaret W. Ferguson, and A. R. Buck. Toronto: University of Toronto Press.

Nagel, Thomas. 2005. "The Problem of Global Justice." *Philosophy and Public Affairs* 33(2): 113–147.

National Intelligence Council, U.S.A. 2001. *Growing Global Migration and Its Implications for the United States.* Washington D.C.: NIE 2001–02D Publication (March 2001).

Nedelsky, Jennifer. 1989. "Reconceiving Autonomy: Sources, Thoughts and Possibilities." *Yale Journal of Law and Feminism* 1(1): 7–36.

———. 1990. *Private Property and the Limits of American Constitutionalism: The Madisonian Framework and Its Legacy.* Chicago: University of Chicago Press.

———. 2001. "Citizenship and Relational Feminism." In *Canadian Political Philosophy: Contemporary Reflections,* ed. Ronald Beiner & Wayne Norman, 131–146. Oxford: Oxford University Press.

Nett, Roger. 1971. "The Civil Right We Are Not Yet Ready For: The Right of Free Movement of People on the Face of the Earth." *Ethics* 81(3): 212–227.

Neuman, Gerald L. 1987. "Back to *Dred Scott*?" *San Diego Law Review* 24(2): 485–500.

———. 1993. "Buffer Zones Against Refugees: Dublin, Schengen, and the German Asylum Amendment." *Virginia Journal of International Law* 33(3): 503–526.

———. 2006. "Discretionary Deportation." *Georgetown Immigration Law Journal* 20(4): 611–655.

Neumayer, Eric. 2006. "Unequal Access to Foreign Spaces: How States Use Visa Restrictions to Regulate Mobility in a Globalized World." *Transactions of the Institute of British Geographers* 31(1): 72–84.

Ngai, Mae M. 2004. *Impossible Subjects: Illegal Aliens and the Making of Modern America*. Princeton, N.J.: Princeton University Press.

North, Douglas C. 1990. *Institutions, Institutional Change, and Economic Performance*. Cambridge: Cambridge University Press.

Nozick, Robert. 1974. *Anarchy, State, and Utopia*. New York: Basic Books.

———. 1989. *The Examined Life: Philosophical Mediations*. New York: Simon and Schuster.

Nussbaum, Martha. 2000. *Women and Human Development: The Capabilities Approach*. Cambridge: Cambridge University Press.

Nygh, P. E. 1963. "Problems of Nationality and Expatriation before English and Australian Courts." *International and Comparative Law Quarterly* 12(1): 175–188.

Ohilger, Rainer. 2005. "Ius Sanguinis." In *Immigration and Asylum: From 1900 to the Present*, vol 1., ed. Matthew J. Gibney and Randall Hansen, 342–345. Santa Barbara, Calif.: ABC CLIO.

Ong, Aihwa. 1999. *Flexible Citizenship: The Cultural Logics of Transnationality*. Durham, N.C.: Duke University Press.

Oppenheim, Lassa. 2008. *Oppenheim's International Law*, 9th ed. Ed. Robert Jennings and Arthur Watts. Oxford: Oxford University Press.

Organization for Economic Co-operation and Development (OECD). 2005a. "Counting Immigrant and Expatriates in OECD Countries: A New Perspective." In *Trends in International Migration 2004: Continuous Reporting System on Migration*. Paris: OECD.

———. 2005b. *Health at a Glance: OECD Indicators 2005*. Paris: OECD.

Orlenticher, Diane. 1998, "Citizenship and National Identity." In *International Law and Ethnic Conflict*, ed. David Wippman, 296–325. Ithaca, N.Y.: Cornell University Press.

Orth, John V. 1992. "After the Revolution: 'Reform' of the Law of Inheritance." *Law and History Review* 10(1): 33–44.

Ostrom, Elinor. 1990. *Governing the Commons: The Evolution of Institutions for Collective Action*. Cambridge: Cambridge University Press.

Ottonelli, Valeria. 2002. "Immigration: What Does Global Justice Require?" In *Global Citizenship: A Critical Introduction*, ed. Nigel Dower and John Williams, 231–243. New York: Routledge.

Pamuk, Orhan. 2007. "My First Passport: What Does It Mean to Belong to a Country?" *The New Yorker*, April 16, 2007, 56–57.

Parekh, Bhikhu. 2003. "Cosmopolitanism and Global Citizenship." *Review of International Studies* 29: 3–17.

Parliament of Canada. 1994. Report of the Standing Committee on Citizenship and Immigration. *Canadian Citizenship: A Sense of Belonging*. Ottawa: Parliament of Canada.

Pastor, Robert A. 2001. *Towards a North American Community: Lessons from the Old World for the New.* Washington, D.C.: Institute for International Economics.

Pateman, Carole. 1988. *The Sexual Contract*. Stanford, Calif.: Stanford University Press.

Peled, Yoav. 1992. "Ethnic Democracy and the Legal Construction of Citizenship: Arab Citizens of the Jewish State." *American Political Science Review* 86(2): 432–443.

Pew Hispanic Center. 2006. "Modes of Entry for the Unauthorized Migrant Population." *Factsheet,* 22 May 2006.

Pikeety, Thomas, and Emmanuel Saez. 2007. "How Progressive Is the U.S. Federal Tax System? A Historical and International Perspective." *Journal of Economic Perspective* 21(1): 3–24.

Pocock, J. G. A. 1995. "The Ideal of Citizenship since Classical Times." In *Theorizing Citizenship,* ed. Ronald Beiner. Albany: State University of New York Press.

Pogge, Thomas Winfried Menko. 1992. "Cosmopolitanism and Sovereignty." *Ethics* 103(1): 48–75.

———. 2002. *World Poverty and Human Rights: Cosmopolitan Responsibilities and Reforms.* Cambridge: Polity Press.

Posner, Richard A. 2007. *Economic Analysis of Law,* 7th ed. New York: Aspen Publishers.

Pound, Roscoe. 1939. "The Law of Property and Recent Juristic Thought." *American Bar Association Journal* 25(12): 993–998.

Pretto-Sakamnn, Arianna. 2005. *Boundaries of Personal Property: Shares and Sub-Shares.* Oxford: Hart.

Price, Polly J. 1997. "Natural Law and Birthright Citizenship in *Calvin's Case* (1608)." *Yale Journal of Law and the Humanities* 9(1): 73–145.

Radin, Margaret Jane. 1982. "Property and Personhood." *Stanford Law Review* 34(5): 957–1015.

———. 1986. "Time, Possession, and Alienation." *Washington University Law Quarterly* 64(3): 739–758.

———. 1987. "Market-Inalienability." *Harvard Law Review* 100(8): 1849–1937.

———. 1993. *Reinterpreting Property.* Chicago: University of Chicago Press.

———. 1996. *Contested Commodities.* Cambridge, Mass.: Harvard University Press.

Radin, Margaret Jane, and Madhavi Sunder. 2005. "Introduction: The Subject and Object of Commodification." In *Rethinking Commodification: Cases and Readings in Law and Culture,* ed. Martha M. Ertman and Joan C. Willams, 8–29. New York: New York University Press.

Rath, Jan. 1990. "Voting Rights." In *The Political Rights of Migrant Workers in Western Europe,* ed. Zig Layton-Henry. 127–157. London: Sage.

Ratha, Dilip. 2007. *Polity Brief: Leveraging Remittances for Development*. Washington, D.C.: Migration Policy Institute.

Rawls, John. 1999a. *The Law of Peoples*. Cambridge, Mass.: Harvard University Press.

———. [1970] 1999b. *A Theory of Justice*. Rev. ed. Cambridge, Mass.: Belknap Press.

Redpath, Jillyanne. 2007. "Biometrics and International Migration." In *International Migration Law: Developing Paradigms and Key Challenges*, ed. Ryszard Cholewinski, Richard Perruchoud, and Euan MacDonald, 427–445. The Hague: T. M. C. Asser Press.

Reich, Charles. 1964. "The New Property." *Yale Law Journal* 73(5): 733–787.

Reisen, Helmut. 2002. "Tobin Tax: Could It Work?" OECD Observer no. 231/232, May 2002.

Rignano, Eugenio. 1924. *The Social Significance of the Inheritance Tax*. Trans. and adpt. William J. Schultz. New York: A. A. Knopf.

Roberts, Maurice. 1975. "The Exercise of Administrative Discretion Under the Immigration Laws." *San Diego Law Review* 13(1): 144–165.

Rodrick, Dani, ed. 2003. *In Search of Prosperity: Analytical Narratives on Economic Growth*. Princeton, N.J.: Princeton University Press.

Rodriguez, Cristina. 2007. "Guest Workers and Integration: Toward a Theory of What Immigrants and Americans Owe One Another." *University of Chicago Legal Forum* (2007): 219–288.

Roemer, John E. 1998. *Equality of Opportunity*. Cambridge, Mass.: Harvard University Press.

Roman, Ediberto. 2006. "The Citizenship Dialectic." *Georgetown Immigration Law Journal* 20(4): 557–609.

Romero, Victor C. 2001. "The Child Citizenship Act and the Family Reunification Act: Valuing the Citizen Child as Well as the Citizen Parent." *Florida Law Review* 55(1): 489–509.

Rose, Carol M. 1990. "Property as Storytelling: Perspectives from Game Theory, Narrative Theory, Feminist Theory." *Yale Journal of Law and the Humanities* 2(1): 37–57.

———. 1994a. *Property and Persuasion: Essays in the History, Theory, and Rhetoric of Ownership*. Boulder, Colo.: Westview Press.

———. 1994b. "'Takings' and the Practices of Property: Property as Wealth, Property as 'Propriety'." In *Property and Persuasion: Essays on the History, Theory, and Rhetoric of Ownership*, 49–70. Boulder, Colo.: Westview Press.

———. 2004. "Economic Claims and the Challenges of New Property." In *Property in Question: Value Transformation in the Global Economy*, ed. Katherine Verdery and Caroline Humphrey, 275–295. Oxford: Berg.

Rose-Ackerman, Susan. 1985. "Inalienablity and the Theory of Property Rights." *Columbia Law Review* 85(5): 931–969.

Rubenstien, Kim. 2002. *Australian Citizenship Law in Context*. Sydney: Lawbook.

Rubio-Marin, Ruth. 2000. *Immigration as Democratic Challenge: Citizenship and Inclusion in Germany and the United States*. Cambridge: Cambridge University Press.

Ruggie, John Gerard. 1993. "Territoriality and Beyond: Problematizing Modernity in International Relations." *International Organization* 47(1): 139–174.

Ruths, Martin. 2005. "Designing Viable and Ethical Labor Immigration Policies." In *World Migration 2005: Costs and Benefits of International Migration.* Geneva: International Organization for Migration (IOM).

Sachs, Jeffrey D. 2005. *The End of Poverty: Economic Possibilities for Our Time.* New York: Penguin Press.

Sadiq, Kamal. 2008. *Paper Citizens: How Illegal Immigrants Acquire Citizenship in Developing Countries.* Oxford: Oxford University Press.

Salyer, Lucy E. 2005. "*Wong Kim Ark:* The Contest over Birthright Citizenship." In *Immigration Stories,* ed. David A. Martin and Peter H. Schuck. 51–85. New York: Foundation Press.

Sandel, Michael J. 1982. *Liberalism and the Limits of Justice.* Cambridge: Cambridge University Press.

———. 2005. "What Money Can't Buy: The Moral Limits of Markets." In *Rethinking Commodification: Cases and Readings in Law and Culture,* ed. Martha M. Ertman and Joan C. Williams, 122–127. New York: New York University Press.

Sangiovanni, Andrea. 2007. "Global Justice, Reciprocity, and the State." *Philosophy and Public Affairs* 35(1): 3–39.

Sapiro, Virginia. 1984. "Women, Citizenship, and Nationality: Immigration and Naturalization Policies in the United States." *Politics and Societies* 13(1): 1–26.

Sassen, Saskia. 1996. *Losing Control? Sovereignty in an Age of Globalization.* New York: Columbia University Press.

———. 2006. *Territory, Authority, Rights: From Medieval to Global Assemblages.* Princeton, N.J.: Princeton University Press.

Satz, Debra. 1999. "Equality of What among Whom? Thoughts on Cosmopolitanism, Statism, and Nationalism." In *NOMOS: Global Justice,* ed. Ian Shapiro and Lea Brilmayer, 67–85. New York: New York University Press.

———. 2005. "What Do We Owe the Global Poor." *Ethics and International Affairs* 19(1): 47–54.

Scott, James C. 1998. *Seeing Like a State: How Certain Schemes to Improve the Human Condition Failed.* New Haven: Yale University Press.

Schuck, Peter H. 1997. "Refugee Burden-Sharing: A Modest Proposal." *Yale Journal of International Law* 22(2): 243–297.

Schuck, Peter H., and Rogers M. Smith. 1985. *Citizenship Without Consent: Illegal Aliens in the American Polity.* New Haven: Yale University Press.

Schwartz, David S. 1986. "The Amorality of Consent." *California Law Review* 74 (6): 2143–2171.

Sen, Amartya K. 1992. *Inequality Reexamined.* New York: Russell Sage Foundation; Cambridge, Mass.: Harvard University Press.

———. 2000. *Development as Freedom.* New York: Anchor Books.

Shachar, Ayelet. 1999. "Whose Republic? Citizenship and Membership in the Israeli Polity." *Georgetown Immigration Law Journal* 13(2): 233–272.

———. 2001. *Multicultural Jurisdictions: Cultural Differences and Women's Rights*. Cambridge: Cambridge University Press.

———. 2006. "The Race for Talent: Highly Skilled Migrants and Competitive Immigration Regimes." *New York University Law Review* 81(1): 148–206.

———. 2007. "The Shifting Border of Immigration Regulation." *Stanford Journal of Civil Rights and Civil Liberties* 3(1): 165–193.

Shachar, Ayelet, and Ran Hirschl. 2007. "Citizenship as Inherited Property." *Political Theory* 35(3): 253–287.

Shafir, Gershon, ed. 1998. *The Citizenship Debates: A Reader*. Minneapolis, Minn.: University of Minnesota Press.

———. 2004. "Citizenship and Human Rights in an Era of Globalization." In *People Out of Place: Globalization, Human Rights, and the Citizenship Gap*, ed. Alison Brysk and Gershon Shafir, 11–25. New York: Routledge.

Shapiro, Ian. 1999. *Democratic Justice*. New Haven: Yale University Press.

Shapiro, Ian, and Casiano Hacker-Cordon. 1999. "Outer Edges and Inner Edges." In *Democracy's Edges*, ed. Ian Shapiro and Casiano Hacker-Cordon, 1–15. Cambridge: Cambridge University Press.

Sharron, Jessica. 2007. "Passing the DREAM Act: Opportunities for Undocumented Americans." *Santa Clara Law Review* 47(2): 599–644.

Shklar, Judith N. 1991. *American Citizenship: The Quest for Inclusion*. Cambridge, Mass.: Harvard University Press.

Simon, Julian L. 1986. "Auction the Right to Be an Immigrant." *The New York Times*, January 28, 1986, A1.

Simpson, A. W. Brian. 1986. *A History of the Land Law*, 2nd ed. Oxford: Clarendon Press.

Singer, Joseph William. 2000. *Entitlement: The Paradoxes of Property*. New Haven: Yale University Press.

Singer, Peter. 1972. "Famine, Affluence, and Morality." *Philosophy and Public Affairs* 1(3): 229–243.

Smith, Anthony D. 1991. *National Identity*. London: Penguin.

Smith, Henry E. 2000. "Semicommon Property Rights and Scattering in the Open Fields." *Journal of Legal Studies* 29(1): 131–169.

———. 2002. "Exclusion Versus Governance: Two Strategies for Delineating Property Rights." *Journal of Legal Studies* 31(2): 453–487.

Smith, Rogers M. 1997. *Civic Ideals: Conflicting Visions of Citizenship in U.S. History*. New Haven: Yale University Press.

Somers, Margaret R. 2006. "Citizenship, Statelessness, and Market Fundamentalism: Arendtian Right to Have Rights." In *Migration, Citizenship, Ethnos*, ed. Y. Michal Bodemann and Gokce Yurdakul, 35–62. New York: Palgrave Macmillan.

Soysal, Yasemin Nuhoglu. 1994. *Limits of Citizenship: Migrants and Postnational Membership in Europe*. Chicago: University of Chicago Press.

Spiro, Peter J. 2008. *Beyond Citizenship: American Identity After Globalization*. Oxford: Oxford University Press.

Spring, Eileen. 1993. *Law, Land, and Family: Aristocratic Inheritance in England, 1300–1800*. Chapel Hill, N.C.: University of North Carolina Press.

Stark, Oded. 1991. *The Migration of Labor*. Oxford: Blackwell.

Steiner, Hillel. 2001. "Hard Borders, Compensation, and Classical Liberalism." In *Boundaries and Justice: Diverse Ethical Perspectives,* ed. David Miller and Sohail H. Hashmi, 79–88. Princeton, N.J.: Princeton University Press.

Stevens, Jacqueline. 1999. *Reproducing the State.* Princeton, N.J.: Princeton University Press.

Stratton, Lisa C. 1992. "The Right to Have Rights: Gender Discrimination in Nationality Law." *Minnesota Law Review* 77(1): 195–239.

Sunstein, Cass. 1988. "Beyond the Republican Revival." *Yale Law Journal* 97(8): 1539–1590.

Tamir, Yael. 1993. *Liberal Nationalism.* Princeton, N.J.: Princeton University Press.

Tan, Kok-Chor. 2004. *Justice without Borders: Cosmopolitanism, Nationalism, and Patriotism.* Cambridge: Cambridge University Press.

Tawney, Richard H. 1964. *Equality.* London: Unwin Books.

Taylor, Charles. 1989. *Sources of the Self: the Making of the Modern Identity.* Cambridge, Mass: Harvard University Press.

Torpey, John. 2000. *The Invention of the Passport: Surveillance, Citizenship, and the State.* Cambridge: Cambridge University Press.

Trebilcock, Michael J. 2003. "The Law and Economics of Immigration Policy." *American Law & Economics Review* 5(2): 271–317.

Trebilcock, Michael J., and Robert Howse. 2005. *The Regulation of International Trade,* 3rd ed. New York: Routledge.

Tronto, Joan C. 1993. *Moral Boundaries: A Political Argument for an Ethic of Care.* New York: Routledge.

U.K. Border Agency (The Home Office). 2007. "Immigration Directorate Instructions." (chapter 6). www.ukba.homeoffice.gov.uk/sitecontent/documents/policyandlaw/IDIs/idischapter6/.

United Nations. 2000. *United Nations Millennium Declaration.* Resolution adopted by the General Assembly, A/RES/55/2. Fifty-fifth Session. September 18, 2000. New York: United Nations.

———. 2002a. *International Migration Report 2002.* New York: United Nations/Department of Economic and Social Affairs, Population Division.

———. 2002b. *Report of the International Conference on Financing for Development: Monterrey, Mexico, 18–22 March 2002.* New York: United Nations.

———. 2002c. *World Population Monitoring: Reproductive Rights and Reproductive Health: Selected Aspects.* New York: United Nations/Department of Economic and Social Affairs.

———. 2003. *Monterrey Consensus on Financing for Development.* Conference on Financing for Development, Monterrey/Mexico, March 18–22, 2002. http://www.un.org/esa/ffd/monterrey/MonterreyConsensus.pdf.

———. 2004. *World Economic and Social Survey 2004: International Migration.* E/2004/75/Rev.1/Add.1,ST/ESA/291/Add1. New York: United Nations/Department of Economic and Social Affairs.

———. 2005. *World Migrant Stock: The 2005 Revision Population Database.* New York: United Nations/Department of Economics and Social Affairs. www.esa.un.org/migration.

———. 2006. *Report of the Secretary-General: World Population Monitoring, Focusing on International Migration and Development.* E/CN.9/2006/3. Commission on Population and Development. New York: United Nations.

United Nations Children's Fund (UNICEF). 2005. *The State of the World's Children: Childhood Under Threat.* Oxford: Oxford University Press.

———. 2006. *Facts on Children: Early Childhood.* www.unicef.org/media/9475.html.

———. 2007. *Progress for Children: A World Fit for Children, Statistical Review,* no. 6, December 2007.

United Nations Development Programme (UNDP). 2002. *Human Development Report 2002: Deepening Democracy in a Fragmented World.* New York: Oxford University Press.

———. 2004. *Human Development Report 2004: Cultural Liberty in Today's Diverse World.* New York: Oxford University Press.

———. 2005. *Human Development Report 2005: International Cooperation at a Crossroads: Aid, Trade and Security in an Unequal World.* New York: Oxford University Press.

United Nations Millennium Project. 2006. "Q&A on the Millennium Project and the Millennium Development Goals." (December 2006). www.unmillenniumproject.org/documents/UNMP-QandA-E.pdf

United Nations Population Fund (UNFPA). 1999. *The State of the World Population 1999: 6 Billion: A Time for Choices.* New York: United Nations Population Fund.

———. 2006. *State of World Population 2006: A Passage to Hope: Women and International Migration.* New York: United Nations Population Fund.

Vachudova, Mildad Anna. 2000. "Eastern Europe as Gatekeeper: The Immigration and Asylum Policies of an Enlarging European Union." In *The Wall around the West: State Borders and Immigration Controls in North America and Europe,* ed. Peter Andreas and Timothy Snyder, 153–171. Lanham, Md.: Roman and Littlefield.

Van den Anker, Christien. 2002. "Global Justice, Global Institutions and Global Citizenship." In *Global Citizenship: A Critical Introduction,* ed. Nigel Dower and John Williams, 158–168. New York: Routledge.

Van Parijs, Philippe. 2007. "International Distributive Justice." In *A Companion to Contemporary Political Philosophy,* 2nd edition, ed. Robert E. Goodin, Philip Pettit, and Thomas W. Pogge, 638–652. Oxford: Blackwell.

Vertovec, Steven, and Robin Cohen, eds. 2002. *Conceiving Cosmopolitanism: Theory, Context, and Practice.* New York: Oxford University Press.

Volpp, Leti. 2007. "Citizenship Undone." *Fordham Law Review* 75(5): 2579–2586.

Waldrauch, Harald. 2006. "Acquisition of Nationality." In *Acquisition and Loss of Nationality: Policies and Trends in 15 European States, Vol. 1: Comparative Analyses,* ed. Rainer Baubock, Eva Ersboll, Kees Groenendijk, and Harald Waldrauch, 121–182. Amsterdam: Amsterdam University Press.

Waldron, Jeremy. 1985. "What Is Private Property?" *Oxford Journal of Legal Studies* 5(3): 313–349.

———. 1988. *The Right to Private Property.* Oxford: Oxford University Press.

———. 1993. "Property, Justification, and Need." *Canadian Journal of Law and Jurisprudence* 6(2): 185–215.

———. 1996. "Property Law." In *A Companion to Philosophy of Law and Legal Theory,* ed. Dennis Patterson, 3–23. Oxford: Blackwell.

Wallace, Paul. 2001. *Agequake: Riding the Rollercoaster Shaking Business, Finance, and Our World.* London: Nicholas Brealey.

Wallace, Tony. 2006. "New Year Brings Changes to Citizenship." *Islands Business,* January 2, 2006.

Walzer, Michael. 1983. *Spheres of Justice: A Defense of Pluralism and Equality.* New York: Basic Books.

———. 1989. "Citizenship." In *Political Innovation and Conceptual Change,* ed. Terence Ball, James Farr, and Russell L. Hanson, 211–219. Cambridge: Cambridge University Press.

———. 2002. "Spheres of Affection." In *For Love of Country?* ed. Martha C. Nussbaum and Joshua Cohen, 125–127. Boston: Beacon Press.

Weber, Max. 1946. "Politics as a Vocation." In *From Max Weber: Essays in Sociology,* ed. Hans H. Gerth and C. Wright Mills. 77–128. Oxford: Oxford University Press.

———. 1947. *The Theory of Social and Economic Organization.* Trans. A. M. Henderson and Talcott Parsons; ed. Talcott Parsons. Oxford: Oxford University Press.

Wedgwood, Josiah. 1929. *The Economics of Inheritance.* London: G. Routledge & Sons.

Weil, Patrick. 1996. "Nationalities and Citizenships: The Lessons of the French Experience for Germany and Europe." In *Citizenship, Nationality, and Migration in Europe,* ed. David Cesarani and Mary Fulbrooke, 74–87. New York: Routledge.

———. 2001. "Access to Citizenship: A Comparison of Twenty-Five Nationality Laws." In *Citizenship Today: Global Perspectives and Practices,* ed. T. Alexander Aleinikoff and Douglas Klusmeyer, 17–35. Washington D.C.: Brookings Institution Press.

Weiler, Joseph H. H. 1999. "To Be a European Citizen: Eros and Civilization." In *The Constitution of Europe: "Do the New Clothes Have an Emperor?" and Other Essays on European Integration.* Cambridge: Cambridge University Press.

Weiner, Annette B. 1992. *Inalienable Possessions: The Paradox of Keeping-While-Giving.* Berkeley: University of California Press.

Weinrib, Ernest J. 2003. "Poverty and Property in Kant's System of Rights." *Notre Dame Law Review* 78(3): 795–828.

Weinrib, Laura. 2002. "Reconstructing Family: Constructive Trust at Relational Dissolution." *Harvard Civil Rights-Civil Liberties Law Review* 37(1): 207–247.

Weinstock, Daniel. 1999. "Building Trust in Divided Societies." *Journal of Political Philosophy* 7(3): 287–307.

Weis, Paul. 1979. *Nationality and Statelessness in International Law,* 2nd ed. Alphen aan den Rijn: Sijthoff & Noordhoff.

West, Max. 1893. *The Inheritance Tax.* New York: Columbia College.

Whelan, Frederic G. 1983. "Prologue: Democratic Theory and the Boundary Problem." In *Liberal Democracy,* ed. J. Roland Pennock and John W. Chapman, 13–47. New York: New York University Press.

Wightman, John. 2000. "Intimate Relationships, Relational Contract Theory, and the Reach of Contract." *Feminist Legal Studies* 8(1): 93–131.

Winters, Alan L. 2003. "The Economic Implications of Liberalizing Mode 4 Trade." In *Moving People to Deliver Services,* ed. Aaditya Mattoo and Antonia Carzaniga, 59–91. Washington, D.C.: World Bank/Oxford University Press.

World Bank. 1994. *Averting the Old Age Crisis: Policies to Protect the Old and Promote Growth.* New York: Oxford University Press.

———. 2001. *World Development Report 2000/2001, Attacking Poverty: Opportunity, Empowerment, and Security.* New York: Oxford University Press.

———. 2005. *World Development Report 2006: Equity and Development.* Washington, D.C.: World Bank.

———. 2006a. *World Bank Global Economic Prospects 2006: Economic Implications of Remittances and Migration.* Washington, D.C.: World Bank.

———. 2006b. *World Development Indicators 2006.* Washington, D.C.: World Bank.

———. *Global Millennium Development Goals,* Goal 4: Reduce Child Mortality. www.go.worldbank.org/1FSX9LB5Vo.

Wright, Sue. 2008. "Citizenship Tests in Europe," *International Journal on Multicultural Societies* 10(1): 1–9.

Yack, Bernard. 1996. "The Myth of the Civic Nation." *Critical Review* 10(2): 193–211.

Young, Iris Marion. 1995. "Mothers, Citizenship, and Independence: A Critique of Pure Family Values." *Ethics* 105(3): 535–556.

Zilbershats, Yaffa. 2002. *The Human Right to Citizenship.* Ardsley, N.Y.: Transitional Publishers.

Zolberg, Aristide R. 2006. *A Nation by Design: Immigration Policy in the Fashioning of America.* Cambridge, Mass.: Harvard University Press.

Zucker, Ross. 2001. *Democratic Distributive Justice.* Cambridge: Cambridge University Press.

Case Law and Legislation

Australia

Al-Kateb v. *Godwin,* 219 CLR 562, 2004 (High Court of Australia).

Pochi v. *Macphee,* 151 CLR 101 (1982) (High Court of Australia).

Australian Citizenship Act 1948 (Cth.).

Australian Citizenship Act 2007 (Cth. No. 20 of 2007).

Canada

Ahani v. *Canada (Minister of Citizenship and Immigration),* [2002] 1 S.C.R. 72.

Canada (Minister of Employment and Immigration) v. *Chiarelli,* [1992] 1 S.C.R. 711.

Charkaoui v. *Canada (Citizenship and Immigration),* [2007] 1 S.C.R. 350.

Re Pourghasemi (1993), 19 Imm. L.R. (2d) 259 (F.C.T.D.).

Romans v. *Canada (Minister of Citizensip and Immigration),* [2001] 281 NR 357; F.C.A; [2004] 3 F.C.R. 139.

Romans v. *Canada (Minister of Citizenship and Immigration)*, [2001] SCCA no. 471.
Baker v. *Canada (Ministry of Citizenship and Immigration)*, [1999] S.C.R. 817.
Benner v. *Canada (Secretary of State)*, [1997] 1 S.C.R. 358.
Anti-Terrorism Act, S.C. 2001, c. 41.
Citizenship Act, R.S.C, 1985, c. C-29.
Citizenship Regulations, 1993, S.O.R/1993–246.
Immigration and Refugee Protection Act, S.C. 2001, c.27.
Immigration and Refugee Protection Regulations, 2002, S.O.R./2002–227.

Finland

Nationality Act 359/2003.

Germany

BVerfG, 83, II, Nr. 3, 1990.
Residence Act of 30 July 2004. (Federal Law Gazette I, p. 1950), last amended by the Act on Implementation of Residence- and Asylum-Related Directives of the European Union of 19 August 2007 (Federal Law Gazette I, p. 1970).

Greece

Greek Citizenship Code.

Ireland

Irish Nationality and Citizenship Act 1956 [consolidated version, as amended by the Irish Nationality and Citizenship Act 2004, no. 38 of 2004].
Twenty-seventh Amendment of the Constitution Act 2004 (Amendment of Article 9 of the Constitution), 2004.

Israel

H.C. 442/71, *Lansky* v. *Minister of the Interior* (1972), 26(2) P.D 337.
C.A. 6182/98, *Sheinbein* v. *Attorney General* (1999), 53(1) P.D 625.
F.H. 1210/99, *State of Israel* v. *Sheinbein* (decision given on March 18, 1999).

Netherlands

Aliens Act 2000.

United States

Abreu v. *Callahan*, 971 F. Supp. 799 (1997).
Adams v. *Slattery*, 156 Texas 433 (1956).

Chan v. *Bell,* 464 F.Supp 125 (D.D.C.1978).
Doe v. *Miller,* 573 F. Supp. 461 (N.D. Ill. 1983).
Klapprott v. *United States,* 335 U.S. 601 (1949).
Landon v. *Plasecnia,* 459 U.S. 21 (1982).
MacKenzie v. *Hare,* 239 U.S. 299 (1915).
Maria Teresa Garcia De Nunez, Administrative Appeal Office, file no. A78264450, U.S. April 10, 2007, 2007 WL 5317484.
Mathews v. *Diaz,* 426 U.S. 67 (1976).
Matter of Andazola-Rivas, 23 I & N December 319 (Board of Immigration Appeals, April 3, 2002).
Matter of C-V-T, 22 I & N December 7 (Board of Immigration Appeals, February 12, 1998).
Matter of Cervantes-Gonzalez, 22 I & N December 560 (Board of Immigration Appeals, 1999).
Matter of Martin, 16 I & N December 581 (Board of Immigration Appeals, August, 4, 1978).
Matter of Monreal, 23 I & N December 56 (Board of Immigration Appeals, 2001).
Matter of Ortiz-Martinez, I & N (Board of Immigration Appeals, May 25, 2007).
Miller v. *Albright,* 523 U.S. 420 (1998).
Nehme v. *INS,* 252 F.3d 415 (5th Cir. 2001).
Nguyen v. *INS,* 533 U.S. 53 (2001).
Olga de Leon v. *Shih Wei Navigation,* no. G-05-CV-579, 2007 U.S. Dist. Lexis 49665 (S.D. Tex. July 10, 2007).
Santos v. *Gonazales,* 2007 U.S. Dist. Ct. (Mass.), Lexis 49417, July 10, 2007.
Schneiderman v. *United States,* 320 U.S. 118 (1943).
Shaughnessy v. *United States ex. rel. Mezei,* 345 U.S. 206 (1953).
Stokes v. *INS,* no. 74 Civ. 1022 (S.D.N.Y. December 1, 1976).
United States v. *Wong Kim Ark,* 169 U.S. 649 (1898).
Weedin v. *Chin Bow,* 273 U.S. 657 (1927).
Zadvydas v. *Davis,* 533 U.S. 678 (2001).
The Border Protection, Anti-Terrorism, and Illegal Immigration Control Act of 2005, H.R. 4437, 109th Cong. (2005).
Child Citizenship Act of 2000, Pub. L. no. 106–395, 114 Stat. 1631 (2000).
Comprehensive Immigration Reform Act of 2006, S. 2611, 109th Cong. S2 (2006).
Comprehensive Immigration Reform Act of 2007, S. 1348, 110th Cong. (2007).
Federal Register, vol. 44, June 21, 1979.
Federal Register, vol. 46, January 28, 1981.
Homeland Security Act of 2002, Pub. L. no 107–296, 116 Stat. 2135 (2002).
Illegal Immigrant Reform and Immigration Responsibility Act of 1996, Pub. L. 104–208, 110 Stat. 3009 (1996).
Immigration and Nationality Act, 8 U.S.C. (2008).
Naturalization Act of 1790, 1 Stat. 103–104(1790).
Personal Responsibility and Work Opportunity Reconciliation of 1996, Pub. L. 104–193, 110 Stat. 2105 (1996).
REAL ID Act of 2005, H.R. 418, 109th Cong. (2005).
USA Patriot Act of 2001, Pub. L. no. 107–56, 115 Stat. 272 (2001).

United Kingdom

Calvin's Case, 77 Eng. Rep. 377 (K.B. 1608).
Duke of Norfolk's Case, 3 Chan. Cas. 1, 2 Swanston 454 (1682).
Taltarum's Case, Y.B. 12 Edw. 4 Mich. 25 (1472).
British Nationality Act 1981 (U.K.), 1981 c. 61.
Land Registration Act 2002 (U.K.), 2002, c. 9.

Regional and International Legal Materials

Abdulaziz, Cabales, and Balkandali v. *the United Kingdom* [European Court of Human Rights]. 7 EHRR 471 (28 May 1985).
Ahmut v. *the Netherlands* [European Court of Human Rights]. 24 EHRR 62 (28 November 1996).
Beljoudi v. *France* [European Court of Human Rights]. 14 EHRR 801 (26 March 1992).
Collins v. *Secretary of State for Work and Pensions* [European Court of Justice]. Case C-138/02. ECR I-2703 (23 March 2004).
Gul v. *Switzerland* [European Court of Human Rights]. 22 EHRR 93 (19 February 1996).
Karassev v. *Finland* [European Court of Human Rights]. no. 31414/96, ECHR 1999-II (12 January 1999).
Kunquian Catherine Zhu and Man Lavette Chen v. *Secretary of State for the Home Department* [European Court of Justice]. no. 84/04, Case C-200/02 (19 October 2004).
Liechtenstein v. *Guatemala* (The Nottebohm Case), [International Court of Justice] 1955. I.C.J. Reports, vol. 1955, 4–65.
Martinez Sala v. *Freistaat Bayern* [European Court of Justice]. Case C-85/96, ECR, I-2691 (12 May 1998).
Nsona v. *the Netherlands* [European Court of Human Rights]. 63/1995/569/655 (28 November 1996).
Romans v. *Canada* [UN Human Rights Committee]. Communication no. 1040/2001, CCPR/C/81/D/1040/2001 (2004).
Convention on Certain Questions Relating to Conflict of Nationality Laws ("1930 Hague Convention"), 179 L.N.T.S. 89 (1937).
Convention Relating to the Status of Refugees ("1951 Refugee Convention"), April 22, 1954, 189 U.N.T.S. 137 (amended by the Protocol Relation to the Status of Refugees, October 4, 1967, 606 U.N.T.S. 267).
Convention on the Elimination of All Forms of Discrimination Against Women ("CEDAW"), December 18, 1979, 1249 U.N.T.S. 13.
European Council Directive 2003/109/EC Concerning the Status of Third-Country Nationals Who Are Long-Term Residents, OJ 2004, L16/44.
North American Agreement on Environmental Cooperation, Canada, Mexico, and the United States, 14 September 1993, 32 I.L.M. 1480 (entered into force January 1, 1994).

Index